THE USES OF OBSCURITY

THE USES OF OBSCURITY
The Fiction of Early Modernism

Allon White

Routledge & Kegan Paul
London, Boston and Henley

First published in 1981
by Routledge & Kegan Paul Ltd
39 Store Street,
London WC1E 7DD,
9 Park Street,
Boston, Mass. 02108, USA and
Broadway House,
Newtown Road,
Henley-on-Thames,
Oxon RG9 1EN
Printed in Great Britain by
Biddles Limited, Guildford, Surrey
© Allon White, 1981

British Library Cataloguing in Publication Data

White, Allon
The uses of obscurity.
1. English fiction - 19th century - History
and criticism
I. Title
823'. 7   PR 830. 0/

ISBN 0 7100 0751 5

To Catherine

CONTENTS

Acknowledgments   ix

Introduction   1

Part I

1   Obscurity and enlightenment   13

2   Obscure writing and private life, 1880-1914   30

3   Truth and impurity   55

Part II

4   'Godiva to the gossips': Meredith and the
    language of shame   79

5   Conrad and the rhetoric of enigma   108

6   'The deterrent fact': vulgarity and obscurity
    in James   130

Notes   163

Select bibliography   181

Index   187

ACKNOWLEDGMENTS

I would like to acknowledge the help of The Leverhulme Trust in its generous award of a European Studentship for the year 1975-6. I would also like to thank the Fellows of Trinity Hall, Cambridge, both for their moral support and for the provision of a Research Fellowship which has given me the best possible environment for my work.

I would also like to thank the Tate Gallery, London, for permission to reproduce the illustration of Wallis's 'Death of Chatterton', and The Ashmolean Museum, Oxford, for permission to reproduce Max Beerbohm's cartoon of Mr Henry James; The Trustees of the late Dylan Thomas for permission to reproduce an extract from 'Out of the Sighs'.

I have received excellent advice, criticism and encouragement from Raymond Williams, Gerard Genette, Gillian Beer, David Lodge and Gabriel Josipovici and I would also like to record my debt to the late Roland Barthes.

My special indebtedness is to Professor John Holloway whose patient supervision of my work has been invaluable. He has always guided my research with kindly and scrupulous critical attention. I would also like to thank Caroline for her ceaseless support at a time when others would have turned away, and Janet Laing, who is quite simply the best typist anyone could wish for.

INTRODUCTION

A midnight door that we are astonished to find we have in our daylight house.

George Meredith

From its earliest moment the voice of modernism has echoed to the lament of its defeated readers. Why is it so obscure? Why so difficult? The obscurity of modern writing is often placed on a scale of disgust which runs from the murky to the mandarin, and it thereby poses a singular problem not only to the common reader but also to the critic and cultural historian. Even sophisticated partisans of the avant-garde may be found loitering at the restful, lyrical oases in these intransigent works of art. Reading 'The Cantos', the temptation is always to linger by 'the marble form in the pine wood', rather than '13,455 ft. up Mount Kinabalu facing Jesselton, Borneo' (Canto CX).

The present book examines the moment when obscurity began to appear as an important, positive aspect of nineteenth-century English fiction. How and why were the novels of the early modernists, and particularly those of the first three in England - George Meredith, Henry James and Joseph Conrad - so obscure and difficult for their readers? In the last decades of the nineteenth century these writers appeared to their contemporaries as producing literature which resisted easy interpretation in quite new ways. This book attempts to analyse their fiction both as part of a deep cultural transformation and as individual literary projects carried through in equivocal relation to this transformation.

It is more than modesty which makes for the tentative and provisional nature of such a project. This is not a full-scale ascent of the peaks of modernist difficulty: by concentrating on the initial phase of this movement and by confining itself to England (always marginal in the development of modernism - and it is not insignificant that of the three novelists examined in detail, two were foreign and the third was educated in Germany), the present study may be said automatically to disqualify itself from analysing the most radical and imposing kinds of new writing. Yet the romanticism of obscure writing emerges powerfully in Meredith, Conrad and James, and the private logic of obscurity in modernism can be seen forming in their work. Which is not to succumb to a myth of origins, but to suggest that to study the earliest phase of modernism is to show what precisely was involved in that momentous shift when certain deep, discursive regularities (clarity, coherence, sincerity, objective representation) began to crack and slide in the 1870s and 1880s. With Henry James and George Meredith we witness the gradual occlusion of Victorian realism in a complex which belies any single or simple explanation. The present study is the first to examine the fusion and confusion of cultural factors informing the new, fiercely difficult kind of writing as it developed in England.

One purpose of the book is to break the closure which has been effected in criticism by the over-familiar phrase 'the break-down of realism'. The central problem is that textual obscurity is both a positive and a negative phenomenon. It is used for good and ill, it is a multiform, functioning element of language which, according to its relationship with more accessible parts of the text, will alter its significance. Its meaning is never purely formal, it is contextual, and therefore never falls outside of representation however opaque or arcane it may appear to be. Like the symptom or the metaphor, it simultaneously reveals and conceals. It 'signifies'. Even when (or often, because) things are unclear or imprecise, they become a source of significance. When realism began to dissolve, it did so in an uneven and partial way such that new elusive orders were produced by the kind of dissolution it proved to be.

The fictions analysed here are, in this respect, mixed and occluded. They shift backwards and forwards clinging to the desire for referential fixity and clarity of representation at the same time as dissolving both of these into the dense 'textualité' of metaphor, obscure syntax, broken narrative and anomic subjectivism. Often, indeed, the novels were constructed upon mutually incompatible principles of truth. Narrated events and linguistic forms troubled and unsettled each other until meaning began to feel self-enclosing and provisional - in James or Mallarmé, writing became an intimation of possibility deliberately withdrawing from the robust indication of fact.

Part I proposes that, in the cultural and literary history of the modern period, the new difficulty of writing was intimately linked to the growth of a new kind of reading. The growth of a distinctively new mode of attention and the growth of the new writing were part of a broad cultural change which included them both. Modern literary obscurity was a 'convergence' phenomenon. That is to say, a number of different ideological transformations occurred such that textual resistance is explicable only in terms of their convergence and interplay. Difficult modern writing, its formal intransigence, is usually described as resulting from artistic alienation or the disruptive effects of the unconscious. In fact what emerges most forcefully is that the dialectics of writing and reading production and reception, were crucially altered by 'alienation' and the discoveries of psychology, and that the form in which these things came together was of major importance. A quite new and complex relation between the act of writing and the act of reading was produced on the basis of a certain cultural movement which created both 'symptomatic' writing and its correlate, 'symp-

tomatic' reading. These grew together in an age which Nathalie
Sarraute was to call the 'Age of Suspicion', and symptomatic reading became the primary institutionalized form of this suspicion.
Its intrusion indelibly inscribed itself on the sensibilities of modern writers. With subtlety and violence it continually transgressed
their defensive privacies, provoking in its turn renewed attempts
at evasion. By tracing its growth in the late nineteenth and early
twentieth century one can see clearly the profound effect of symptomatic reading upon artistic production, and, in turn, the stim-
ulus that the new writing gave to this kind of reading. Part I is
an account of this double relationship with respect to the growth
of modern fictional practice.

Part II concentrates on the novels of Meredith, Conrad and
James, looking at the individual role of obscurity in each. Moving
on from the general preconditions outlined in Part I, it looks at
the specific mediation of textual obscurity in their work - obscurity
not simply of style, but of narrative, of symbolic and metaphorical structure, and of scene. What fears were allayed, or what
desires fulfilled, by the evasion, equivocations, enigmas, and
obliquities of these novelists? It becomes apparent that textual
difficulties tend to cluster around areas of fecund imaginative
production for each writer. Novelists tend compulsively to return
to moments and episodes which haunt or hurt them, but it is precisely this painfulness which coaxes forth their written elaborations
and misremembrances. This occurs not simply because such areas
are intrinsically complex, contradictory or deep (although they
are usually all of these), but because the energy or conflict of
energies which engender the fiction rarely speak directly: displacement is the price paid by the imagination for its purchase on
reality. Literature without displacement is unthinkable, but literature written for readers alerted to this fact is inevitably self-
obscuring. This, in the full breadth of its implication, is a major
theme of the study.

However, what is valuable and instructive in it perhaps emerges
from a contradiction which, even by the end, I have been unable
to resolve to my satisfaction. The problem is essentially one of
method, though it is not narrowly nor neutrally methodological. It
is concerned with the kind of criticism the book attempts when seen
in relation to the cultural history which it describes. Indeed, were
it not for the changes in the nature of reading, writing and authorship which are detailed below, then my own critical procedure
would have been impossible. Essentially I have carried out precisely
the sort of critical reading of Meredith, Conrad and James against
which they guarded so carefully. Even if it has been done with
tact and sensitivity, as I hope, nevertheless the critical method itself has treated their obscurities as defences against exactly the
kind of reading which is used here. I have consistently stressed
that these obscurities cannot be treated as merely defensive: they
were a crucial guarantee of creative possibility in a period of particular vulnerability for the writer; they were a positive aspect of
sublimation and displacement at a time when the writer felt

insufficiently covered by the forms of realism. Yet, even with this emphasis, I have been aware throughout the book that the kind of understanding which I seek of these authors contains within it the possibility of harm against them, and that has not been my intention. This is a real difficulty, for, given that the obscurities are, to a certain extent, a kind of semiotic defence, then in order to understand fully we are forced to penetrate them: for it is otherwise impossible to see why and how they operated. The irony is that if it is correct that textual opacities often serve to prevent a certain kind of knowledge, it is often only that kind of knowledge which can be used to understand them.

The kind of knowledge in question is what I have called, following Althusser,(1) 'symptomatic reading'. At its crudest and most general, symptomatic reading treats a literary utterance as a surface sign of something that could not be said directly. In this very general sense, it is an idea which goes back at least as far as Savonarola, who believed that each work of art was a revelation of its creator's spiritual state. However, once the idea of an unconscious replaces that of the soul, then the work of art is considered increasingly as an index of the psychological conflicts of the author. Ideological and psychological forces engender conflicts in a writer which then appear displaced in the particular forms, scenes, and issues of his fiction. Indeed, this is the freedom and pleasure that creative writing allows - the setting forth and prospective resolution of fear and desire in the domain of the 'as if'. This process can be most clearly seen, for a particular writer, at the level of the 'oeuvre'. Indeed, my analyses have necessitated a constant return to the apparently compulsive repetition of certain patterns in the overall sequence of a writer's work. Certain habitual dispositions of the text only become visible when seen repeated in different works. The 'turned back' in Henry James for example, which I explore in chapter 6, when encountered for the first time in a single work, will be read as a detail of realist embellishment, a piece of 'vraisemblance'. But when it is repeated over and again, its recurrence cannot be accounted for by its apparent realism. It suggests that other things are happening which are more closely related to the activity of the writer engaged in producing his fiction than to the specific character (Densher, Milly or Strether) whose turned back it may happen to be.

Thus what seems to be part of the 'code of the real' in a single work may well become a 'symptom' when seen repeated in different works. It is important to stress however that it is both of these things simultaneously, both a symptom and a specific item in the codes of the fiction. If the code is realist, then it is because of the item's realism, its mimetic plausibility, that it can be used by the writer at all. Realism is the most secure and spacious realm for the deposition of forces which contend in the deep subjectivity of writing. Realism accommodates the pressures of fantasy, desire and ideological conflict and thereby enables the writer to display them with innocent pleasure, to disperse them among characters and neutralize them in the local detail of a world elsewhere. Realism

in this important respect afforded a maximum of creative privacy,
it was the discursive place in which a sensitive imagination could
play itself out in freedom and security. In doing this, it mini-
mized that overt psychic stress which has often shown itself in
more subjectivist literature.

This is not to say that nineteenth-century realism always successfully contained the psychological and ideological forces which
might be contending within the realm of imaginative production:
many of the violent gothic episodes which erupted out of that
fiction are sufficient witness to the fact that containment was
never more than provisional.(2) But realism was the negation, the
conjuring away, of subjective immediacy for the writer, and the
symptoms of his repeated imaginary encounters could be dispersed
almost invisibly into the plausible features of the story. The
'symptom' melted into place among the objective images of the text.

In the late nineteenth century the guarantee of creative privacy
afforded by a robust realism was slowly failing. As one might expect, in those areas where this happened it was accompanied by
the growth of symptomatic reading, a refusal to accept the prof-
fered legitimation of the fiction – its 'sincere intention' – at face
value. Amongst those authors who continued the traditional realist
practice (Wells, Galsworthy, Bennett, Gissing, Gosse) the indi
cations of symptomatic reading by them or their public critics,
were negligible. As will become apparent, the prototypical symptomatic readers were Nordau, Lombroso, Nisbet, Mallarmé and
Vernon Lee, as well as the characters in the novels of Meredith,
Conrad and James. The decay of realism and the growth of symptomatic reading were inexorably linked and between them the
writer was left oddly vulnerable to the public gaze. (Meredith's
recurrent metaphor of public nakedness was one of the most
evident signs of a writing left unprotected by the gradual loss of
faith in the form of realism.) The new, obscure writing and the
new symptomatic reading emerged together through the fractures
of realist fiction.

The narrator in Henry James's 'The Sacred Fount', for example,
is a sophisticated symptomatic reader, cleverly suspicious of all
and every act and utterance of those around him, constantly read
ing his fellow guests for the hints, signs and symptoms of an
underlying 'malaise'. His obsessive desire to see and to know is on
the borders of madness and he is considered half insane by other
guests. Yet his unpleasant prying and refusal to take anyone at
face value are not just the bad habits of a gossip-monger. He sus-
pects a deep and complicated psychological relation which will
explain the behaviour of the guests, and his attitude to them is
based upon the attempted recovery of this relation. In this respect
he represents the most corrosive and insidious aspect of the new
reader. He is possessed of a distinctively modern 'knowingness' a
refined suspicion, akin to that of the psychologist, which per-
vades modern literature. 'We have no longer', wrote Symons in
1898, 'the mental attitude of those to whom a story was but a story,
and all stories good.'

Symptomatic reading has become an intellectual reflex of our age. By refusing to take an utterance at its word it treats it as the symptom of a hidden 'problematic' or 'sub-text'. Its initial gesture is one of suspicion or refusal, and above all it refuses to treat a work of literature or a conscious utterance as complete. There is always something further which has been disavowed, repressed, or avoided. Nothing can be taken at face value. In this important respect, there is a direct line from the guilty duplicities and sense of compromise informing the stories of Meredith, Conrad and James which leads to the iterated proclamation by so many modern critics that 'no text is innocent.'

At the very least, the notions of intention, sincerity, and integrity ('wholeness') are made equivocal by this practice. ('A man's most open actions have a secret side to them,' Conrad wrote, and he was not referring to villains alone.) The practice displaces attention away from 'a man's most open actions' towards his 'secret side'. It consequently links the assertions of truth made by a writer to an underlying complex of motives and drives. Again it was Symons who felt this to be happening in the late 1890s when he said that it was no longer possible 'for a writer, at the present day, to be quite straightforward with the old, objective simplicity, in either thought or expression'. Symptomatic reading is the result of an attitude which, when it became widespread, undermined the robust values of objective clarity and reason in the production of literature. Sartre perceived the nature of its attack and the insidiousness of its power in 'What is Literature?' There he discussed the modern critic's tendency to play off the truth-value of the text against its author's underlying desires, and the consequent apparent elevation of the critic over his dead victim:(3)

behind the reasons of reason, which wither, we perceive the reasons of the heart, the virtues, the vices, and that great pain that men have in living.... If we are a bit versed in psychoanalysis, our pleasure is perfect. We shall explain the *Social Contract* by the Oedipus complex and *The Spirit of the Laws* by the inferiority complex. That is, we shall fully enjoy the well-known superiority of live dogs to dead lions.

In a parallel movement there is a tendency in symptomatic reading to confine Goethe's 'open spaces of thought' to the region of servile obsession. The fiction is often read as nothing more than a substitutive formation, and the result is inevitably a denial of the specificity of the literary object. The problem which symptomatic reading poses is the relation between the literary text and its ideological and psychic sub-text; yet, for the reasons that have been outlined, the predominant move is to reduce the former to an inessential mask of the latter. The single most arduous task of the present work has been the attempt to preserve the insight of symptomatic reading without reducing and degrading the specific value of the literary text. It is insufficient for a critic simply to penetrate the phenomenal form of a work in order to reveal its psychological and ideological generative matrix. This is a crucial aspect of the critical labour, but it is what Hegel would call 'a one-sided abstraction'. It falls prey to the old idealist notion that the 'form of appearance' (in this case, the literary work itself) is an inessential husk to be discarded once we penetrate beneath it.

Thus it is simply wrong for Terry Eagleton - one of the most aggressive of all symptomatic readers - to infer that his reading requires the rejection of the surface form of the work in order to elucidate its sub-text. He writes, 'Beneath the "phenomenal" coherence of the literary text lies what we might call the mutilated "sub-text" of its true desires, strategies, operations; and ... literary criticism consists above all in the *refusal* of the "phenomenal" text....'(4) Whilst granting the truth of the sub-text, its discovery does not require the 'refusal' of the 'phenomenal' form of the text itself. Indeed, once Eagleton does this, he is faced with enormous difficulty in accounting for the specific value and pleasure of the text.(5) If a work is treated as nothing but symptom, then indeed this is a valuation of it which makes it the literary equivalent of a sore throat. The critic is privileged by distance, just as the psychoanalyst is. He does not suffer from that myopic distortion which was necessary for the creating of the work of art, his 'blind spot' will be of a different kind (though interestingly enough, to the degree to which the critic shares an inner blindness with the writer, the sub-text will remain invisible to him as well as to the writer).

But the critic must never therefore suppose that the symptom could not have issued in other, useless or destructive kinds of activity. The remarkable and unrepeatable thing is that the contending, subjective forces enter into combination with the modes of art made available by the culture so that the symptom may be wrought into, say, 'The Golden Bowl'. It is insufficient, in my view, for a critic simply to perform the first, negative part of symptomatic reading, which consists in locating the sub text. He must also show what was made of this in the specific aesthetic production of the writer. Thus, in my analysis of George Meredith, I have striven to show the relation between his obsessive, personal preoccupation with shame (the 'mutilated sub-text', in Eagleton's phrase) and the acute sensitivity of his feminism, which was a positive, enduring, and valuable transformation of the sub-text in his novels. A full critical reading is a double process which moves back to the artistic product once it has explored the matrix of its production.

A distinctive mark of symptomatic reading, then, is the way in which, all too often, it collapses the objective content of a statement back into its subjective, ideological moment. Reading in this way, the critic looks for what writers reveal in what they say, rather than what they claim to be true. Sartre understood this perfectly:(6)

But since we find pleasure in foiling the ruses of Chateaubriand or Rousseau, in surprising them in the secret places of their being at the moment they are playing at being the public man, in distinguishing their private motives from their

> most universal assertions ... let them reason, assert, deny,
> refute, and prove; but the cause they are defending must
> be only the apparent aim of their discourse; the deeper goal
> is to yield themselves without seeming to do so.... Let them
> not presume to think in earnest; thought conceals the man,
> and it is the man alone who interests us.

Sartre's irony here is as applicable to Conrad's Marlow as it is to
the modern critic. Both are part of a wide cultural movement in
which attention shifts from the truth-value or verisimilitude of a
statement to the dark motive of its utterance. The symptomatic
reader is always reading between the lines for the ideological complicities and unconscious conflicts of the writer. The kinds of
knowledge acquired in this way are substantial and undeniable –
nostalgia for the old dispensation is useless. Nevertheless, there
remains something Faustian in the price paid for the acquisition of
such knowledge.

It is in constant danger of cynicism, it is a knowledge which
imposes a rigorous testing of scruples if it is not to appear too
'knowing'. Kate Croy, in 'The Wings of the Dove', embodies both
its remarkable perspicuity and its moral ambivalence as she reads
every public word and gesture for hidden complicities and sub-
merged contracts. In the end she finds – like Marlow – that she
has become enmeshed in her own knowing, denied the chance of
happiness by the compromising privilege of her insight. Kate
Croy probes, pushes, guesses all she can about Milly by 'scan-
ning' her for symptoms – and in this case the symptoms are quite
literally those of her terminal illness as well as those of her
desire for Densher. Symptomatic reading in 'The Wings of the
Dove' achieves a macabre literalism, and for Kate Croy it is both
a liberation and an indictment.

'Every portrait that is painted with feeling', wrote Oscar Wilde,
'is a portrait of the artist, not of the sitter.'(7) This, in the
coolness of its negation and displacement, is the classic over-
simplification of symptomatic reading. The portrait is not the
mimetically accurate representation of another, it is indirect self-
expression. Its portrayal is betrayal, both of the sitter (who is
as nothing, a mere vanishing mediator) and of the artist (who
betrays himself and his art by painting a self-portrait instead of
the sitter). The statement also reveals clearly the interconnection
between the loss of faith in realism and the assumption which follows it that representation is now of the artist himself. The act of
symptomatic reading constantly effects this double betrayal, and
it is surely why the smell of treachery attends the demise of realism. Not yet confidently subjectivist or confessional, transitional
novelists were in danger of failing in both the objective and subjective spheres. (Wilde's remark also goes some way to explain the
'decadence' of the period, since it posits a purely self-regarding
art: the other is reduced to the insignificant mediation of one's
own appearance and creativity, and the result is a purely formal
narcissism with no significant objective moment.)

In an important sense, symptomatic reading is constitutive of what it means to be a modern, and the things which made it historically possible were also, crucially, things which made for the increasing difficulty of modern literature. What is revealed in the study of late-nineteenth-century fiction is an accelerating dialectic whereby the growth of this sophisticated kind of reading hastened the collapse of realism, and the collapse of realism reconfirmed the validity of the new kind of reading. Conrad's 'Heart of Darkness' is a remarkable response to, and confirmation of, a constructive circularity in the relationship. It is an enigmatic vindication of the underlying complicity between the new writing and the new reading. Thus, as well as having an important place in the history of modern literature, symptomatic reading has a perfect appropriateness to it. There is a kind of decorum between them which constitutes their positive moment, and it is this which I have tried to express in the following pages.

Part I

1 OBSCURITY AND ENLIGHTENMENT

D'abord la clarté, puis encore la clarté, et enfin la clarté.
Anatole France

We wait for light, but behold obscuritie.
Isaiah 59:9

Strange that the metaphor of light should simultaneously organize
the axes of morality, knowledge, and discourse. At the height of
the Renaissance, a certain J. Smith (what better name for a paradigm of common usage?) wrote in his 'Discourses' of 'The intellectual world being ... made all lucid, intellectual, and shining
with the sunbeams of eternal truth.' The dialectic of light and
darkness has dominated the theological discourse of Europe and in
turn marked those of morality, understanding, and language itself; the light and the dark, the good and the evil, the true and
the false, the 'lucid' and the 'obscure'. A consequence of the same
metaphorical organization of these different fields has been an
identification, through the symbolic opposition of light and darkness, of their respective terms. Truth, goodness and lucidity fall
together in the sunlight, just as falsehood, evil and obscurity
fall together in the shade. These two opposed, contiguous orders
compound their major terms. They promote an insidious identification of lucidity, truth and goodness on the one hand, and
obscurity, falsehood and evil on the other.

Thus, despite elevation to the status of apparently free concepts,
'lucidity' and 'enlightenment' are *radically* aligned by their shared
metaphorical origin. Metaphor engrains the concepts before we
even begin to think about them, and yet so subliminal is this residual metaphorical order that it hardly registers when we use these
words to consider the question of 'clarity', 'obscurity', 'lucidity'
and 'illuminating' or 'enlightened' thinking. In other words, the
question of textual obscurity can never be purely formal nor
purely neutral. The terms are already aligned and grouped into
distinct ideological unities before we begin.

It thus becomes impossible to separate the degree of intellig-
ibility of a text from moral and epistemological considerations.
'Prose', John Middleton Murry tells us in 'The Problem of Style',
(1) 'is the language of exact thinking; it was made for the purpose;
and I suppose that a proposition in Euclid is an elementary example of good style, though in an absolutely non-creative kind.'

Lucidity is a powerful virtue and obscurity a sin. The darkening
or dimming of intellectual light, of the mental vision and the sense
of words is simultaneously felt to be a loss of truth - and the loss
of truth a loss of goodness. This theological equation is made
manifest in both a puritan and utilitarian(2) textual economy: the
chaste pleasure of clear thinking and speaking is a matter of
purity, propriety and economy. 'Proper words in proper places
make the true definition of a style,' and Swift's prose, tried and
tested for clarity against the patience of his two celebrated foot-
men, is taken as exemplary when viewed from within the critical
tradition which it helped to inaugurate. Plain speaking, at one
with the puritan hatred for frills and ornament, for the luxury of
excess, unites the desire for moral strenuousness with a contempt
for obscure discourse. And if ratification of these links and
oppositions were required, then their genesis can be found in
God's first 'fiat' pronounced across the face of darkness when the
obscure was made lucid in the Word.

'That absolute precision of statement which is the mark of excellent prose' is not only a Puritan, but a pragmatic requirement.
An act of verbal clarification was not only God's preliminary to
the creating of the Universe, it was the Royal Society's preliminary to the scientific understanding of the world. In the seven-
teenth century, considered as the high point of English prose
style, the juxtaposition of Puritanism and scientific endeavour
placed the highest premium on lucidity: both began to turn their
back upon 'the conceits and vicious tropes' of classical languages
in order to develop the ideal of a clear, simple vernacular, 'a
close, naked and natural way of speaking'. This rationalist dem-
and for clarity is what underpins Middleton Murry's ideal of good
style as a proposition in Euclid. Behind the powerful desire for
clarity there is all the combined force of the moral and pragmatic
indictment of obscurity.

In this respect the combination of Augustan *claritas*(3) with
Cartesian 'clarté' lent formidable strength to the idea that, in all
areas of discourse, precision is the proof or guarantee of truth.
In the 'Third Meditation',(4) Descartes proposes that clarity of
conception is the condition of validity of the concept itself:

Je suis certain que je suis une chose qui pense; mais ne sais-
je donc pas aussi ce qui est requis pour me rendre certain de
quelque chose? Dans cette première connaissance, il ne se
recontre rien qu'une claire et distincte perception de ce que
je connais; laquelle de vrai ne serait pas suffisante pour
m'assurer qu'elle est vraie, s'il pouvait jamais arriver qu'une
chose que je concevrais ainsi clairement et distinctement se
trouvât fausse. Et partant il me semble que déjà je puis
établir pour règle générale, que toutes les chose que nous
concevons fort clairement et fort distinctement, sont toutes
vraies.

In this respect we can recognize Cartesian thinking in critical
thought about language and literature as far as the present.
Nicely marked in the very title of Noam Chomsky's 'Cartesian

Linguistics', the deep association of precision with truth and the correlative idea that self-consciousness, 'self-transparency', can furnish us with fundamental truths, might well be termed 'Cartesian' criticism, that is to say, a criticism which assumes a normative criterion of exactitude as the indication of the 'truth' and the value of literature. Such a notion was obviously at work behind F. L. Lucas's early attack on 'The Waste Land' for what he called its 'Alexandrianism': 'Disconnected and ill-knit, loaded with echo and allusion, fantastic and crude, obscure and obscurantist - such is the typical style of Alexandrianism.'(5)

Modernist literature, breeding its own kinds of criticism and revaluations, has of course revolutionized our attitude towards the resistance and inaccessibility of difficult literature, and few would now agree with Lucas's judgment on Eliot. Our critical responses have become more 'hermeneutic', even enthusiastically so. Following the institutionalization of literary study, the explosion of interpretations of fictions and poems has raised a fundamental question about 'precise' meaning. We can no longer be content with the transparency theory of prose: that at its best literature can make itself into some kind of invisible medium, a clear medium through which Berkeley saw the 'bare notions and naked, undisguised ideas ... [that are] separated from all that dress and encumbrance of words.' Such a notion of transparency underlies Sutherland's following definition of good prose (and although Cartesianism still has enough residual cultural power to make the definition attractive, the experience of critical practice gives us pause): 'It is good prose when it allows the writer's meaning to come through with the least possible loss of significance and nuance, as a landscape seen through a clear window.'(6)

The undermining of this idea has come from a variety of directions, but undoubtedly the considerable and rapid literary transformations which took place towards the close of the nineteenth century play the crucial part. It became increasingly difficult to hold simply to the received definition and valuations of clarity and obscurity. As early as 1878 the famous American philosopher C. S. Peirce wrote:(7)

> That much-admired 'ornament of logic' - the doctrine of
> clearness and distinctness - may be pretty enough, but
> it is high time to relegate to our cabinet of curiosities the
> antique *bijou*, and to wear about us something better
> adapted to modern uses.

Peirce was not about to abandon totally the ideal of clarity but his uneasiness with the traditional thinking about it is significant. In Europe, in specific modernist forms, the compacted identification of moral, epistemological and discursive orders structured metaphorically upon the opposition of darkness and light began to fall apart. Partly decaying under diverse cultural changes and partly prised open by identifiable literary and philosophical iconoclasms, the dissolution of this triple alliance of terms was, in my view, a most important cultural shift. The period

between the 1870s and the turn of the century produced kinds of
difficulty and obscurity in form, style, technique and vision
distinct from earlier periods and from more traditionally minded
contemporaries.

Our critical vocabulary, within which types and levels of difficulty, forms of imprecision and semantic resistance can be
discriminated, is not a rich one. It is only very recently – and
then only in a programmatic and tentative way – that critics have
endeavoured to produce a 'theory of difficulty', but attention
addressed to the 'blocage' of meaning has been infrequent and
uncoordinated until the last few years. Thus George Steiner poses
the question in terms which require a beginning almost from first
principles:(8)

> After Mallarmé nearly all poetry which matters, and much of
> the prose that determines modernism, will move against the
> current of normal speech. The change is immense and we are
> only now beginning to grasp it. One consequence is an
> entirely new, ontologically motivated, order of difficulty.

The phrase which Steiner uses here, 'ontologically motivated
order of difficulty,' does not seem to me altogether felicitous, but
I think it indicates correctly that difficulty and obscurity become
constitutive of the very being of the art work. In modernism, a
kind of textual resistance emerges which cannot be resolved by
dictionaries, nor ascribed to the cultural remoteness of the text,
nor to the tactics of defamiliarization adopted by a poet to freshen
and renew the language used. As Jürgen Habermas notes:(9)

> Where difficulties of comprehension are the result of cultural,
> temporal, or social distance, we can say in principle what
> further information we would need in order to achieve under-
> standing: we know that we must decipher the alphabet,
> become acquainted with lexicon and grammar, or uncover
> context-specific rules of application. In attempting to explain
> unclear or incomprehensible meaning-associations we are able
> to recognize, within the limits of normal communication, what
> it is that we do not – yet – know.

The obscurities of early modern fiction are not of this sort. We
cannot, even in principle, specify the 'keys' or missing information which will enable us to find the meaning of 'Heart of Darkness', 'The Golden Bowl' or 'One of Our Conquerors'. The
obscurity of modernism is not susceptible to simple de-coding. It
is usually not a matter of information suppressed or omitted which
the critic can patiently recover. It is rather that, despite a remarkable diversity of intent and effect, modernist difficulty
signifies in and by the very act of offering resistance. The formal,
structural difficulties of a text, the kinds of de-formation that it
uses, are inseparable from the way it produces significance, from
its mode of signification. That is to say, the wide range of textual
obscurities which become so formidable in modern writing have
positive functions. They are productive of meaning at the same
time as (apparently) concealing meaning.

It will be objected that all important works of art are in some way difficult and obscure when they first appear, and that modern obscurity is really no different from that of Donne's verse or of Impressionism: the great work of art educates its consumers, and what at first seems incomprehensible soon becomes commonplace: 'First it seems obscure, gnomic, perversely inaccessible; next illuminating, masterly, classic; finally obvious, familiar and traditional. These seem to be the three stages in the growth of any key work of art.'(10) It is certainly true that, in so far as a radically new work of art systematically opposes or disrupts traditional rules and values, then once the public has mastered and internalized the systematic nature of the disruption, consternation gives way to comprehension. But this view of the matter, popularized by the Russian formalists, is a partial and misleading truth. Modernist obscurity is not due simply to the unfamiliarity of the protocols upon which it is based. It is rather that a key protocol upon which it is based is obscurity. Modernism not only attacks this or that particular artistic tradition (such as naturalism), but also the general preconditions of precise and coherent forms of representation. The fascinating thing is that it never ceases to represent or to mean, but that a major means of its representation is obscurity. Obscurity is used, in a wide range of different ways, to produce new kinds of significance. Again this is the opposite of many previous moments when a new way of seeing gave rise to charges of obscurity from contemporaries. Only in the analysis of diverse forms and uses of obscurity can we understand this fundamental aspect of modern writing. Even though the word 'obscurity' is obviously obscure in itself, a non-technical term handicapped by carrying the 'inappropriate suggestion that clear matter has been wantonly and artificially darkened,'(11) I have preferred it to 'difficulty' and 'ambiguity' for various reasons: obscurity is the indispensable word for a literature which begins positively to adopt darkness as a primary organizing metaphor, an 'écriture d'ombres'. Furthermore, neither 'difficulty' nor 'ambiguity' would centre the discourse in quite the way I wish. Not all the areas of hesitation, vagueness and concealment in these authors are areas of difficulty: difficulty applies largely to the language of a text, its style or syntax, but often in these novels the obscurity is of a visual nature, a matter of oblique point of view or concealed vantage within a scene, and this is not a matter of 'difficulty' but rather one of obscured vision.

Neither is 'ambiguity' a sufficient term to cover the diversity of semantic imprecision and textual opacity in Meredith, Conrad and James. Ambiguity takes its place alongside other subversive modulations of meaning such as lying, secrecy, equivocation, ellipsis, enigma and euphemism, all of which are found as important and determining structures in the novels. In addition, ambiguity from Empson through New Criticism to the present has within it a determining critical history which takes the term away from the area under consideration. This is particularly true of criticism on Henry James, where the traditional choice of ambiguity as the focal

category to describe structures in his fiction has led to a significant failure to analyse their full range of opaque kinds of
significance.(12)

Indeed, this 'New Critical' cherishing of ambiguity is no more
than an inversion of the equally cherished ideal of total clarity,
and as such offers a purely numerical, or economical superiority
(ambiguity as 'richness'). It failed to analyse the function of
obscurity as a structure of meaning rather than a subtle multiplier
of sense. Even in Empson, where there is an exhilarating sense of
the collaborative choice between writer and reader, a feeling of
open-endedness and potential variety in the reading process,
there is no real discussion of the semantics of imprecision, 'blocage', and concealment: instead meaning is subsumed beneath the
idea of complexity (complex words, types of ambiguity).

Meredith, Conrad and James have all been accused of obscurity
(13) in the sense that some clear matter had been artificially and
incompetently darkened. This common accusation of muddle, with
its Laurel and Hardy connotation of textual confusion, is a rare
sort of obscurity in these writers. Most of the sorts of unclear
meaning in their novels and stories are not amenable to retrospective rearrangement into a 'correct' text, which muddle implies.

The problem is in the way obscurity has been traditionally conceived as a contingent and avoidable surface effect in a text which
prevents us reaching an already constituted, pure message under-
neath. This is the 'dark filter' notion of obscurity - take it away
and behind it there is a pre-existing, luminous meaning, a lucid
content which the inadequacy of style or presentation has made
hard to 'make out'. It assumes the possibility of paraphrase, that
someone else (or even the same author in a more intelligent or
perceptive moment) could have written the same message with
conciseness and lucidity.

But modes of obscurity are important signifying structures in
literature and carry distinct and distinctive kinds of meaning
which are not secondary to an anterior obscured content. Obscurity signifies in the very act of obscuring, and in a rich variety of
ways which are linked to its contexts of appearance (narrative,
cultural, psychological). Concepts with blurred edges, as Wittgenstein pointed out in his 'Philosophical Investigations', are not just
second-rate 'clear' concepts. There are several points where
Wittgenstein's thinking comes very close to the concerns of these
three novelists (particularly in relation to the ideas of private
language, language-games and 'blurred' concepts). He writes:(14)

   - 'But is a blurred concept a concept at all?' - Is an
   indistinct photograph a picture of a person at all? Is it even
   always an advantage to replace an indistinct picture by a
   sharp one? Isn't the indistinct one often exactly what we
   need?

In these three writers, the indistinct is often 'exactly what we
need.' It is not necessarily a case of two terms, precise/imprecise,
placed in an exact and unalterable relation to each other, for, as
Husserl remarks in 'The Paris Lectures', clarity is a function of

context and level. In his introductory essay to 'The Paris Lectures', Peter Koestenbaum writes:(15)

There is no absolute criterion of precision. Precision is a
function of context and subject-matter. Already Aristotle,
in his *Nichomachean Ethics* and Mill, in his *Utilitarianism*,
refer to what might be called the 'principle of contextual
precision'. To accept Husserl's analyses we must grant that
vague experiences are legitimate objects of philosophic
scrutiny. We cannot restrict our efforts to the simple, the
clear, and the distinct. For example, the structures of
experience that are analysed under 'ego', 'intersubjectivity',
'horizons', 'transcendental subjectivity', 'Lebenswelt',
'intentionality', and the like, are neither clear, simple, nor
distinct. Quite to the contrary, the *analysandum* consists of
obscure, fuzzy, and cloudy clusters of experience. Therefore the present premise is that precision, i.e., clarity and
distinctness, is a variable, one that is a function of context.
The same premise is prerequisite to accepting, even in
principle, the existentialist analyses of guilt, anxiety, death,
my body, encounter, freedom, boredom, Mitsein, self-
deception and transcendence.

My approach is not phenomenological, but this long quotation is
worth giving in full. The list of intrinsically unclear material cited
includes several of the central notions related to obscurity in
Meredith, Conrad and James. Meredith's relations to the image of
his own body and to self-deception; Conrad's relation to the idea
of 'transcendent horizon'; James's relation to intersubjective
encounter and anxiety; all these relations are productive of
textual obscurity. Since the opposition of precision to imprecision
is not absolute but provisional, the kind and degree of difficulty
or vagueness in these novels is decided by contextualization:
obscurity, as Husserl remarks, is a variable. Not all the novels
under discussion are unclear all the time or in the same way;
there are zones and registers of semantic indecidability which
depend for their meaning upon relations with clearer parts of the
text. Meaning in a novel rests upon the relation of the explicit to
the implicit, the obvious to the hidden, and not upon one side or
the other of this barrier.

The powerful and insidious metaphor of light and dark which is
invoked so often in relation to a piece of discourse is thus significant in determining thinking about a wide range of perplexing
structures, and it becomes difficult to think against the grain of
this metaphor. But unless we do so, the real nature of the problem involved is itself obscured. How a thing is obscured in a text
is itself significant. It carries meaning such that, to believe only
the 'clear' truth 'behind' the difficulty to be the 'actual' meaning,
is to produce a partial (and inadequate) reading. There is usually
no pre-existing, homely version of the passage. Its significance
arises from a structured interrelation of three elements: its con-
text(s); the specific form, trope, or type of obscurity; the
imputed information content seen in relation to the degree of

difficulty and the exact nature of its de-coding. The articulation
of these three axes delimits the semantic field of obscureness and
frames the area of its interpretation. It must be added that, in
the three novelists looked at here, and in much of 'difficult' modernist prose generally, the third element, the 'imputed information
content' or denotative axis, may be of marginal significance or
disappear altogether ('Finnegans Wake'), so that one is left only
with the interplay of contexts and tropes.

When this happens as a general principle of construction in the
text, without guilt or nostalgia for the loss of denotation (as in
'Finnegans Wake'), then obscurity itself becomes an inadequate
term: we are not being tricked, beguiled or led into a search for
the concealed message (or at least we should not be: much Anglo-
American criticism of 'Finnegans Wake' still insists upon trying to
read it quite anachronistically as possessing some final deep narrative beneath the dark surface of paronomasia.)(16) In this
sense it would be wrong to call 'Finnegans Wake' an obscure work.
The use of the term is much more suitable for novelists like Meredith, Conrad and James where the desire for denotation is still
strong, and where its eclipse is partial or incomplete. In their
novels there is little opportunity for an abandoned and guiltless
'jouissance' in the luxury of infinite connotation. They are
occluded or mixed fictions in which a traditional respect for truth,
sincerity, and mimetic accuracy vies with deep uncertainty and
difficulty. Even though there are places where denotation and
reference seem to be slipping away, the narrative quest (and the
correlative referential quest of the reader to 'see what happens'
to X or Y) is still of central importance. Indeed, in Conrad this
uncertain slippage of referential fixity provokes a metaphysical
quest for meaning in a world where signs have become sinister
and enigmatic. An unsettling, almost Borgesian feeling of 'ficciones'
gathers round those hazy coastlines and dark continental interiors.

Just as the traditional notion of obscurity makes it difficult to
understand that the opposition of precision to imprecision is not
absolute but relative and contextually determined, so also it per-
plexes the matter by opposing exterior form to interior content in
a similar, absolute way. What I have termed the trope or type, it
calls the 'envelope', and its activity is simply to recover the message from its enigmatic envelope: 'mais pour extraire ce message
de son enveloppe énigmatique, il faut de la patience, de la
délicatesse et du temps.'(17) By casting the matter in this form,
the only significant thing is the enveloped message, what I have
called the imputed information content of the text or passage. But
often the 'message' only takes on significance in relation to its
'envelope', to the way it is contained. The form of enclosure may
be as important as, or more important than, the enclosed.

We have no better representation of this than the letter - or what
James calls the 'communication' - sent to Merton Densher from
Milly Theale at the end of 'The Wings of the Dove', and which
Kate Croy burns unopened. Those last few chapters of 'The Wings
of the Dove' are as oblique and elliptical as anything which James

ever wrote, and it is very difficult indeed for a reader to fathom
exactly what is taking place. In this respect Densher's received
'communication' is a perfect index of the way in which communication as such operates in the novel. The contents of that letter
are never revealed: it is probable, from the narrative context,
that it contains a gift of immense wealth, from Milly to Densher,
a fabulous fortune which will enable him to marry Kate, yet he
refuses to open it, and James refuses to affirm to the reader that
this is what it contained: its 'message' remains a tantalizing promise of a Victorian romance ending, the content of Milly's letter
is quite probably the traditional magical gift of money which
enables hero and heroine to marry - signed, sealed and delivered.
But throughout 'The Wings of the Dove' James has signalled his
rejection of that kind of narrative certainty, with its concomitant
public affirmations - the novel begins to exclude the type of
reader who expects and demands these things in his reading: the
refusal to open communication is fundamental to the narrative and
authorial positions inscribed within it.

This applies in equal measure to the second letter, from Milly's
New York lawyers, which Densher also refuses to open and which
he wanted to send back to them with seal unbroken, 'intact and
inviolate'. The communication if opened reveals an object of desire,
immediate material gratification, but it also degrades and defiles
the receiver, who is a fallen and ashamed man. This is pursued
more fully in the chapter on James below, but Densher's desire
that the communication stay closed perfectly illustrates a wider
narrative linkage in James's later works, between desire, obscurity and knowledge - that if communication remains closed this is
because an object of desire which may defile and contaminate, is
'enclosed' within it, and by keeping such information sealed, the
receiver remains uncompromised. Obscurity contains desire. A
receiver who hurries to open the letter (Kate Croy) reveals herself by that very act of seizure as vulgar and 'previous'. This is
a replay in tight symbolic form of a repeated movement in James.
Densher uses the sealed message as a test ('You wanted to measure the possibilities of my departure from delicacy,' as Kate
remarks) of the most subtle and oblique kind. Densher may well
guess what is within the envelope, as indeed may the reader, but
to open it up is to fall. His integrity is guaranteed by the envelope and the flames, by his refusal of certainty, by his willed
desire to live on the threshold of positive knowledge but not to
grasp that knowledge. To know is to fall (made explicit in James's
story 'The Tree of Knowledge') and James subtly rewrites his own
version of the Genesis myth in a particular modernist idiom. I
believe it can be shown in James's novels that he associates, at
some deep level, the idea of obscurity of information with purity:
that if meanings are so elliptical that they remain 'intact and inviolate', then this containment of desire guarantees the integrity
and 'virginity' of the receiver. Overt representation becomes a
source of moral danger, and it is only by staying as far outside
communication as possible, by remaining outside the letter, that

one might 'get off'. Innocence in the late James is not granted by
simplicity of utterance but by an almost impenetrable reticulation
of surface which envelops that which is desired and feared, the
'message' which brings satisfaction and contaminating vulgarity.

It is insufficient then, when dealing with imprecise material, to
ascribe its meaning only to an anterior message which has been
muddled up in the telling (though of course under certain circumstances this may well be exactly the sort of obscurity involved,
but with modernist fiction it is not common). Reading does not
consist in de-coding some primary, pure sense established before
the writing came and covered it over. As Jean-Noël Vuarnet remarks:(18)

> Que lire ne consiste pas à déchiffrer un sens institué, un
> sens premier pur et propre établi avant que ne se produise
> l'écriture, que lire ne consiste pas à reconstituer l'image
> réelle ou fictive d'un supposé auteur identique à soi, voilà
> ce qu'il convient de n'oublier plus jamais.

The referent is not separable from its literary language, it is a
component of that language in all its complexity. The latter part
of Vuarnet's remark - that reading does not consist in recon-
stituting some real or fictional image of the author whom we
suppose to be always some self-identical being behind the text -
relates closely to the third opposed pair of terms which a discussion of obscurity necessarily involves: intention/contingency.
Thus, 'Did he really mean that or was he just muddled?' always
resolves its own question with respect to the imputed conscious
intention of the author.

Subject as are all questions of authorial intention to the ancient
blunderbuss of Wimsatt's 'intentional fallacy',(19) the opposition
between an underlying, private intention and a messy surface
transcription needs very careful scrutiny. There is on record an
apposite anecdotal exchange between Alphonse Daudet and
Mallarmé:(20)

> 'My dear Mallarmé', said Daudet, 'you should write and tell
> us - it would be most interesting - whether it is of your own
> accord that you withdraw into darkness, where only an *élite*
> can follow you, or whether your obscurity is involuntary.'
> The poet had no intention of being drawn into discussion
> 'Mais est-ce', he replied, 'que l'opération même d'écrire n'est
> pas mettre du noir sur du blanc?'

However arch Mallarmé's reply appears to be, it is not just a witty
rejoinder to an inept question. It was precisely the intention of
the author, and the concomitant authority which this gave him
over his own work, which modernist obscurity brought into doubt.
For a sophisticated writer like Mallarmé (or like James - the closeness of this anecdote to James's stories 'The Figure in the Carpet'
and 'John Delavoy' is most striking) it became increasingly apparent that the words on the page only ever operated by indirection
- they necessarily covered something up in the process of un-
covering. Fiction or poetry often had its roots in aspects of the
psyche which were not fully conscious and therefore not clearly

'intended' - though always amenable to a host of simultaneous or subsequent intentions. Obscurity within literature is one way of signalling the subversion of purposive reason (particularly in a period dominated by quasi-scientific naturalism).

At this point it is necessary to say that there are different but interrelated kinds of intention. As Alastair Fowler has written in his sane and persuasive essay 'Intention Floreat'(21) there is the 'fore-idea', the pure and germinal idea of this or that novel or poem: Virginia Woolf's 'It will never be so good as it is now in my mind - unwritten.' This 'fore-idea' or preliminary kind of intention can change during the act of composition and become altered by a variety of other intentions: by a specifically 'literary intention', the kind of aesthetic aspiration (to seriousness, lightness, to achieve something of *that* level of seriousness, the kind of thing Conrad dwells upon in his Author's Notes); by 'generic intention' which Fowler describes as overlapping the former sort and intending to 'present a piece of discourse as a work of art, or as a particular kind of work (such as the kind whose artifactual status is deliberately ambiguous)' - and this is obviously of particular relevance to the three authors discussed here; by 'semantic intention', the localized intention of sentence, word or paragraph interacting in the endeavour to realize the initial fore-idea modified by the feedback mechanisms of writing. This overall intention, subject to such modifications as the above, is also subject to what Fowler calls, in defiance of some theorists, 'unconscious intention'. He adds:(22)

We need not suppose that literary intention is always deeply buried; but it always includes an unconscious or spontaneous component. Every honest writer will confess to effects happier than he meant; no writer knows all of the purpose he reaches out to fulfil. Indeed, he may know almost none of it. That is not important: it is for the author to intend, for the critic to discover and know that intention. The critic may be far better able to rationalize about the work, just as an analyst may be more aware of the motives governing his patient's dream.

Despite Fowler's assurances, there is something too pat about treating unconscious motivation as a variety of intention. As well as making it seem that the unconscious is simply a less accessible kind of consciousness (a bland and passive 'not-yet-conscious') it means that the problem of textual production can be resolved into the notion of a 'family' of intentions - preliminary, literary, generic, semantic and unconscious. But (as Oedipus might have remarked) the unconscious is not 'one of the family'. Fowler's domesticated unconscious is conceived as simply the last addition in a sequence of intentions which he imagines to be like a row of editors, compositors and readers all participating creatively. The sense of an heterogeneous set of drives which may disrupt and interrupt conscious production is completely absent. As with so many intentionalists (especially those who advocate a strong form of intentionalism like E. D. Hirsch, Jr.)(23) literature is made to sound like philosophy, that Cartesianism of which I spoke at the outset in which self-consciousness and agreeability to reason furnish the process and material of its production. Fowler's essay, though analytically superior to much intentionalism in usefully discriminating generic and semantic intention (which I find valuable in relation to Conrad and Meredith) is a kind of redaction criticism which views the writing of poetry or fiction as something carried out by a small, and scrupulously polite committee which is always in agreement with itself.

The fictions examined here are not like that, nor can their obscurities be 'cleared up' by appeal to a sophisticated concept of authorial intention. Certainly, different levels of motivation are visible in the novels, letters, prefaces and essays of all three writers, and these are both fairly accessible and important in understanding the composition of the works. But it emerges very quickly that the problem of obscurity here has something fundamental to do with the absence of self-conscious intention (24) and it is precisely this absence which is important as a creative element in the writing. It is because certain things are opaque to the novelists themselves that the novels are written. This may not be generalizable beyond the three writers here, but it is something which has forcefully emerged in these three cases. There is a kind of doubleness in their obscurities, a Janus quality which looks in towards the novelist with reassurance and out towards his public with composure. The obscurities are neither 'contingent' (off-days, slips, lapses, decline in writing power) nor 'intentional' (the self-conscious fulfilment of a previously constituted plan). They are, rather, moments when knowledge threatens to destroy something so fundamentally constitutive of the fiction-making that its clear and direct revelation would silence the discourse. Put more positively, it is this 'blindness' which drives the writer on to fictional creation and its creative insight.

The metaphor which comes to mind to describe this is the retina of the eye. Obscurity is like a 'yellow spot' in the text, at the centre of which we find the blind point where the optic nerve joins the retinal surface enabling one to see. Without this opacity at the centre of the retina where nerves and vision conjoin, there is no sight. Writers (all writers?) have areas of opacity, of troubled vision which exist because they are areas of difficulty and sensitivity for the writer concerned and hence partly resistant to self-conscious exposure.

But this would be to say simply that obscurity in Meredith, Conrad and James was quasi-defensive, and I want to claim something rather different and rather more positive than this: that these three men could only write their novels on the basis of both fundamental and localized opacities in their texts, and that these opacities become a fecund source of exploratory understanding about the place and nature of subjectivity and culture on the threshold of modernism. That total clarity, even had it been possible in these intensely private and resistant areas, would have engendered a lesser achievement.

The energies of concealment in Meredith, Conrad and James, conflicting with the traditional communicative norms and sincerities of the genre, charge the field of encounter between subject and language with unexpected potential. Stable and traditional responses to sincerity, honesty, openness, fluency and exactness crumble into uncertainty. Secrets, lies, hesitations, enigmas and equivocations flood the texts, washing away many of the existing boundaries between public and private, true and false.

My understanding of these novels could thus be described as closer to a modern rewriting of Pascal ('Le coeur a ses raisons que la raison ne connaît point') than to Descartes. Different sorts of conscious intention operating locally and globally in the text are traversed by unconscious desires and ideological (25) forces within the culture. The text is the resulting disposition or 'settlement' of these different forces coming together. I do not think that the widely noted obscurity of these three most important 'English' novelists of the turn of the century can be sufficiently explained by reference to any one of these forces. The narratives are modes of bringing together on a single discursive ground the more or less dispersed intentions of the author and the ideological and psychic forces within which he is held. The novels can be seen as textual dispositions of these vectors in the structure of writing in a way which is analogous to the concept of *Geistesbeschäftigung* (mental disposition) used by the Dutch critic André Jolles.(26) From this perspective, narrative is formed under the pressure of desire, intention and ideology, the interaction of all three of these offering the site of a discursive solution to their disruptions, conflicts and combinations. In this sense, narrative is the most omnivorous, greedy kind of discourse in its desire to satisfy need: psychic material and ideology, the position of subjectivity (both specifically and generally) are taken up and drawn together, disposed in the single configuration of the text. The novelist's procedure is much more opportunistic and heterogeneous than the strict intentionalist would allow. Jean Cocteau's remark that 'La poésie trouve d'abord et cherche après' seems to me closer to the truth of much literary composition.(27)

Obscurity in this respect is often a boundary function within a fiction, marking a point of interdiction or contradiction (a 'confusion of tongues and gainsaying') between these different elements, like those ever-recurrent coastline fogs in Conrad between the land and the sea. Cryptic and indefinite forms often eclipse the boundary between unconscious desires and conscious intention and between cultural norms and subjective need: they are the occluded frontiers between contradictory formations in the novel, areas like those in 'The Ambassadors' where 'parts were not to be discriminated nor differences comfortably marked ... and what seemed all surface one moment seemed all depth the next.'

This goes some way towards making sense of obscure fiction which appears to be the result of an 'interference' with the message:(28)

In such a model 'difficulty' would, presumably, be an
interference-effect between underlying clarity and
obstructed formulation. This, roughly, is the classical and
Cartesian reading of opaqueness, a reading whose inference
is necessarily negative.
I have suggested that such a classical idea of opaqueness is subject to many qualifications, but there are kinds of disrupted
communication for which the metaphor of interference-effect is
accurate. Nevertheless, the question of what is interfering with
what has usually been avoided. The interference has been thought
of as a kind of 'noise' which introduces meaningless, external
crackle into the basic message. Although this has been adopted as
a conscious procedure in certain aleatory music by John Cage, the
interference-effect in fiction usually concerns a conflict between
distinct semantic energies, and both of them 'internal' to the
creation of the fiction. In this sense there is no outside to the
text from which 'noise' could be introduced, except in the sense
of historical and cultural remoteness referred to in Steiner's description of 'contingent difficulties': noise in this sense accumulates
in the intervening historical distance, it is the static crackling on
the lines of cultural transmission. But within a fiction there is
often interference between contradictory movements in the structure, the conflict of (sometimes radical) differences.
   This is particularly visible in Meredith's later novels. Time and
again Meredith introduces dual narrators who battle over the telling of the story. In 'Sandra Belloni' he struggles against the
interruptions of The Philosopher, a figure who tries to introduce
a new level of analytical seriousness into the romantic drama. Even
though he knows such a move is likely to reduce his appeal to a
mass audience ('The which is naturally resented, and away flies
my book back at the heads of the librarians, hitting me behind
them a far more grievous blow'), the conflict actually enables him
to say things - at the risk of a fragmented and disrupted narrative - which he could not otherwise do. Meredith's long, mock-
eighteenth-century chapter headings are always of significance,
and in the same novel we find chapter XXX entitled: 'Of The
Double-Man In Us, And The Great Fight When These Are Full-
Grown.' This warring doubleness is of great importance not only
in Meredith but also in Conrad (especially his story The Secret
Sharer), James (The Private Life) and the period generally. It is
explored at much further length below (pp. 48-52), but its
importance in connection with fictional obscurity in the period
cannot be over-estimated. It relates both to the concept known in
linguistics as the doubling of the speaker (first introduced by
Charles Bally as 'dédoublement de la personnalité')(29) and to the
long tradition of 'Doppelgänger'. As early as the 1820s, Friedrich
Schlegel related the idea of internal division of self to the idea of
'an eddying stream of speech and counter-speech', the conflicts
of an inner dialogue undermining then rebuilding subjectivity:(30)
   So tief und fest [ist] übrigens diese innre Zwiefachheit und
   Duplicität - welchen Ausdruck ich aber hier nicht in dem

gewöhnlichen moraiischen Verstande [brauche], sondern in
einem rein psychologischen und höhern, mehr metaphysischen
Sinne nehme - in unserm Bewußtseyn eingewurzelt, daß wir
selbst dann, wenn wir allein sind, oder allein zu seyn glauben,
immer eigentlich [noch] zu Zweyen [denken und dieß auch so]
in unserm Denken finden, und unser innerstes tiefstes Seyn
als ein wesentlich dramatisches anerkernnen müssen.

In another Meredith novel, ''The Amazing Marriage', the battling
narrators struggle to censor and retell each other's version of the
story with vociferous energy: parts of the narrative remain un-
told, other parts are narrated twice, and once again the values of
unity and lucidity are usurped by the emergence of an uncertain
'dialogic' relation of public and private self. In Meredith we can
find many such moments of obscure duality, splitting voices,
inner and outer selves, schizoid representation and cleavage of
subjectivity which reveal him as at times closer to Maurice Blanchot than to his Victorian contemporaries:(31)

   ... et pourquoi un seul parlant, une seule parole ne
peuvent-ils jamais réussir, malgré l'apparence, à le nommer?
  - Il faut être au moins deux pour le dire.
  - Je le sais. Il faut que nous soyons deux.
  - Mais pourquoi deux? Pourquoi deux paroles pour dire
une même chose?
  - C'est que celui qui la dit, c'est toujours l'autre.

Meredith's 'dialogical novels'(32) are full of the most unexpected
eruptions and diversions which can be traced back to a conflict of
domains and authority in the writing. He is witness to a 'legitimation crisis' in which the traditional, easily assumed mantle of
single author/ity would no longer quite fit. Partly - as in 'Sandra
Belloni' - this is to do with the increased division of labour and
intellectual discourse at the end of the nineteenth century: the
uneasy, self-conscious partnership of philosopher and novelist in
'Sandra Belloni' betokens the irrevocable splitting of these two
domains, the passing of the age of George Eliot. But also it is a
result of a rapid transformation in the relationship between reader
and writer and, correlatively, a destabilized conception of what
constitutes one's public and private self. The crossing of textual
surfaces in Meredith, the interrupted dialogues and sudden
plunges from one sort of writing to another can be understood in
relation to this separation and inmixing of the domains of subjectivity. Interference indexes the painful incompatibility of some
of these domains in the absence of a fixed subject, creator of a
univocal and totally unified narrative 'sense'. Many of the vertiginous swoops and leaps in Meredith's prose are the sudden movement from one level to another, a textual 'alpinisme' to match the
physical self-image that he created for, and of, himself.

The tendency in all three writers is to write such problems and
conflicts into the form of their work rather than simply write
about them. When the afflicting anxiety is a dualism of authorial
role, or a feeling of chronic isolation from certain public realms
of meaning and communion (as in Conrad), then it is inevitable

that this should be so. All three writers felt they occupied a difficult and distanced position with respect to the idea of sincere and open communication, and to have written about that in a sincere, open, and communicative way would have been either impossible or a grotesque act of bad faith. Such things are not spoken but shown in the difficulty of speaking and the not-said. This 'not-said' (the 'yellow spot' of my earlier metaphor) is not an absence to be supplied, some insufficiency which the reader must replenish. It is not a provisional 'unsaid' that one can permanently eliminate, it is rather the necessary not-said of the text, it is on account of its not being clearly articulated that the novel establishes its distinctive power and reality.

It can be shown in the work of James for example that there is a deep, unresolvable contradiction which centres on the idea of 'vulgarity' (see chapter 6, pp. 140-6). On the one hand James is sexually haunted by a scene of intimate liaison, his novels hover on the threshold of wanting to represent affairs and weekend encounters. But at the same time, such a desire, which animates so many of his scenes and narratives, is to him horribly 'vulgar': it would immediately compromise this fastidious and sensitive New Englander with the unpalatable evidence of his predilections. Both private desire and public fear centre on the idea of vulgarity, it both attracts and repels. Now this as such cannot be clearly said - never is clearly said - in the novels, but it is silently shown as their production, it is the repeated playing out of this conflict of meaning and desire which becomes the fiction. The radical division in the idea of vulgarity produced by the contradictory desire and fear is not resolved or absorbed by the books, but shown by them. Thus the more or less complex opposition which gives structure to the work cannot be effectively spoken by it, even though it is that which constitutes its statement and gives it flesh. The work shows in its form what it cannot say, and it is the silence of the unsaid which gives it existence. James could never say, 'I have a voyeuristic fascination for sexual intrigue which I mediate into the most refined and sophisticated forms of discourse,' but the novels and stories obliquely show this again and again. And further, that this is never clearly said is surely right and proper: for out of the silence which replaces that banal and embarrassing confession emerge 'The Sacred Fount' and 'The Ambassadors'. In this respect James seems to me exemplary of Pierre Macherey's aphoristic statement that one only manages to say something because other things cannot or must not be said ('car pour parvenir à dire quelque chose, il y en a d'autres qu'il ne faut pas dire').(33)

These writers, then, considerably modify the inherited conception of lucid writing. The traditional identification of unclear discourse with moral failure and truthlessness is challenged and deposed. The three absolutes upon which the interference model of obscurity had always rested were either recast or cast out: technical precision as the sole guarantee of truth dissolves at those boundaries where vagueness, darkness and contradiction

are foregrounded as structures of meaning in the fiction; the
opposition between a pure internal message and a murky external
linguistic envelope cannot be maintained in a period when communication alters significantly with respect to all its terms -
sender, receiver, code and contact - where communication in
fiction no longer endeavours to be just a transparent bearer of
fact or feeling but imbricates the form with the narrative, erasing
the distinction between something said and saying something in
such a way that 'the' or 'a' meaning has to be searched for at
more than one level; and the opposition between intended meaning
and contingent interference, the belief that the final arbitration
of significance is the intended meaning of the author 'behind' the
confusion, also comes to seem one-sided and inadequate. The
period in question problematized the traditionally conceived unities
of author, genre and audience. Authorial intentions are still evident and important, but undermined and challenged by cultural
and unconscious forces which subvert the sense of total authorial
control and legitimation in the process of writing. The result is a
distinctive incompleteness to the narratives, like one of Marlow's
'inconclusive experiences', which hints that the 'real' significance
of the story is elsewhere and not given as an identifiable part of
the whole.

Frequently, then, the creative process in these fictions seems
to emerge from things that cannot be directly said but which are
shown by and in their opacities. Reading these novels means
attending to their 'darkening forms' without a nostalgic and
offended desire for Cartesian clarity, for it is precisely the Car
tesian ego as source of that clarity which comes under pressure
in this period. The complex cultural shifts and slips which mark
this change are explored in the following chapter.

2 OBSCURE WRITING AND PRIVATE LIFE, 1880-1914

If I were to talk to myself out loud in a language not understood by those present my thoughts would be hidden from them.

Ludwig Wittgenstein

Seek discourse with the shades.

Joseph Conrad

In his essay on culture, first published in 1883 and immensely popular in England and America, Ralph Waldo Emerson wrote: 'I must have children, I must have events, I must have a social state and a history, or my thinking and speaking want body or basis.' (1) Emerson had two simple things in mind: that social standing imparts weightiness and value to one's words; and that language is social. Unless one is fully part of society, integrated into the heart of its public and private life, linked to it by family relations, by participant action, by social status and by history, then one's discourse is alienated, it is without fixity or firm social origin and is therefore rendered somehow insubstantial. Emerson's is a classic expression of the idea that communication is the possession of the tribe, and that to speak clearly and effectively, with 'body and basis' one must be indisputably of the tribe, speaking to it in its own language. Although he would not have put it in this way, Emerson is making plain a basic socio-linguistic postulate about origins and effective communication - that community and communication share more than a common etymology, and that distance from the norms and values of a language community increases the difficulty of immediate and clear communication with it:(2)

Familiarity more than any other one thing, would seem to determine clarity. Clarity's model of models, the prose of John Dryden, seems far from clear to a student whose prose reading has started at Thomas Hardy and soared to Ernest Hemingway. Conversely, a psychological report incomprehensible to me opens like a flower to a psychologist ... Familiarity means reassurance. Clarity's first job is to make us feel at home. We want to see where we are.

For the innovative artist, this pact between the community and communication has to be broken. Formal innovation, the infraction of syntactic and narrative rules, the forging of a new lexicon and style, the breaking of established boundaries of genre and

judgment, any of these things is simultaneously a removal of self
and art from the normative matrices of the language. This is of
course a double process, for social alienation makes it correspondingly difficult to adopt the language of the other. Publication
under these circumstances becomes a central problem. The recip-
rocity of values which is understood to guarantee the exchange
process underlying publication is thrown into jeopardy by the
author's separation from the realm of his addressee, the 'public'.
The author has to confront the question of how to communicate
without being compromised by the predictable or insidious structure of expectation and value held in the language. The problem
of reception - who exactly is one writing for? - raises itself more
acutely the further the writer feels himself from the mainstream
of the reading public. It is this relation of artistic idiolects to
the dominant bourgeois expectations, responses and judgment
which became so complicated towards the end of the nineteenth
century.(3)

We still have no standard, detailed history of the publication
and reception of fiction after the collapse of the three-decker
under pressure from the circulating libraries in the decade 1887-
97.(4) The circulating libraries, especially the two giants, Mudie's
and W. H. Smith, had kept authors, readers and publishers tied
into an extremely stable and predictable structure of expectation
about novels and novel-reading from the 1840s to the 1880s, and
in that period the form flourished.(5) 'We have become a novel-
reading people, from the Prime Minister down to the last-appointed
scullery-maid,' declared Anthony Trollope in 1870, '... all our
other reading put together hardly amounts to what we read in
novels.' And in 1892 Edmund Gosse wrote that the tyranny of the
novel has never been 'more irresistible', and he added 'the Victorian has been peculiarly the age of the triumph of fiction.'(6)
In the 1860s, writers like Bulwer-Lytton, Thackeray, Trollope and
George Eliot were receiving four figure sums for their novels in a
period of immense commercial prosperity for fiction.

We are inclined to think of Meredith, Conrad and James as the
natural successors to the mid-century novelists, with perhaps a
slightly 'elevated' public, but not substantially different from that
of their predecessors: the end of the three-decker was more than
compensated by the drastic reduction in book prices from 31s.6d.
to 6s., which the move to cheap, one-volume novel publication
involved.

But there is evidence to show that, by the late 1880s the fiction-
reading public had begun to split into two different groups. Of
course the so-called 'reading public' is never entirely homogeneous,
and as Louis James, Michael Sadleir and Richard Altick (7) have
shown, the Victorian novel market was already polarized to a
certain extent around the 'respectable' novel and the yellowback.
The former was usually published in parts (Dickens's preferred
method of publication, and 'Middlemarch' was also sold initially in
eight parts) or as a three-decker; the yellowback was either a
reprint of the most popular 'respectable' novels or cheap (and often
lurid) romances and mystery fiction.

But with the end of the three-decker the market for the 'respectable' novel seems to have split internally into an 'élite' or
reviewers' public and the more traditional Victorian public. Again
and again in the reviews of Meredith, Conrad and James we meet
the same distinction (which to a great extent was in itself formed
around these three novelists) between an élite and popular
audience:(8)

> Whosoever knows them knows that Mr Meredith's novels are
> marked by great and rare qualities; but that he makes so
> constant, so urgent a demand on the imagination, his thought
> is so subtle and penetrating, and his modes of expression
> are sometimes so dark with excess of light that he does not
> succeed very well with the 'ordinary reader'.

> The appearance of a new work from his [Meredith's] pen is
> hailed by every journal that occupies itself with literature
> as the great literary event of the day ... [yet] Popular, in
> the sense in which Dickens and Walter Scott on the one hand
> were popular, or on the other in which Miss Braddon and
> Mr Rider Haggard are popular, he is not and never will be.

The paradox of the position in which Meredith found himself
applied with equal force to Conrad and James: that they were 'too
intellectual to be popular', that the higher the quality of their
work, the less likely they were to appeal to the mass market. This
is of no novelty to us, for whom the divorce between a mass culture and high culture is a familiar lament, but at the end of the
nineteenth century, with the examples of George Eliot and Dickens
so close in the memory, it was a puzzling and sometimes distres-
sing phenomenon. Some reviewers of the time were quick to discern the effects of such a split in the reading public. H. M. Cecil,
in an intelligent essay in the 'Free Review' of August 1894, placed
Meredith with Wagner and Ibsen as examples of great artists who
will never be 'popular', and he uses the idea to account for Meredith's secretiveness and his inclination 'to retire inward upon
himself':(9)

> To blame Mr Meredith for his perversities, indeed, would
> be sometimes to blame the innocent. The guilt for much of it
> must lie on the shoulders of the public. Cordial recognition
> of his work in the beginning would have made him less
> secretive, less inclined to retire inward upon himself, and
> would have spared us that conviction that he is writing for
> the select few, whose contempt for the long and hairy-eared
> public is as great as his own.

Isolation and a lack of recognition from 'the novel-reading public' whilst at the same time being hailed as genius (as 'Shakespeare in modern English' by George Gissing; as 'the most
obviously Shakespearean in a certain sense of modern authors' by
Percy Lubbock; as 'out and away the greatest force in English
letters' by the admiring R. L. Stevenson) became a most trying
and bitter paradox for Meredith - the 'Ordeal of George Meredith'
as one of his biographers has put it.(10) By the 1880s the British

public was beginning to appreciate his work more widely, but
even when his reputation was at its highest at the turn of the
century, the public remained divided, the majority quite convinced, as one critic put it, that 'Mr Meredith does not write the
vernacular.' In a letter to Morley, Swinburne remarked how he
thought that Meredith was deliberately reacting to the values of
the Victorian novel in a way which necessarily (but, to Swinburne's mind, wrong-headedly) equated the ideal of lucidity with
artistic failure:(11)

> By dint of revulsion from Trollope on this hand and Braddon
> on that, he seems to have persuaded himself that limpidity of
> style must mean shallowness, lucidity of narrative must imply
> triviality, and simplicity of direct interest or positive incident
> must involve 'sensationalism'.

This alienation from the bourgeois public is not in any sense a
simple cause of Meredith's obscurity, nor is the problem solved by
suggesting that it was a result. The two things interpenetrate
throughout his career: Meredith's particular psychological
estrangement from the public and dominant values held by it in
respect of literature made it very difficult for him to write fiction
which was both popular and acceptable to himself. He felt con-
stricted by the demands of the public ('The English public will not
let me probe deeply into humanity. You must not paint either
woman or man: a surface view of the species flat as a wafer is
acceptable'). Thus his desire for success (12) conflicted with the
conditions necessary for success: Meredith found himself writing
for a 'dual addressee', for two different groups with different
expectations and values, and his work bears the marks of the
compromise which this condition engendered.

This is particularly visible in the conflict between narrative and
analysis in his novels, the felt incompatibility between conventions
of plot and depth of psychological penetration. For Meredith,
stories and plots could not reveal in their sequence of actions the
inner secrets of his characters. I do not think that this was merely
an inexplicable 'defect', that 'Meredith lacked the sense of construction which should have warned him that he was going wrong.'
(13) It is rather that the contrivance of plot seemed to Meredith,
much earlier than to most others, a fetter to fiction and not a
vehicle for it. His novels bear witness to the modernist mistrust of
'plot', a modernism which either plays up its fabulation and contrivance or neglects it altogether. Meredith did both of these: he
was quite conscious that the pressure upon him to tell a good tale
conflicted with his inner conviction that 'tales' and 'fiction' were
not at all the same thing. The division between novelist and philosopher in 'Sandra Belloni' testifies as much. The novelist is in
antagonistic partnership with 'a fellow who will not see things on
the surface, and is blind to the fact that the public detest him.'
(14) The one preoccupies himself with the public events, with the
'field of action, of battles and conspiracies, nerve and muscle,
where life fights for plain issues,' the other protests that such
fluency and motion in external events is itself a falsehood, that

'a story should not always flow, or, at least, not to a given measure.' The former then protests that this halting of the story, its
hesitation and interpolation will, in itself, destroy the illusion of
the fiction, that the characters will be revealed as puppets, their
'golden robe' of illusion reduced to tatters.

This explicit debate on the status and nature of the fiction (in
the middle of the fiction) looks back to Sterne and forward to
Beckett, Pynchon and Fowles. It is anything but 'Victorian' and
it explicitly rejects the contract of illusion between author and
reader, that the events are to be seen through the transparent
medium of the text. Author, a kind of estranged double, has
entered his fiction to reveal himself as a sly manipulator and
inept conjuror, like the Rajah and his minister, whom Meredith
introduces in chapter 5 of 'One of Our Conquerors' with a satir-
ical double-act to explain the farce of London commuters. In that
passage Meredith explicitly associates the self-conscious and
elaborate subversion of the story with the accusation of obscurity
it will inevitably bring ('princes and the louder members of the
grey public are fraternally instant to spurn at the whip of that
which they do not immediately comprehend'). In the first chapter
of 'The Egoist', Meredith implicitly ironizes this public preference
for action by opening the novel with an abstract and essayistic
discussion of comedy, leaving the 'real' opening of the story, the
mention of the egoistic English gentleman, until the last page of
the chapter: he entitles it 'A chapter of which the last page only
is of any importance'. It is a technique employed by Robert Musil
in the first volume of 'The Man Without Qualities'; chapter 28 is
entitled 'A chapter that can be skipped by anyone who has no
very high opinion of thinking as an occupation'. In both cases,
the self-deprecation is actually at the reader's expense. (15) Yet
direct presentation of the action is a function of unity and stability in the act of communication; it requires and projects a
unified sender, receiver, code and contact. Communication in
Meredith's novels was disintegrating with respect to all of these
elements. The receiver was doubled as was the sender; the generic stability of the fiction was in question, and the 'contact', the
social relation of the novel's production, was in the process of
change.

Meredith's strong sense of being pitted against the public had
far-reaching consequences. It was more than just the fact that he
had lost faith in the efficacy of narrative continuity and yet the
general novel-reading public had not. In his best novels (which
for me are 'The Ordeal of Richard Feverel', 'Evan Harrington',
'Beauchamp's Career', 'The Egoist', 'The Tragic Comedians',
'Diana of the Crossways' and 'One of Our Conquerors') Meredith
conceives of his characters as victims damaged by public life,
sometimes even destroyed by it. His heroes and heroines are
either intensely and nervously combative in public, performing
desperate feats of verbal warfare, or they hide their inner feelings behind a 'ritual mask of sociability'. His characters are
always on the defensive against the public and its opinions.

This tends to split them internally into private, 'natural' beings and public figures covering up their vulnerabilities. In a marvellous phrase, Meredith says that they tend to take refuge in 'that subterranean recess for Nature against the Institutions of Man'.(16) Particularly for his women, 'the Institutions of Man' present a constant threat. The rules of courtship, marriage, propriety and finance Meredith found both offensive and indefensible, and what is striking is that he felt dishonesty and evasion to be morally justified when used to protect oneself from them. Abstract 'truth' is less important than the protection of men and women from the wounding gossip, horrible marriages and powerful social snobberies to which they are subjected in his novels.

The most moving and intensely realized narrative of this opposition between public and private life is Meredith's late novel 'One of Our Conquerors' (1891). In it Victor Radnor has, as a young man, married a rich widow much older than himself and subsequently fallen in love with her companion, Natalia. Victor leaves his wife and lives with Natalia, and they have a fine and courageous daughter, Nesta Victoria. The novel describes the gradually increasing pressure on all three of them under the threat of public exposure; the daughter's relations with her friends and prospective lover are threatened by the knowledge of her illegitimacy and her friendship with Mrs Marsett, a woman of some notoriety but 'more sinned against than sinning'.

Victor and Natalia adopt the two paths which we see taken repeatedly in Meredith's work: combat and withdrawal. Victor, who has become immensely prosperous, 'fronts out' the danger of public attack by building opulent houses and entertaining on a lavish scale, defying scandal with his wealth. Natalia, a timid and sensitive woman, withdraws further into herself, suffers from a progressive nervous exhaustion under the pressures of public encounter and malicious scandal. Finally, the pressures burst these twin defences, Natalia dies and Victor suffers severe mental breakdown. Only their daughter survives the corrosive power of public insinuation and Grundyism.

The novel is one of Meredith's most obscure, and Lionel Johnson was quite correct in saying 'that with Mr Meredith style and subject change or grow together.... In 'Beauchamp's Career', and 'Diana of the Crossways' and 'One of Our Conquerors', it is not too much to say that "the world", or "society", or "the public", or "the nation", seems to rank among the *dramatis personae*.'(17) And they rank as forces to be excluded, to be kept away from the chief characters in the fiction. Open and honest communication in Meredith's world leads to suffering. The world must be kept out: (18)

> Behold! I looked for peace, and thought it near.
> Our inmost hearts had opened, each to each.
> We drank the pure daylight of honest speech.
> Alas! that was the fatal draught, I fear.

The 'pure daylight of honest speech' is the bringer of death and

mental breakdown in Meredith, whilst obscurity of language and
self-presentation bring the possibility of inner safety. Obscurity,
then, is the linguistic defence of vulnerable offenders against
public codes. The contract of sincerity between these offenders
and the wider society is the key to their failure, it becomes a
source of terrible anxiety. Self-revelation in the process of communication almost inevitably brings condemnation and suffering,
from Evan Harrington's revelation of his class origins at Beckley
Court to Natalia's writhing shame at Lakelands.

This inner connectedness of pain and communication is a major
source of obscurity in Meredith and is discussed fully in chapter
4; but the antagonism between an inner and outer language which
results from defensive introversion is of paramount importance in
the period. In it are rooted the seeds of that fearsome isolation
and solipsism which afflict Conrad's characters and later Thomas
Mann's Leverkühn and Kafka's Hungry Artist: the dialectic of
withdrawal and rejection force one further into the wasteland or
wilderness.(19) This modernist phenomenon of what Bradbury and
Fletcher have called 'narrative introversion'(20) and 'an internal
crisis of presentation', triggers off in the author a dialectical
process of increased distance and obliqueness. Both Meredith and
James, like James Joyce (and perhaps like Browning before them)
become increasingly difficult and resistant in their work with age.
The style and the subject grow together inwardly, less concerned
with openness towards a public which is felt to be corrosive of
one's integrity and alien to one's private desires and needs.(21)

Some of Meredith's difficulty is in the endeavour to catch this
mixture of self, never quite in control, never quite 'together'.(22)
'The Tragic Comedians', as the title suggests, required a deliberate collapse of the traditional opposition of tragedy and comedy
to describe its protagonists, and the calculated impurity of mode
is invoked to express 'a stature and a complexity calling for the
junction of the two Modes to name them'.(23) Alvan (taken from a
description of the socialist Lassalle upon whose history the novel
is based) is described at his death as 'profusely mixed', 'a house
of many chambers':(24)

> That mass of humanity profusely mixed of good and evil, of
> generous ire and mutinous, of the passion for the future of
> mankind and vanity of person, magnanimity and sensualism,
> high judgment, reckless indiscipline, chivalry, savagery,
> solidity, fragmentariness, was dust.

Underlying this profuse mixture is that recurrent doubleness
of which I have already spoken, for Alvan is not one but two men,
'the untamed and the candidate for citizenship, in mutual dissension'. The proximity to certain characters in Conrad is unmis-
takable (one thinks of that mixture of savagery and civilized
accomplishment in Kurtz); but whereas in Conrad the incommensurability of these dissenting voices is figured as radically
incomprehensible, as 'enigma', in Meredith the duality produces
paradox and bizarre juxtapositions. This modal and generic ambiguity in 'The Tragic Comedians' is a confusion of masks, of

principles, and processes of reading. Meredith strenuously endeavours to maintain the ludicrous and the elegiac in Alvan, his
contradictory drives towards life and death, his private eroticism
and public altruism. Our reading is held between the tragic and
comic in a way which challenges purity of response and simplicity
of affective reception. The reader is placed exactly in the position
of those people in Henry James's 'The Sacred Fount' when they
discover the picture of the young man holding a mask. The passage is worth quoting in full, for the similarity to the underlying
structure of presentation in 'The Tragic Comedians' is striking.
(25)

'.... It's the picture, of all pictures, that most needs an
interpreter. *Don't* we want,' I asked of Mrs. Server, 'to
know what it means?' The figure represented is a young
man in black – a quaint, tight black dress, fashioned in
years long past; with a pale, lean, livid face and a stare,
from eyes without eyebrows, like that of some whitened old-
world clown. In his hand he holds an object *that strikes the
spectator at first simply as some obscure, some ambiguous
work of art*, but that on a second view becomes a representation of a human face, modelled and coloured, in wax, in
enamelled metal, in some substance not human. The object
thus appears a complete mask, such as might have been
fantastically fitted and worn.
'Yes, what in the world does it mean?' Mrs. Server replied.
'One could call it – though that doesn't get one much further
– the Mask of Death.'
'Why so? ... Isn't it much rather the Mask of Life? It's
the man's own face that's Death. The other one, blooming
and beautiful – '
'Ah, but with an awful grimace!' Mrs. Server broke in.
[My italics]

The disagreement between Mrs Server and the narrator continues
unresolved, we never learn which is the face and which the mask,
which life and which death, and the word 'fantastical' which
James uses of the mask/face is chosen by Meredith as the key
word for 'The Tragic Comedians', it is used to open the novel in
an endeavour to reclaim the word from mere pejorative usage.(26)
The idea of a fantastical sad clown used to express character as
motley and mysterious, as essentially *bizarre*, is common not only
to Meredith and James but to Conrad as well. That strange and
unlikely harlequin who suddenly emerges from the forests in
'Heart of Darkness' is surely an extravagant and enigmatic symbol
of the same kind:(27)

I looked at him, lost in astonishment. There he was before me,
in motley, as though he had absconded from a troupe of mimes,
enthusiastic, fabulous. His very existence was improbable,
inexplicable, and altogether bewildering. He was an insoluble
problem.

All three writers thus adopt the harlequin figure to give an
emblematic form to the essential and constitutive obscurity of

personality, of the self as divided, enigmatic, presenting itself
to the world in the form of a question or riddle ('Yes, what in the
world does it mean?' asks Mrs Server; 'He was an insoluble problem,' remarks Marlow; 'Oh! she's a riddle of course. I don't pre-
tend to spell every letter of her,' remarks Alvan of Clotilde, the
other 'tragic comedian'). Half magus and half clown, the solitary
and romantic figure of the harlequin juggles his illusions for a
public from which he is always estranged, he crystallizes a fluid
and indistinct sense of self. It is used in precisely this sense in
the 'Esthétique',(28) of Jules Laforgue, who invented the neologism 's'arlequiner', to behave like or become like a harlequin,
and the emblematic adoption of the figure reveals the three novelists at their closest to the symbolist imagination, turning on that
remote and haunting image of 'Pierrot Lunaire'. It brings together
in one 'fantastical' but determinate cipher, Meredith's sense of a
fragmentary self, at once wry and mystical in its inner evasions;
James's expression of the 'obscure, the ambiguous work of art',
and Conrad's powerful sense of life as infinitely 'questionable',
proposing and never answering its own conundrums. It is also an
image expressive of the isolation and idiosyncrasy of the artist,
his sense of awkwardness with respect to his public. Towards the
end of his life Meredith told an interviewer:(29)

> The press has often treated me as a clown or a harlequin -
> yes, really! and with such little respect that my fellow
> citizens can scarcely put up with me. Do not cry out!
> Certainly at this late hour they accord me a little glory:
> my name is celebrated, but no-one reads my books.

In his short story The Informer, Conrad uses the same structure of the 'double comedian' as Meredith had used for Lassalle.
In a remarkably similar narrative, Conrad uses the idea to describe that 'genius of betrayers', Sevrin, the traitor to an anarchist group who is himself betrayed by his love for a dilettante
young woman who is flirting with political activism (the similarity
to 'The Princess Casamassima' and 'The Tragic Comedians' is
striking). Sevrin, like Lassalle and Hyacinth Robinson, is destroyed by an inner doubleness or 'duplicity' which is not mere
surface hypocrisy but an internal, 'mutual dissension' which
obscures his vision and robs him of his lucidity at the critical
moment. He is betrayed by that 'unconscious comedian' hidden
within:(30)

> An actor in desperate earnest himself, he must have
> believed in the absolute value of conventional signs. As to
> the grossness of the trap into which he fell, the explanation
> must be that two sentiments of such absorbing magnitude
> cannot exist in one heart. The danger of that other and
> unconscious comedian robbed him of his vision, of his per-
> spicacity, of his judgement.

Sevrin is a tragic clown perplexed by the turmoil of private love
and political hate, an 'informer' caught between the dangers of
conventional signs outside and unconscious desire within. His
sudden loss of self-possession tokens the double threat posed to

lucidity by the unconscious and by an intrinsic treachery located in the very nature of linguistic communication.

This double insecurity seems to me fundamental to Conrad's writing and his relation to the separation of public and private experience. In his most successful work conscious control, directed energy and concentrated intention in his characters become narrowed to a fragile shell between external and internal hostilities. Cartesian clarity and that solid self-confidence which supports it has almost melted away in his work. Like Sevrin, his characters often feel like actors trapped in their roles, unable to do anything else except act (Marlow feels as though he is trapped in 'some sordid farce acted in front of a sinister back-cloth' in 'Heart of Darkness'). The vertigo of infinitude and endless repetition afflict the actors (and the reader) with a sense of dizzying emptiness. The sinister insubstantiality of categories, signs and rational decisions means that darkness for Conrad was of particular significance, like that primordial darkness which folds round the narrator of 'The Shadow Line', where 'every form was gone... spar, sail, fittings, rails; everything blotted out in the dreadful smoothness of that absolute night.' In his book 'The Metaphysics of Darkness'(31) Raymond Roussel has traced the pervasive importance of darkness in Conrad's work and amasses impressive evidence that, 'Although it is itself without weight or dimension, [for Conrad] this darkness lies behind all the distinct forms of creation.' He described it in a letter to Cunninghame Graham as 'une ombre sinistre et fuyante dont il est impossible de fixer l'image.'(32)

It is precisely the difficulty of 'fixing the image' which is so terrifying. The agonies of writing, which he recalls endlessly in his gloomy letters to friends and fellow writers, become a torment which in mid-career charted his mental breakdown, it led to him being trapped in the darkness of his own metaphor:(33)

> I see how ill, mentally, I have been these last four months.
> ... This horror ... has destroyed already the little belief
> in myself I used to have. I am appalled at the absurdity of
> my situation .... Most appalled to feel that all the doors
> behind me are shut and that I must remain where I have
> come blundering in the dark.

This was in 1898, and, by late May, Conrad's close friends had become most concerned about his sanity. His complaints strongly recall Emerson's diagnosis quoted above, that an absence of social identity produces a language wanting 'body or basis'. Not only did Conrad share with Meredith a fearful intuition of inward divisiveness, he also felt a cultural isolation which manifested itself as a fading of subjectivity, an evaporation of anything distinctive either in himself or his writing:(34)

> I feel nothing clearly. And I am frightened when I remember
> that I have to drag it all out of myself. Other writers have
> some starting point, something to catch hold of ... they lean
> on dialect - or on tradition - or on history - or on the pre-
> judice or fad of the hour; they trade upon some tie or

conviction of their time – or upon the absence of these
things – which they can abuse or praise. But at any rate
they know something to begin with – while I don't. I have
had some impressions, some sensations – in my time –
impressions and sensations of common things. And it's all
faded – my very being seems faded and thin like the ghost
of a blonde and sentimental woman, haunting romantic ruins
pervaded by rats. I am exceedingly miserable.

This tragic sense of timelessness, of being a ghost or wanderer
outside of any culture, expresses Conrad's anxious sense of exclusion as a literary refugee. Polish, Russian, French, English,
remote from any origin and uncomfortably separated from his
audience, there are no terms adequate to 'fix the image' and no
one close enough for whom it might be clarified.

The bond of familiarity between author and reader which we
find in Thackeray and Dickens had almost completely vanished for
Conrad. Serial publication had fostered, in Thackeray's words, a
'communion between the writer and the public ... something con-
tinual, confidential, something like a personal affection'.(35) It
meant that the writer could be immediately responsive to the
desires of his reader, even to the point of changing the plot or
characters if he felt the public demanded it (as in Thackeray's
decision that Clive Newcome might marry Ethel – 'What could a
fellow do? So many people wanted 'em married'). The familiarity
of the bond is striking. In his prefatory note to the concluding
number of 'Dombey and Son' Dickens wrote:

> I cannot forego my usual opportunity of saying farewell to
> my readers in this greeting-place, though I have only to
> acknowledge the unbounded warmth and earnestness of their
> sympathy in every stage of the journey we have just con-
> cluded.

And in Thackeray's preface to 'Pendennis', this closeness is given
as a primary reason for the sincerity of the author, it accounts
for his 'frankness of expression':

> in his constant communication with the reader the writer is
> forced into frankness of expression, and to speak his own
> mind and feelings as they urge him .... It is a sort of con-
> fidential talk between writer and reader.

For Conrad, this confidential talk was impossible; indeed the
very idea of such public confidentiality is a threat. In 'The Return'
the London public is leaving a West End station:(36)

> Outside the big doorway of the street they scattered in all
> directions, walking away fast from one another with the
> hurried air of men fleeing from something compromising;
> from familiarity or confidences; from something suspected
> and concealed – like truth or pestilence.

The linking of compromise with confidence, truth with pestilence,
is symptomatic: the image which Conrad uses to describe the process of writing is that of addressing a void. 'The work itself' he
complained to Sanderson, 'is only like throwing words into a
bottomless hole.' And again, writing to Sanderson, 'I've taken to

writing for the press, ... More words, - another hole.'(37) The
commonplace of artistic alienation which operates with such evident force in Conrad reaches to the roots of the 'new crypto-
graphic style'. The more that the addressee of fiction appears
dispersed or remote, the more solipsistic the act of writing seems
to become. In his essay on Daudet, Conrad speaks of the road for
the writer of fiction (38) which

> does not lie through the domain of Art or the domain of
> Science where well-known voices quarrel noisily in a misty
> emptiness; it is a path of toilsome silence upon which travel
> men simple and unknown, with closed lips, or, may be,
> whispering their pain softly - only to themselves.

The degree of withdrawal is closely linked to a failure to penetrate the broad community of common readers, and the more the
writer feels himself to be whispering only to himself, or at best to
a small group, the more vulnerable he becomes to the act of publication. Narrative exposition becomes self-exposure. Thackeray's
'confidential talk' between writer and reader becomes Conrad's
'compromising familiarity'. It is not surprising that the figure of
the anarchist agitator became both an attractive and repulsive
subject for these novelists: The anarchist is cut off from all those
linkages of which Emerson spoke (Conrad writes 'Anarchists, I
suppose, have no families - not, at any rate, as we understand
that social relation'), and the conspiratorial intimacy of the political subversive or the informer is an appropriate parallel to the
writer's nervous introversion. The Victorian sense of shared
language (perhaps quaintly modified by dialect) withers in the
absence of the enriching power of social cohesion. Conrad writes:
(39)

> we, living, are out of life - utterly out of it ... we don't
> even know our own thoughts. Half the words we use have
> no meaning whatever and of the other half each man under-
> stands each word after the fashion of his own folly and
> conceit. Faith is a myth and beliefs shift like mist on the
> shore; thoughts vanish; words, once pronounced, die; ...
> only the string of my platitudes seems to have no end.

As the sense of belonging to a single, enfolding culture becomes
relativized and distant, all forms of thought and belief lose their
substantiality.

This modification in the status of the subject is simultaneously
a modification of his relation to communication as such. The
shared referentiality of language available to him seems to de-
crease as the origins and ends of his verbal activity recede into
difficulty. Subjective depth gradually replaces both the instru-
mental and consummatory functions of language, it becomes more
and more difficult to gauge when and where the language should
stop, how far one can go in interior exploration. The mechanisms
of embarrassment (James), shame (Meredith) and guilt (Conrad)
are easily triggered by this increasingly personal reference, the
risk of self-exposure in forcing the boundary between public and
private discourse. I think it no accident that these three men

were so reticent about their private lives, even to the point of deliberately misleading people about incidents in their past.(40) Changes in the social relations of production of the fiction combined with the specific trajectories of their lives made novel-writing a constant risk of self-revelation. For Conrad, the art of writing novels was 'the most liable to be obscured by the scruples of its servants and votaries, the one pre-eminently destined to bring trouble to the mind and the heart of the artist.'(41) He felt a strong need to remain hidden within his fiction, to conceal himself behind a veil. E. M. Forster put this most succinctly in his review of Conrad's coy and reticent autobiographical work:(42)

The character [of Conrad] will never really be clear, for one of two reasons. The first reason has already been indicated; the writer's dread of intimacy. He has a rigid conception as to where the rights of the public stop, he has determined we shall not be 'all over' him, and has half contemptuously thrown open this vestibule and invited us to mistake it for the private apartment if we choose. We may not see such a character clearly because he does not wish us to see. But we also may not see clearly because it is essentially unclear. This possibility must be considered. *Behind the smoke screen of his reticence there may be another obscurity, connected to the foreground by wisps of vapour, yet proceeding from another source*, from the central chasm of his tremendous genius. This isn't an aesthetic criticism nor a moral one. Just a suggestion that our difficulties with Mr. Conrad may proceed in part from difficulties of his own. [My italics]

Indeed the difficulties do proceed from 'another obscurity' anterior to the manifest forms of the elusive fiction, an obscurity of authorial voice talking too loudly and insistently amongst the voices of his characters. Conrad's difficulties relate closely to his fear of self-exposure at a time when the nature of fiction somehow altered the relation between writer and the written so that the latter always referred back with uncomfortable rapidity to the former. In 'A Personal Record', Conrad describes how the writer appears to write about the world but in fact only succeeds in writing out himself as that world:(43)

a novelist lives in his work. He stands there, the only reality in an invented world, among imaginary things, happenings and people. Writing about them, he is only writing about himself. But the disclosure is not complete. He remains, to a certain extent, a figure behind a veil, a suspected rather than seen presence – a movement and a voice behind the draperies of fiction.

Conrad is explicit here about the discernible link between the forms of fiction and a new reticence on the part of the author, an unwillingness or inability to communicate himself which upsets the contract of openness between reader and writer. Yet that is perhaps expressing it too simply: communication still takes place but it has a changed relation to the information it bears, it no longer

feels able to keep up the fiction of its realism, that it is 'about'
something 'outside' and for which the novelist is just a kind of
perspicacious and sensitive observer. For Conrad, the author is
always writing about himself even when he writes about invented
and imaginary things, and his remark is of the utmost significance, not simply for the anxiety it betrays about the visibility
of the author in his work, but for the assumption it makes that a
reader will consider the fiction a revelation of the psychic state
of the author rather than a subjective description of reality.

This vulnerability is connected to a new kind of reading, a new
kind of critical attention in the period, whereby the sophisticated
read through the text to the psychological state of the author.
This was the growth of 'symptomatic reading', an analysis of literature not so much for the accuracy or truth of its rendering of
reality, but for the mental disposition of the writer. 'A writer of
imaginative prose stands confessed in his work,'(44) Conrad
wrote, in writing fiction he writes himself. Literature could thus
seem a jejune kind of displacement whereby an author shuffled off
his own preoccupations and fantasies into a make-believe world
which appeared, precisely, as 'make-believe'. It became increasingly difficult to maintain that heroism of sincerity which had
underpinned the desire of the Victorian novelist to be 'honestly
transcriptive, veraciously historical'.

This growth of symptomatic reading is inseparable from the
growth of psychological understanding in the period. The increasing belief in the existence of the unconscious (or 'subconscious'
as it was usually called in the 1880s and 1890s) was linked to a
growing revaluation of irrational experience and abnormal mental
states. William James's classic book, 'The Varieties of Religious
Experience', was taken as arguing strongly for the value of
irrational and paranormal states of mind. When Oliver Elton reviewed it in 1904, he made a casual remark which, in the light of
the subsequent development of modern literature should be treas-
ured as a prescient understatement:(45)

> Professor James seems to imply that in such a state there
> may be true revelation, especially from those latent parts
> of the mind, for which the word 'subconscious' has been
> found as a metaphor for their imagined sphere or receptacle.

There was a variety of intellectual works appearing in books and
periodicals which tended to problematize the barrier between
rational and non-rational states of mind. The boundaries of 'true
knowledge' were more and more difficult to define or defend. In
the same volume of the 'Fortnightly Review' which was serializing
Meredith's novel about mental disintegration 'One of Our Conquerors',* E. L. Linton wrote an article called 'Our Illusions', and

---

* Meredith's novel provoked an interesting correspondence about
  the precise medical form of Victor Radnor's mental illness, and
  whether it begins with the fall (both physical and mental)
  which he sustains right at the outset of the novel.

it is as remarkable a condensed statement of the dissolving boundary between true and false, rational and irrational, that can be found anywhere before 1900, not only because it captures so succinctly a variety of 'fin de siècle' anxiety prevalent at the time, but because of the way it challenges all absolute notions of truth - moral, historical and aesthetic. In it she compares the state of mind of a fervent Christian believer with that of a man suffering from persecution mania. She concludes that there is essentially no difference between the two:(46)

> When the very presence of Satan is realised by the trembling Christian sinner, is he in any way differently held from the malefactor pursued by the Furies? The state of mind is the same - but the objective truth of the appearance? Was not that maya, illusion, in each case alike? If this be not so, *then we have no line of boundary between madness and sanity. If we affirm the truth of spiritual impressions, however we may name them, we open the doors of Bedlam and make its haunted inmates free citizens like the rest.* [My italics]

There was indeed genuine social alarm in the period that insanity was increasing. A serious debate in the 'Fortnightly Review' in 1896 voiced fears, supposedly supported by statistical evidence, that there had been a dramatic increase in the number of insane people in Britain towards the end of the century,(47) and this had the strange effect of providing a material image of madness encroaching upon sanity, a statistical and generalized metaphor of the changing boundary between rationality and irrationality in favour of the latter. It was of course not only an imputed quantitive change, but, far more importantly, a qualitative change in the attitude to the irrational. Bearing in mind that Meredith, Conrad and James all suffered from periods of mental illness and wrote fictions in which madness is of central importance,(48) the publication of enormously influential, contemporary work which connected the psychic condition of the writer with literary creativity is of special interest.

Two books which were of paramount importance in this respect and achieved something of a 'succès de scandale' were Professor Lombroso's 'The Man of Genius' (1891) and Max Nordau's 'Degeneration' (1895) which some years earlier than William James's book had generated enormous interest. Although she was over-estimating somewhat, Helen Zimmern in a review of Lombroso said that his book had an influence as 'immediate and decisive' as 'The Origin of Species'.(49) If she had been talking of the general approach to mental phenomena employed by Lombroso, she would not have exaggerated. Nordau's book even stimulated a riposte from A. E. Hake called, predictably enough, 'Regeneration' (50) and despite the fact that Nordau's belligerence often overshadowed his judgment and that Professor Lombroso was not renowned for the accuracy of his scholarship (he was not allowed to forget his statement that 'Milton studiously avoided marriage' by English reviewers!),(51) the books of these men contributed centrally to the debate on the abnormality of genius, the decline of reason and

the uncertain psychical bases of intellect. Nordau dedicated his
book to Lombroso, and in his dedication wrote:(52)

> Degenerates are not always criminals, prostitutes, anarchists,
> and pronounced lunatics; they are often authors and artists.
> These, however, manifest the same mental characteristics
> and for the most part the same somatic features, as the
> members of the above-mentioned anthropological family, who
> satisfy their unhealthy impulses with the knife of the
> assassin or the bomb of the dynamiter, instead of with pen
> and pencil....

> Thus this book is an attempt at a really scientific criticism,
> which does not base its judgement of a book upon the purely
> accidental, capricious and variable emotions it awakens -
> emotions depending on the temperament and mood of the
> individual reader - but upon the psychophysiological elements
> from which it sprang.

Nordau became notorious for his attacks on Ibsen ('not wholly
diseased in mind but only a dweller on the borderland - a
"mattoid" '); Nietzsche ('insane drivel'); the Parnassians ('ego-
mania of degenerate minds'); and all forms of symbolist aestheti-
cism from Baudelaire to Wilde. Although it is mainly in connection
with his violent and malicious attack on decadence that he is now
remembered by literary historians, the above extract is an indication of an entirely serious side to his work, symptomatic of an
intellectual shift reaching far beyond his bludgeoning criticism of
particular literary movements. Nordau did not read these writers
for their representation of reality, but read 'through' their work
back to the psychic life of the author; he was not so much inter
ested in the mimetic plausibility of the work of art as in the
evidence it provided for 'the psychophysiological elements from
which it sprang.' Thus he read works of literature as if they were
transcriptions of the fantasy life of psychically disturbed patients,
and not descriptions, by earnest and rational persons, of some
external order of fact and sentiment.

It is difficult to over-estimate the importance of this shift in
attention and its concomitant change in the act of reading. It had
of course always been a common notion that genius and madness
were 'near allied', but within a few years in the 1880s, under the
influence of proto-psychology, literary texts were transformed
into primary evidence of the inner private fantasies of the author.
The sincerity of the relationship between author and middle-class
reader (even when the former strongly attacked the latter as,
say, George Eliot did in 'Daniel Deronda'), their mutual interest
in the honest transcription of the emotional life, was supplemented
by a new kind of relationship which made the old contract extremely difficult to keep. The author was suddenly placed at a
disadvantage by the sophistication in reader response, he became
vulnerable to a certain kind of knowing smile which found in his
words the insufficiently disguised evidence of his most intimate
preoccupations. As more and more intellectual readers began to

regard fiction as a transformation of fantasy by various quasi-defensive devices, the notion of the 'truth' of the text, and the relations between text, author and reader, swiftly changed.

A series of works was published in the 1890s to the effect that, to quote the phrase of a French intellectual Guernsen, 'Genius is a disease of the nerves.' The works of Nordau and Lombroso were central, but to them may be added others also positing the strongest possible link between artistic ability and mental abnormality. J. F. Nisbet's 'The Insanity of Genius' (London, 1891), A. G. Bianchi's 'La Patologia del Genio e gli Scienziati Italiani' (Milan, 1892), Vernon Lee's Beauty and Sanity (1895), P. Radestock's 'Genie und Wahnsinn' (1884), Clifford Allbut's Nervous Diseases and Modern Life (1895), purported to prove the basis of genius in psycho-physiological disorders and erase the boundary between 'delinquency' and artistic production. The assimilation was not always in one direction. Not only was genius considered a (fortunate) kind of insanity, but the work of many insane people was adduced to show how frequently madness was a form of genius. Lombroso in Part III of 'The Man of Genius' (chapter 1: Insane Genius in Literature) quotes over a dozen examples of work executed by inmates of asylums which show the temporary appearance of 'real genius' among the insane. The emphasis of course varied. Whereas Lombroso wished to teach 'respect for the supreme misfortunes of insanity' as well as caution in confronting 'the brilliancy of men of genius', Nordau vociferously attacked modern literary writers as dangerous degenerates, but in both cases one can find, in more or less exaggerated or programmatic form, the explicit statement of a new kind of attention to literature. Lombroso writes:(53)

What I have hitherto written may, I hope (while remaining within the limits of psychological observation), afford an experimental starting-point for a criticism of artistic and literary, sometimes also of scientific, creations.

Thus, in the fine arts, exaggerated minuteness of detail, the abuse of symbols, inscriptions, or accessories, a preference for some one particular colour, an unrestrained passion for mere novelty, may approach the morbid symptoms of mattoidism. Just so, in literature and science, a tendency to puns and plays upon words, an excessive fondness of systems, a tendency to speak to one's self, and substitute epigram for logic, an extreme predilection for the rhythm and assonance of verse in prose writing, even an exaggerated degree of originality may be considered as morbid phenomena. So also is the mania of writing in Biblical form, in detached verses, and with special favourite words, which are underlined, or repeated many times, and a certain graphic symbolism.

Lombroso's list is an artful compilation of many of the characteristics - given in a remarkably economic and convincing form - of what is now called modernist literature, and among the writers

whom he cites as 'suspect' we find Walt Whitman, Hoffman, De
Musset, Nerval, Dostoevsky, Poe, Kleist, Baudelaire, Flaubert,
the Goncourts and Darwin! Looking even further back to the
period of Lamb and Southey, J. F. Nisbet's book 'The Insanity
of Genius' (54) which went through six editions by 1912, claimed
of its investigation that:

> The result is to place upon a solid basis of fact the long
> suspected relationship of genius and insanity. Apparently
> at the opposite poles of the human intellect, genius and
> insanity are, in reality, but different phases of a morbid
> susceptibility of, or want of balance in, the cerebro-spinal
> system.

Although the first of these studies,(55) contending that exceptional intellectual ability was organically much the same thing as
madness, was written as early as 1859, it was not until the German,(56) French and Italian work on the subject began to flood
into the country in the 1880s that English writers began to take
the notion seriously. It involved a change of critical regard as to
what was understood to be the 'origin' of the literary text. It was
less and less a case of looking at these texts as either a reflection
of the truth or an illuminating source throwing light upon it, but
a case of looking through the semi-transparency of the words to
the 'real origin' which was the psycho-physiology of the author.
This is not the same as simple biographical criticism, which
aspired to clarify or amplify the meaning of certain passages in
an author's work by a supplement of personal details; this had
traditionally endeavoured to be a charitable activity, based upon
a sympathetic understanding for the subject on the part of the
biographer. There was a direct threat in this new form of attention which shifted the understanding of literature itself, for, to
the degree that the source of literature was increasingly located
in neurosis, hysteria, hallucination, mattoidism, perversion and
other psychological traits, the less 'reality' and 'transcribed
truth' could be maintained as the real source of literary production.
Even further, if writers persisted in claiming that pure mimesis
was their goal and that honest and sincere copying of observable
social and emotional events was the novelist's primary activity,
then they were either insincere or did not sufficiently understand
themselves - the origin of their work was literally 'unconscious',
from sources to which rationality was completely secondary. As
early as 1895, Vernon Lee (pseud. of Violet Paget, acquaintance of
James) wrote in a remarkable article in the 'Fortnightly Review',
(57) based on a review of Lombroso:

> When, for instance, shall we recognize that the bulk of our
> psychic life is unconscious or semi-unconscious, the life of
> long-organized and automatic functions; and that, while it
> is absurd to oppose to these the more new, unaccustomed and
> fluctuating activity called *reason*, this same reason, this
> conscious portion of ourselves, may be usefully employed in
> understanding those powers of nature (powers of chaos
> sometimes) within us, and in providing that these should

turn the wheel of life in the right direction, even like those other powers of nature outside us, which reason cannot repress or diminish but can understand and put to profit. But instead of this, we are ushered into life thinking ourselves thoroughly conscious throughout, conscious beings of a definite and stereotyped pattern; and we are set to do things we do not understand with mechanisms which we have never even been shown!

In another of the major periodicals the same year, T. C. Allbut wrote on the increase in nervous disorders, suicide and insanity in modern life and succinctly summarized the new critical attitude: 'The young poet, who gets rid of the stings of passion by throwing them into verse, is set down as a "sexual pervert".'(58) For writers who had not infringed the prurient code of Victorian morality, to be indicted in this way was really quite new, and to describe a poet in these terms immediately made the act of writing love poetry without guilt or shame a more difficult task. It meant that literature was being read not for its manifest content, which might be quite conventional, but for the 'symptoms' from which could be read off the particular psychic malady of the poet. What it assumed was a certain inner blindness on the part of the writer, whereby what he wrote about, and what the work was 'really' about, were two separate things, and the critic could discover the latter in a way that was impossible for the writer himself because of the unconscious origins from which it sprang. It assumed, in other words, that the novelist or poet could not, by the very nature of artistic production, 'know' the meaning of his own work. Arthur Machen, the novelist and writer of strange 'doppelgänger' stories at the turn of the century, put the argument thus in this acute passage from his 'Hieroglyphics', written in 1899:(59)

In truth, the problem is simply a problem of the consciousness and sub-consciousness and of the action and interaction between the two. I will not be too dogmatic. We are in misty, uncertain and unexplored regions...but I am strangely inclined to think that all the quintessence of art is distilled from the sub-conscious and not from the conscious self: or, in other words, that the artificer seldom or never understands the ends and designs and spirit of the artist.

It is a remarkable statement of its time, and in positing a dual voice behind artistic production, the voice of the (unconscious) artificer or constructor (Conrad's 'unconscious comedian') and the voice of the (conscious) artist or designer, it is one of the very few contemporary statements which began to make sense of an obscure 'blurring of voices' in Meredith, Conrad and James. Machen is proposing a 'disjunctive' relation, a relation of non-knowledge at the heart of literary work, 'misty, uncertain and unexplored regions' in the creative space between the twinned makers of a literary text. For the relation of mystery, deception, repression and deceit par excellence is that boundary between the conscious and the unconscious, the boundary between the artistic intent and the psychic origin described by Nordau, Lombroso,

Nisbet and Lee (compared with these writers, Freud had almost
negligible influence in England before the turn of the century).
(60)

By the beginning of the twentieth century, writing showed
clear signs of these antagonistic voices, the controlling poet with
his conscious beliefs and designs struggling against the insistent
and disruptive mysteries of the unconscious:(61)

> Get hence, you loathsome mystery! Hideous animal get
> hence!
> You wake in me each bestial sense, you make what I would
> not be.
>
> You make my creed a barren sham, you wake foul dreams
> of sensual life,
> And Atys with his blood stained knife were better than
> the thing I am.

For Oscar Wilde in these verses from The Sphinx, secrecy and
mystery, symbolized in the sphinx-enigma, have become internalized as an overt threat to creed, the menace of sexuality within a
destabilized psyche, and it is remarkable confirmation of this
identification that Wilde's flight from 'loathsome mystery' should
find its climax in the figure of Atys, the self-castrator.

The regions of rational control and of honest, sincere description in literature had thus suddenly shrunk. ('How little of the
sapiens there is in the bulk of humanity, how dependent the
sapientia is on muscles, nerves and disposition of internal parts..
..')(62) When literary genius was characterized as a form of
psychical abnormality the ability of the artist to tell the truth was
thrown into doubt. The Genius was, as Nordau put it, a kind of
'involuntary charlatan' never quite aware of the roots of his own
productions. And for Nisbet literary men were 'an enigma even to
themselves'. We may recall the words of the great novelist St
George in Henry James's story The Lesson of the Master when he
says, 'I am a successful charlatan ... most assuredly is the artist
in a false position.' And in 'Under Western Eyes' Conrad remarks:
(63)

> The falsehood lies deep in the necessities of existence, in
> secret fears and half-formed ambitions, in the secret con-
> fidence combined with a secret mistrust of ourselves ... It
> seemed to him bizarre that secrecy should play such a large
> part in the comfort and safety of lives ... A man's most
> open actions have a secret side to them.

At the same time as anthropology cast doubt upon the universal
authenticity of social reality, these early forms of proto-psychology cast doubt upon any literary quest for Truth. The possibility
of finding the truth of a literary work passed from the artist to
the critic, and between author and critic a sort of mistrustful
game of cat-and-mouse develops, whereby the author seeks to
make his work opaque to the probing, subtle suggestion of the
critic who attempts to see through the artifice.

Henry James came back to this problem several times and it is most perfectly expressed in two stories which he published in the periodical 'Cosmopolis' which flourished between 1896 and 1898, The Figure in the Carpet (1896) and John Delavoy (1898). Both stories relate the close but competitive relationship between a novelist and a young critic and in both, significantly, the critic is frustrated in his passionate aim to reveal the 'essential truth' about the novelist.

John Delavoy is 'the wonderful writer, the immense novelist: the one who died last year.' The characteristic which James insists upon, after Delavoy's genius, is his extreme reticence, his deter- mination that his private life should not be violated. He was, says the young critic, 'my great artist, on whose consistent aloofness from the crowd I needn't touch, any more than on his patience in going his way and attending to his work, the most unadvertised, unreported, uninterviewed, unphotographed, uncriticised of all originals. Was he not the man of the time about whose private life we delightfully knew least?' The young critic produces a critical analysis of Delavoy's work which he feels to be the perfect ex- pression of the novelist, the most penetrating and accurate account of his secretive, intractable subject, and indeed it is an essay of such distinction that it totally wins the approval of the novelist's sister, a woman of exceptional sensitivity and judgment. But to his mortification, the brilliant article, having been at first accepted by the most important journal of the age, 'The Cynosure', is rejected by the editor as 'indecent' and 'indelicate': 'Did you candidly think that we were going to print this? ... We didn't at any rate want indelicacy.'

Two things are at issue here. First, the critic and the novelist's sister subscribe to a completely different moral and aesthetic order to that of the editor, Bullen, and the readership of 'The Cynosure'. Certain paragraphs of the critical article would lose the journal 'five thousand subscribers'. This division of readership between a small intellectual group, the coterie of initiates with its daring explicitness about sexuality and its sophisticated manner of read- ing, was incompatible with the majority standards of 'ordinary readers'. It was the proof-reader who, with his blue pencil, had first drawn the attention of the editor to offending passages in the essay, and, in this attempted censorship of the writer of the pas- sage by the proof-reader, we have a perfect expression of the conflict between two different readerships.

Second, however, the relationship between the great novelist and the young critic goes back to the game of cat-and-mouse; even though Delavoy, the titular character, is dead throughout the story, in the struggle to preserve his privacy he wins a posthumous battle. The young critic eventually gains the novelist's sister, but she is clearly a sort of compensation prize for his enforced silence. His article is not published, but in its place a small portrait sketch, 'conventional but *sincere*'. The contrast between the original crit- ical essay with its psycho-sexual reading of the novelist (infring- ing the boundary of 'delicacy') and the 'sincere' portrait sketch which replaces it, gives us a perfect index of the new criticism and

the old belle-lettrist biographical tradition which it was beginning
to threaten. James spoke of 'our marked collective mistrust of
anything like close or analytical appreciation' and he loathed the
prying and poking into his private life which seemed a part of
this:(64)

> the artist's life's his work, and this *is* the place to observe
> him. What he has to tell us he tells us with *this* perfection...
> The best interviewer is the best reader.... Admire him in
> silence, cultivate him at a distance and secretly appropriate
> his message.

In the story The Death of the Lion (1894) Paraday, the very
talented novelist, is hounded to death by the 'universal menagerie'
of admirers, he is 'pulled to pieces on the pretext of being
applauded.' John Delavoy escapes this fate, his integrity remains
unviolated to the end, and neither the readers of 'The Cynosure'
nor, more significantly, the readers of Henry James's story John
Delavoy get to discover those indelicate revelations which the
critic had produced in his analysis of Delavoy's last great novel.

The Figure in the Carpet of two years earlier, provides a very
similar situation, but with a more teasing, exasperating relation
between the young critic and Vereker, the great novelist. Vereker,
hardly concealing his disappointment that the critic has completely
missed the essential point of his novels, 'the particular thing I've
written my books most *for*', sets his oeuvre before the ardent
young man as a fascinating enigma, containing, in all its parts, a
most marvellous and tantalizing secret which runs through the
whole like a pattern in an intricate carpet:(65)

> 'You fire me as I've never been fired', I returned 'you
> make me determined to do or die'. Then I asked, 'Is it a
> kind of esoteric message?' His countenance fell at this
> he put out his hand as if to bid me good-night. 'Ah,
> my dear fellow, it can't be described in cheap journal-
> ese.'

Literary criticism is described in the story as an 'initiation' and
Vereker's novels are 'only for the initiated'. The relation the novelist creates between himself and his young critic is one of priest
to acolyte, Vereker binds the critic to him through a kind of hermeneutic mystery by initiating a search for the word of the master
in the myriad patterns of the text. Indeed, at one point the idea of
the novelist's work and the creating of a secret are taken as one
and the same thing;(66)

> 'And now you quite like it,' I said.
> 'My work?'
> 'Your secret. It's the same thing.'
> 'Your guessing that', Vereker replied, 'is a proof that
> you're as clever as I say!'

The inscrutable novelist behaves exactly like a Taoist master to
his noviciate, answering his questions with oblique, parabolic
phrases, fending off his direct approaches to the object. The
writer refuses his reader. He rejects all proposals that the young

man makes to share the meaning of the work, and indeed eventually what seems to give the work value is precisely its esoteric
inviolability, its unbroken code. And once more it is the novelist,
who dies during the course of James's story, who wins the battle
(for the relation has become an intellectual battle to possess the
meaning of the text). The pattern remains still undetected to the
end.

Many things are implied in the story. The metaphor of the
earnest search for truth so beloved of the Victorians is invoked
only to be dismissed with disparaging irony:(67)

'Have I got to *tell* you, after all these years and labours?'
There was something in the friendly reproach of this -
jocosely exaggerated - that made me, as an ardent young
seeker for truth, blush to the roots of my hair.

We are in a world where the 'ardent young seeker for truth' suddenly appears gauche and out of place, like an awkward adoles-
cent amongst sophistications he does not understand, and indeed
the way in which Vereker places the critic at such an acute disadvantage is important. By obscuring the structure of his work
he has turned tables on the new critics, the 'rising young men'
who were reading Wagner as a 'neurotic', Mallarmé as 'a nerve-
sufferer', Verlaine as a mattoid, Ibsen as 'ego-manic' and Zola as
a 'neurasthenic and hysteric'.(68) James employs a rhetoric of
enigma to defend the art of the novelist from the many forms of
criticism which arose once the trust between reader and author
began to break down, and he replaces this trust with the bonds
of Tantalus, 'faint wandering notes of a hidden music. That was
just the rarity, that was the charm'.

It is manifestly an aesthetic strategy which is taken from Symbolism and Art for Art's Sake, an ideology of rarity which endeavours to value the art object by placing it beyond the reach
of the multitude. Vereker even echoes Pater's famous definition of
art - 'to burn always with a hard, gem-like flame' in describing
the hidden pattern in his novels as 'the very passion of his passion, the very part of the business in which, for him, the flame of
art burns most intensely....' By indicating that there is a deeply
concealed meaning in the work of art and then denying the reader
access to it, the modern novelist solicits a hermeneutic attitude
towards his work which, as with Symbolism, fends off a direct,
immediate assimilation of its meaning. It makes the work more and
more densely opaque to the reader, more difficult to see through,
constantly eluding the imposition of one fixed and certain meaning.
In a letter to Barrett Clark about 'Victory', Conrad consciously
adopted this symbolist aesthetic:(69)

I ... put before you a general proposition, that a work of
art is very seldom limited to one exclusive meaning and not
necessarily tending to a definite conclusion. And this for the
reason that the nearer it approaches art, the more it acquires
a symbolic character... all the great creations of literature
have been symbolic, and in that way have gained in complexity, in power, in depth and beauty.

Arthur Symons, in an essay on Mallarmé published in 1898,
brought together these two ideas, the vulnerability of the modern
writer and the impossibility of writing in the old manner, when he
wrote:(70)

> But who, in our time has wrought so subtle a veil, shining
> on this side, where the few are, a thick cloud on the other,
> where are the many? The oracles have always had the wis-
> dom to hide their secrets in the obscurity of many mean-
> ings, or of what has seemed meaningless; *and might it not,
> after all, be the finest epitaph for a self-respecting man of
> letters to be able to say, even after the writing of many
> books: I have kept my secret, I have not betrayed myself
> to the multitude?* [My italics]

In a marvellous phrase, Mallarmé expressed precisely the dilemma
of Vereker and Delavoy (or James, Conrad and Meredith), the
dilemma of risking, by the act of writing, some shameful or embarrassing exposure, when he wrote that all publication is 'almost a
speculation, on one's modesty, for one's silence'. Symons adds:(71)

> And I, for one, cannot doubt that he was, for the most part,
> entirely right in his statement and analysis of the new con-
> ditions under which we are now privileged or condemned to
> write....is it possible for a writer, at the present day, to
> be quite simple, with the old, objective simplicity, in either
> thought or expression? To be naif, to be archaic, is not to
> be either natural or simple; I affirm that it is not natural to
> be what is called 'natural' any longer. We have no longer
> the mental attitude of those to whom a story was but a story,
> and all stories good.

This dialectic of revelation and concealment dominates the literature of Meredith, Conrad and Henry James. There is in their
work the feeling that inner privacies are being cruelly probed and
exposed in a way that was quite new. It is sometimes like the distress and fear which the music of Wagner evoked in Victorian
listeners, the fear of public 'nakedness', of 'baring one's soul',
and not the soul only, but extreme passions normally kept so
heavily covered that their existence had been hardly suspected
by the persons themselves. Vernon Lee, listening to 'some modern
German songs' (probably Wagner or Richard Strauss), wrote that
they were a 'violation of the privacy of the human soul'. She continues:(72)

> It is astonishing, when one realizes it, that the charm of
> music, the good renown it has gained in its more healthful
> and more decorous days, can make us sit out what we do
> sit out under its influence; violations of our innermost
> secrets, revelations of the hidden possibilities of our own
> nature and the nature of others; stripping away of all the
> soul's outward forms, melting away of the soul's active
> structure, its bone and muscle, till there is revealed only
> the shapeless primaeval nudity of confused instincts, the
> soul's vague viscera.

Wagner, it was felt, had made music morbid, shameful, excessive.

He had gone beyond boundaries which should not have been ex-
ceeded (far beyond them), creating the unhealthy, pudic excite-
ment of forbidden indulgence: 'Wagner est une névrose.' For
Wagner was also taken as archetypically modern, 'the *modern
artist* par excellence, the Cagliostro of modernism', and in London
by 1899 one reviewer could write that 'in our capital city at all
events, we are now haunted by a kind of Wagner-madness.'(73)
It is no accident that 'One of Our Conquerors' adopts the music
of Wagner as a fundamental motif, that it should be through Wagner that Victor Radnor can express the depth of his guilt in the
confrontation with his peers and that Meredith can express the
violation of innermost secrets which eventually destroy Radnor.(74)

The movement from James to Mallarmé, to Meredith and Wagner
is not arbitrary. 'Carry the theories of Mallarmé to a practical
conclusion, multiply his powers in a direct ratio, and you have
Wagner', wrote Symons, who also remarked (as indeed others had
done), 'some of Mr Meredith's poems, and occasional passages of
his prose, can alone give in English some faint idea of the later
prose of Mallarmé.'(75) The mutual adoption of deflective strategy
and enigmatic method by so many writers during this period, the
exploratory use of secrecy, lying, obscurity, impression and
withdrawal, form an interconnection of cultural concern and activity which became a generative complex of modernism.(76) This
frequently involves the decision not to tell the truth and the
decision not to strive, or perhaps not to hope, for sincere and
easy communication with the reader. 'Do you understand me?'
asked R. L. Stevenson. 'God knows, I should think it highly improbable.'

3 TRUTH AND IMPURITY

Were vaguenesses enough and the sweet lies plenty
The hollow words could bear all suffering
And cure me of ills

Dylan Thomas

- and noble stories are replaced by chambering talk.

George Moore

For the modern literary mind there is a certain degree of embarrassment about the word 'truth' signified in the tendency since
the Victorian period to deny it the dignity of an initial capital
letter. This orthographic demotion may even extend to placing it
in inverted commas, indicating such a degree of dissatisfaction
that the word is granted only a provisional presence within a
sentence. The sort of respect, even reverence, which the Victorians accorded the word Truth and which led them to mark it
out as special has changed so much that we too must mark it out
from its written context, but rather as a self-conscious index,
anxious or ironic, that the word cannot be allowed to retain an
unremarked authority.

This distance from Truth to 'truth' is one measure of the distance between Victorian and modern literature. The epistemological
shift which is given away in these small typographical changes is
the complex movement, not merely of what constitutes the truth in
literature, but of all the associations of cultural attitude and res
ponse which are bound up with it. Thus nothing appears more
dated in verse, more thoroughly Victorian, than those earnest
exhortations to strive for abstract, capitalized Truth:(1)

O Youth whose hope is high
Who dost to Truth aspire,
Whether thou live or die
O look not back nor tire.

The disappearance of a dominant religious discourse is certainly
the main reason why such a strident apostrophe today appears a
quaint anachronism. We do not know to what this Truth appeals,
there is no object or even objective text, which can be aspired to
or aimed at in the sense assumed by the verse.

Victorian writing is marked in a massive way by this ideal of
Truth as an ultimately pure and unified field. The 'inner verities'
of feeling and religion and the outer laws of nature and social

system often conflicted with enough force to pull the sensitive
mind to the edge of insanity with contradictory intellectual demands, but what was in question was a choice of different orders
of truth, not the idea of truth as such. The belief was powerful
and enduring that even if the road to knowledge were almost
impossibly difficult and narrow, it was an unquestionable duty to
attempt the journey. It is epitomized in the popular verses of
Lewis Morris:

> For knowledge is a steep which few may climb
> While duty is a path which all may tread

This earnest metaphorical expression of a journey towards some
object or place, the 'true', is worth examining in detail. I will
risk saying that I think it the single most important organizational
metaphor in Victorian fiction. On it depends not only the inner
structure of all nineteenth-century 'Bildungsroman', of which
'Great Expectations' may be taken as paradigmatic, but also those
narratives which characteristically chart the progress of someone
who is the prisoner of illusion and (self) deception, and who
finally achieves - in sadness or in joy - a 'true' conception of
himself and the world. The demystification of personal capabilities
and qualities from Emma to Isabel Archer is articulated upon this
metaphorical journey through illusion and falsehood to a true conception of self. Such a journey, and the numerous narratives
which organize biographical development on the model of this
journey, are only made possible by a faith in the clear distinction
of the false from the not-false, and the inestimable value of winning through - or in its more pessimistic form, attempting to win
through - to this latter. The necessary corollary of this journey
towards an objective idea of Truth is the faith in sincerity, and
Trilling was undoubtedly correct in seeing sincerity as a central
and enduring moral counterpart to the search for truth which
engaged the 'honest consciousness' of literature from at least the
period of the sixteenth century.(2) J. S. Mill's praise of 'sincere
earnest, and truth-loving' persons,(3) like Carlyle's characterization of the hero ('Sincerity, a deep, great, genuine sincerity,
is the first characteristic of all men in any way heroic') is an
extension into the moral sphere of the epistemological journey
towards true knowledge which models the ideal progression of
human life.

What strengthens the metaphor and prolongs its use in the nineteenth century is the fact that the forms of understanding common
to both a religious and a positivist comprehension of the world
underpin the idea of a journey from illusion to knowledge, with a
clearly visible distinction of the one from the other. What is
affirmed is the invaluable and necessary development of character
and plot towards knowledge, even if this knowledge shared at
last with the reader produces only the autumnal sadness of disenchantment. It is in this respect that what we know at the termination of a novel is, for the purposes of generic analysis, less
important than the fact that we know. It is this which makes the
late novels of George Meredith, together with those of Joseph

Conrad and Henry James, identifiably distinct from those of
Thackeray, Dickens, George Eliot and Trollope. The stoical optimism which inhabits logic itself, the optimism of control and understanding predicated by a rationally organized and knowable world
(or the stoical optimism of the Christian) is not contradicted by
scientific rationalism but strengthened by it. The word Truth
changes its signification in the process of secularization but it
does not lose it.

In Meredith's work we can trace very clearly a movement away
from this ideal and the growth of a more complex, mixed notion.
His first prose work, 'The Shaving of Shagpat: An Arabian Enter-
tainment' (1856), is purely an allegorical treatment of the quest
for truth, the journey of the sincere soul, and indeed the novel
could be called a commentary upon all the other fictions which
adopt the structural opposition (and it is the 'clarity' of the
opposition which is precisely in question) between false and true
in order to launch the questing soul across the abyss between
them. 'The Shaving of Shagpat' is an extravagant and fantastic
allegory of the quest for truth which unites Meredith's Victorian
interest in self-improvement, integration and education ('Bildung')
with the biographical development of personality; a journey
through the dangers of illusion and falsehood to beyond them, to
a state of 'rightness' and understanding. McKechnie's commentary on the hero, Shibli, notes that, 'On his starting out from
Shiraz there was round his soul, screening it from life's realities,
a cosy cloak of illusion, woven of self-love and inexperience.'(4)

Shibli's adventures and his quest to 'master The Event' become
not merely loosely related episodes in a picaresque extravaganza,
but the progressive stages of an education which leads ultimately
to the defeat of Rabesqurat, Queen of Illusions. Shibli had never
been more lost than when his soul had been 'blinded by Rabesqurat in the depths of the Enchanted Sea', and his final great
battle against evil reaches its climax of difficulty when the Queen
of Illusions fights against him. The equation of evil and illusion
fundamental to nineteenth-century narrative becomes the essential
informing principle, and in this respect Meredith's story is largely
a convention of nineteenth-century thought which has been lav-
ishly ornamented and allegorized:(5)

> Power, on Illusion based, o'ertoppeth all;
> The more disastrous is its certain fall!

George Eliot called the story a work of genius, and in so far as
the narrative of Shibli gives a sort of allegorized version of the
moral development of Dorothea Brooke, held between the gravi-
tational pull of the powerful principles of truth and illusion, one
can see clearly why she so admired it. Dorothea has much in common with Shibli, who begins by 'ever flying at false game';(6)

> A follower of misleading beams
> A cheated soul, the mock of dreams.

Whatever the agonies and errors suffered by the hero or heroine in their deluded state, this is ultimately a quite reassuring,
settled form of understanding. It presupposes, among other things,

that eventually a person can capture and know, in some moment
of fullness, their own personality: that the development of character is an unfolding dialectic of two principles, falsehood and
truth, and that at some point (which is often made coincident with
the termination of the narrative) the dialectic is halted by the
removal of one of the cardinal terms (falsehood). The varieties of
falsehood may range from the outright deceptions of Becky Sharp
to the subtle pressures of a devious and incompletely understood
egoism, but they are defined, not only by their difference from
truth and self-knowledge, but even more by the clarity of the
difference, the space between true and false, which is the space
of potential movement in character development. The more powerful the self-delusion, the more painful, but also more potentially
triumphant, its transcendence: the circumscribed, identifiable
state of delusion is the perilous ground upon which the dramatic
risk of self-destruction is played out. It is a pattern of 'development' (and progress is evidently the standard kind of narrative
movement, as in 'Pilgrim's Progress') which is repeated frequently
in the great nineteenth-century fictions, a pattern which finds in
the provisional achievement of self-knowledge a 'unity' of self-
hood and an end to alienation, and in these two a willed closure of
narrative and subjective identity which is both a parallel of, and
alternative to, the closure imposed by death.

It is only when Shibli fully and finally comprehends his own
nature, after alternating periods of error and increasing knowledge, that a period of unrivalled prosperity and natural harmony
comes to the city. Whilst illusion persists, so too does strife; but
in the defeat of the Genie Karaz, a shape-shifting deceiver, and
Rabesqurat, Queen of Illusions, knowledge restores social unity.
Though new deceptions may in time arise, this period of social
integration and happiness can be re-established by the brave
struggle of future youth against falsehood:

Some doubt Eternity: from life begun,
Has folly ceased within them, sire to son?
So, ever fresh illusions will arise
And lord creation, until men are wise.

The pre-condition for social order, then, is wisdom. The battle
for a united and contented commonwealth turns, perhaps sur-
prisingly, on a battle for knowledge, the battle to which Thackeray urged Arthur in 'Pendennis':(7)

If seeing and acknowledging the lies of the world, Arthur,
as see them you can with only too fatal a clearness, you
submit to them without any protest farther than a laugh; if,
plunged yourself in easy sensuality, you allow the whole
wretched world to pass by you unmoved; if the fight for the
truth is taking place, and all men of honour are on the
ground armed on the one side or the other, and you alone
are to lie on your balcony and smoke your pipe out of the
noise and the danger - you had better have died, or never
been at all, than such a sensual coward.

'Praevalebit Veritas' was not the banner of Newman alone. Nor was

Shibli's battle only Arthur's, for it was also the one to which
George Eliot pledged herself when she announced: 'For my part,
I wish to be among the ranks of that glorious crusade that is
seeking to set Truth's Holy Sepulchre free from a usurped domination.'(8) This famous declaration nicely illustrates the degree
to which the same metaphor (battles encountered on the pathway
to some distant fixed realm of truth) is carried across from a
religious to a rationalist discourse in such a way that the difference is hardly registered: the questing subject remains fixed in
the same position with relation to wisdom and illusory error in
both realms.

This is partly a question of a characteristic attitude (perfectly
expressed by Mill, of whom Carlyle wrote that he felt the highest
duty was to 'see facts as they actually were, and, if that was
impossible, at least to desire to see them, to be sincere with his
own soul'),(9) the counterpart of Meredith's injunction 'To fight
the false, O youths, and never spare!' But it is also more than a
matter of attitude, it is more than simply a common belief in the
value of complete sincerity. It is a compounding of narrative and
biographical progression with the acts of revelation and penetration, with the coming-to-consciousness of knowledge, which in
the end may be no more than a kind of faith in the categorical
'separation' of truth from illusion. That is to say, characters and
plots mix truth and illusion together constantly, but always under
the controlling knowledge of author and reader of the difference
between the two; we can tell them apart, temporary confusion
between their principles are always resolved on this basis. What
George Lukács has termed in reference to Flaubert's 'Sentimental
Education' the 'romance of disillusionment' is only possible upon
the basis of an ironic or compassionate incommensurability between
actual and illusory, between the protagonist's conception of the
real and the author's conception of the 'real', which is an extension of the same structured opposition. The irony or compassion
are functions of a distance, which in the last instance the author
and reader both 'know', and which extends between, and keeps
separate, the false and the true.

In one sense this is no more than a 'Sartor Resartus', a clothes-
philosophy, an aesthetics of sham, exploring at length the multitude of diverse relations between the illusory surface and the
real essence. It is the epistemology of 'Vanity Fair'. In a paper to
the 'English Institute' Wolfgang Iser, in an attempt to account for
the 'observable increase of indeterminacy' in narrative literature
since the eighteenth century, wrote that:(10)

> The aesthetic effect of *Vanity Fair* depends on activating
> the reader's critical faculties so that he may recognize the
> social reality of the novel as a confusing array of sham
> attitudes, and experience the exposure of this sham as the
> true reality. Instead of being expressly stated, the criteria
> for such judgements have to be inferred. They are the
> blanks which the reader is supposed to fill in, thus bring-
> ing his own criticism to bear.

Thackeray's text covertly solicits the judgment of the reader in
'the exposure of sham as the true reality,' which again is only
possible on the basis of a confidence in the irreducible difference
between sham and reality. Of 'The Fair Frankincense' Meredith
wrote that it had 'altogether a new kind of villain, being Humbug
active - a great gun likely to make a noise if I can prime him
properly,' and the words 'humbug' and 'sham' are merely exten-
sions, into the realm of character, of an essentially epistemological distinction: a vertical separation of surface from depth which
never substantially loses track of the relation between them.

But by the 1880s Meredith no longer held to this simple, essential model of 'sham' and 'humbug'. Obscurity of characterization
became more like a 'horizontal' mixing and fragmenting of personality, never subject to the cunning control implicit in a term like
'sham'.(11) The clarity of presentation and consistency of
emotional and moral response which we find in George Eliot's
characters began to appear as a convention of the fiction, inadequate to the unstable inmixing of registers which Meredith found
more appropriate to the comprehension of character. Comprehension is always imperfect in this sphere, for personality is reflected
only in 'a cracked glass' and mirrored best in 'intershifting tales'.
(12) Meredith increasingly noted the ways in which purity of
thought and unity of motive were fractured and twisted by obscure
mental processes, 'that little twist of brain' as he termed it. Indeed his sense that personality is not transparent (to the self, to
others) nor straight, nor unified, became central in his later
poetry and fiction. The images he employs to describe this are
often strained, quirky and defiantly difficult but as such perfect
analogues of his conception of the mind's processes. The world is
not straight, it has 'a curved spine', and the lines of thought
within us are like 'the inebriate's track at night', the mind's
ascent a 'spiral'. Nothing in Meredith is quite straightforward: by
rejecting a faith in direct progression whilst at the same time un-
willing to reject progress as such, he figures the world's advance
as a zig-zag, a flattened spiral or 'the way of worms'. Thus, wisdom endures in Meredith, but only just:(13)

Tis true the wisdom that my mind exacts
Through contemplation from a heart unbent
By many tempests may be stained and rent:
The summer flies it mightily attracts.

There is something wounded and malodorous about this wisdom,
stained and fly-blown. In Meredith, intelligence loses its sentimental translucence and the wisdom of Age speaks with 'a rudder-
less tongue/Turning dead trifles, like the cock of dung'.(14) The
mind is always warring with the senses and can never free itself
from the demands of sensual desire (these two realms are usually
referred to as the Ideal and Earth (or Nature) in Meredith's
writing). The conflict is never clear. It produces division, riddle,
endless circling round inside one's head and Meredith's poems
seek to discover some point of equilibrium, some state of 'vision
and solidity' in the violence of the movement. The need to find

mental stasis is desperate, for until it is found 'we go distraught,/
At best but circle-windsails of a mill.' Desire ('An ardour that
desires, unknowing what')(15) trammels the mind with its obscure
needs. This unknowing realm perpetually troubles and compromises an intelligence which is always hybrid, yet which even in its
mongrel impurity strives for some kind of perfection, some kind
of 'form'.

In one place Meredith shows that the poetics of obscurity are
intimately related to this version of mind as compromised – a
domain unclearly divided between fallen wisdom and unknowing
desire. A Later Alexandrian (1883) sets out subtly to undercut
the pure categories of traditional aesthetic and moral judgment.
It is a poem which places itself off-centre, using calculated dis-
sonance to mark out the dubious and multiform sources of its own
literary conception. It is a justification of Alexandrianism on the
grounds that there is 'subtler promise' in the poetic sensibility
used and compromised by contradictory and disjunctive experience:
(16)

> An inspiration caught from dubious hues
> Filled him, and mystic wrynesses he chased;
> For they lead further than the single-faced,
> Wave subtler promise when desire pursues.
> The moon of cloud discoloured was his Muse,
> His pipe the reed of the old moaning waste.
> Love was to him with anguish fast enlaced,
> And Beauty where she walked blood-shot the dews.

The 'discoloured' syncretism of the verse falls between the
heartfelt celebration of the unique and motley which we find in
Hopkins ('all things counter, original, spare') and that distinct
ively modernist partiality for the used and the second-hand,
Apollinaire's 'poésie de brocante' and Yeats's 'rag-and-bone shop
of the heart.' Dubious, discoloured and bloodshot, Meredith's
muse speaks of a subtly adulterated purity. Yet the literature
which she inspires possesses a wry authenticity which the ideal-
ism of traditional lyric verse had usually lacked. The poem is an
imputation, and in its refusal of the perfect and 'single-faced', it
reveals an inner connection of poetic obscurity with a fractured
intellectual integrity.

The poem is symptomatic, not only of this post-lapsarian sense
of the dignified imperfection of a fallen world mediated into a consciously obscure poetic, but also of the equivocal, 'two-faced'
nature of literary authority, the feeling of dubiousness which
gradually infiltrates the creative process.

This subtle 'discolouration' of traditional moral and aesthetic
purities is of importance in Conrad and Henry James as well as
Meredith. In all three cases, obscurity appears to be related to
an insidious, intensely private fear that however brave or sophisticated one might be, the complete integrity and sincerity of the
'single-faced' will always eventually be compromised or betrayed.
In all three novelists, the honest consciousness drifts into trouble.
The place and function of sincerity in these fictions is uncomfortable,

almost at times an embarrassment. In 'Heart of Darkness' dishonesty to the Intended is preferable to Marlow's usual blunt
truth: the alternative would be 'too dark, too dark altogether'.
Densher, Strether and Amerigo are so placed that sincerity is of
no use at all. The world in which they find themselves has no
secure role for sincerity, and even Milly Theale, that purest of
Jamesian characters, finds it unavoidable to lie.(17)

Indeed, Meredith, Conrad and James were fascinated by liars.
They persistently return to explore situations in which people
are forced to lie to defend themselves or to defend others. Their
lies are rarely malicious or calumniating, they are defensive, often
so vague or subtle that their relation to the truth is hopelessly
perplexed. Lies are as old as the fictions to which they have been
assimilated, but in late nineteenth-century fiction lies and liars
focus some complex issues of literary obscurity. Lies took on a
special significance in a period when it was often felt that neither
culture nor individual expression could be entirely sincere.
Rationality, social forms, language and objective representation
began to seem like fictional constructs, and untruth could not be
clearly and explicitly separated from the true and labelled as 'bad'.
Falsehood seemed not so much an occasional isolated lapse on the
part of an individual but constitutive of representation itself. In
Conrad there is often a desolate sense that language always lies
and that speaking does not portray but betrays its object. His
remark in 'Victory' that 'words, as is well known, are the great
foes of reality,' with the sour irony of its implication for any
novelist, connects with a passage from Nietzsche which precisely
captures this unease about the inseparability of true and false:(18)

> The erroneousness of a concept does not for me constitute
> an objection to it; the question is - to what extent is it
> advantageous to life.... To admit untruth as a condition
> of life - this does indeed imply a terrible negation of the
> customary valuations.

In the tensions of early modernism, lying takes on a metaphysical importance, it becomes an index of the ubiquitous untrust-
worthiness of once familiar and dependable responses. It was
indicative of the period, but unnecessary in fact, for Wilde to
plead against realism and naturalism and in favour of 'lying in art'.
(19) The solidarity between truth and goodness neither dissolved
nor remained intact, it became a suspended and obscure relation,
now the source of confidence, now of anxiety. Characters in the
novels try to live between truth and falsehood, in a compromised
and dubious space between veracity and its disintegration. Marlow, Jimmy Wait, Razumov, Clara Middleton, Diana Merion, Rose
Jocelyn, Natalia Radnor, Maggie Verver, Kate Croy, Densher,
Strether, Capadose, Peter Brench, Milly Theale - the list of
characters who cling to evasive falsehoods and yet also try to tell
the truth in Meredith, Conrad and James is striking. They conceal and obscure their feelings and desires in narratives which
are complexly occluded, which retain contrary and even conflicting conceptions of truth and which may even appear to be

constructed on mutually exclusive premises. Marlow in 'Heart of
Darkness' remarks:(20)

> You know, I hate, detest, and can't bear a lie, not because
> I am straighter than the rest of us, but simply because it
> appals me. There is a taint of death, a flavour of mortality
> in lies - which is exactly what I hate and detest in the world
> - what I want to forget. It makes me miserable and sick, like
> biting something rotten would do.

And yet, of course, Marlow lies. The alternative, as we have seen,
would be 'too dark, too dark altogether'. Even though lying in-
fects words with the taint of death, it is to be preferred to some
sorts of truth. Marlow is compromised. In order to suppress the
depraved horror that Kurtz saw and became, Marlow chooses to
endorse a fictitious, idealized image of Kurtz in the full and sick-
ening knowledge that it is a romantic sham, a coercive substitution
of poetic cliché (the lover's name) for the unnameable horror.
This substitution simultaneously indicates their opposition and
hollow equivalence. The power with which this subverts the
romance ending is an almost brutal rejection of the traditionally
sanctioned coincidence of enlightenment and narrative fulfilment.
There is no dénouement, no explanation, no unravelling of the
hermeneutic code:(21)

> I pulled myself together and spoke slowly. 'The last word
> he pronounced was - your name.' I heard a light sigh and
> then my heart stood still, stopped dead short by an
> exulting and terrible cry, by the cry of inconceivable
> triumph and of unspeakable pain. 'I knew it - I was sure!'
> ... She knew. She was sure.

The romance commonplace of the warrior who dies with the name of
his lover on his lips is deliberately placed so as to be seen by the
reader as a lie, so as to reveal through and through the emptiness
of its signification, the inner deception of its sentimental gesture.

Jimmy Wait, the 'Nigger' of the 'Narcissus', also lies. He pretends that he is pretending to die, so as not to face the truth of
his approaching death. Jimmy's sham existence is a reversal of
the usual situation of a malingerer, he pretends to be work-shy to
obscure the real fact of his illness, both from himself and the other
crew members. But this reversal still has the same objective as all
lies, to conceal the truth by telling a story. He creates a fiction,
a sentimental lie, the real mechanism of which operates to protect
the subject of the lie by repressing a secret. The disturbance and
near anarchy which Jimmy's impending death brings to the crew of
the 'Narcissus' once it is public, is repressed (yet not resolved)
by the reassuring double-think of Jimmy's yarn. Even when a
crucial point is reached when the yarn, the lie, appears as what it
is - utterly false - the loyalty of the liar to his fiction inspires
respect: 'Jimmy's steadfastness to his untruthful attitude in the
face of the inevitable truth had the proportions of a colossal enigma - of a manifestation grand and incomprehensible that at times
inspired a wondering awe.'(22)

An unexpected complexity has crept in: a liar may be 'true' to

his lie. He may remain steadfast and loyal to an untruth with such
tenacity that eventually the demand for the honest facts itself
appears unworthy, 'a perfidious desire of truthfulness'. The lie
thus continues to exert its power of repression even after it has
been discovered to be untrue, and for the liar, to be 'true' to
the story is preferable to a double betrayal, a betrayal of the
fact and of its subsequent fiction. Jimmy Wait's tenacious loyalty
to his lie maintains a continuous falsehood at the heart of the
shipboard community which preserves its safety and ensures its
integrity. It is only upon the basis of this founding deception that
the social group avoids disintegration.

But what is at stake is more than a pragmatic acceptance of untruth. In Meredith, social life confronts his characters like a false
accusation. They have usually breached some social code in the
past (in 'The Ordeal of Richard Feverel', 'The Adventures of
Harry Richmond', 'Diana of the Crossways', 'One of Our Conquerors', 'Lord Ormont and his Aminta' and 'The Amazing Marriage'
this 'crime' is the betrayal of marriage – the relation of this to
lying and obscurity in Meredith is explored at length in chapter
4) and yet the social indictment of his characters becomes a grotesque distortion of their feelings and motives. At the same time
(reluctantly and with some bad grace), Meredith realized that
some degree of social accommodation with the flock was necessary
for the growth and success of language and thought. He was
always afraid that disdainful aloofness might quickly turn to eccen-
tricity:(23)

Who sweats not with the flock will seek in vain
To shed the words which are ripe fruit of sun.

Subjectivity revalued against social codes which in themselves
appeared more and more arbitrary and untruthful gave protective
lies and personal obscurity an apparent justification. Mrs E. L.
Linton in Our Illusions (1891), an article Meredith almost certainly
knew, remarks:(24)

A graver illusion than any of these lies in those counsels
of perfection which form part of the mythic morals inculcated
on the young.... Even verbal truth itself would sometimes
be more dishonouring than a lie.... Try any virtue that can
be named, and the result is the same. Each and all change
according to the angle, like shot-silk or a Brazilian butter-
fly's wing. There is no such thing in the whole of life as the
one unchangeable absolute. And what is relativity but the
illusive character of law?

This last sentence is striking. Relativity for the modern would
suggest a diversity of standards and opinions, but I doubt that
it would be defined, as here, as making law itself 'illusive' – for
there is in our time the contrary argument that relativity makes
all law equally valid, a democratization of standards which no
longer necessarily implies that law itself is false. But at the end
of the Victorian period there is the strong sense that relativism
and increasing subjectivism had made all things false, revealed
the old standards and forms as so many hollow idols. Much of the

art of the end of the century takes its distinctive form from a
positive adoption of this attitude. In an article reviewing the work
of Maupassant in 1888, Henry James quoted from the former's
preface to 'Pierre et Jean' with approval:(25)

How childish, moreover, to believe in reality, since we each
carry our own in our thoughts and in our organs.... Each
one of us therefore forms for himself an illusion of the world,
which is the illusion poetic, or sentimental, or joyous, or
melancholy, or unclean, or dismal, according to his nature.
And the writer has no other mission than to *reproduce faithfully this illusion*, with all the contrivances of art that he
has learned and has at his command.... The great artists
are those who make humanity accept their particular illusion.

This is a distinctive remove from traditional mimetic theory and
it reverses the normal terms: the work of art is not here considered an illusory copy of a true and real object, but a true and
real reproduction of an illusory reality. James's narrative art,
which depends totally on the disjunctive play of subjective realities one against the other, misunderstanding and misrecognizing
what each separate illusion intimates about the value of its possessor, is part of a more general epistemological shift in the
intellectual culture of the period. The definition of the artist
given by Maupassant and endorsed by James is crucial to the
understanding of this shift in that it defines the aim of the artist
as a strategic act of persuasion in the presentation of that which
is not: 'the great artists are those who make humanity accept
their particular illusion.' The sincerity involved in artistic production has shifted from the object to the art work: it is no
longer a case of sincere and faithful truth-to-reality, but rather
a fidelity to the work of art which can give a 'real' and 'true'
representation of what is largely the interplay of illusion. The
fetishization of the art object which we find in the last decades of
the century, not only in self-styled Art for Art's Sake but in
James, George Moore and Gosse, was in part a response to the
devaluation of the earnest search for Truth which had hitherto
made 'reality' the ultimate intellectual goal.

The combination of subjectivism with generalized fictional construction obscured the lines between truth, fiction, conventional
codes and private languages. In 'Lord Jim' the pursuit of the differences hardly seems worth the effort when Marlow says, 'some
such truth or some such illusion - I don't care how you call it,
there is so little difference, and the difference means so little.'
This is indeed a weary dismissal of that energetic and earnest
quest for Truth which had been of paramount importance thirty
years earlier. It anticipates the claim that Yeats was to make that
'All civilization is held together ... by artificially created illusions':
this pervasive sense of general social falsehood conspired with a
growing criticism of inflated and pretentious claims for Imperialism.
The air of darkening unreality in Conrad's An Outpost of Progress
and 'Heart of Darkness' is closely related to the moral indignation
which his close friend Cunninghame Graham expressed at the

exploitation of men and the false, deceiving nature of the dominant ideology upon which it was predicated:(26)
> His detestation of *society's collective hypocrisy*, whether
> of privileged classes or of masses of men, and of the cant
> of 'civilization', brought him to shiver many a lance against
> the triple brass of British Industrialism, commercialism and
> Imperialism.

When civilization or culture itself appears false then the problems of mimetic transcription immediately become complicated - for
if reality is false then what is fiction? Contemporary fictions began
to manifest a strange unease about the insubstantiality of collective meanings. Marzio Pandolfi, the central character in Marion
Crawford's 'Marzio's Crucifix' (1887), opens the novel with a
bitter exclamation which epitomizes the extreme rejection involved:
'"The whole of this modern fabric of existence is a living Lie!"
cried Marzio Pandolfi, striking his little hammer upon the heavy
table with an impatient rap.(27) Granville, in W. H. Mallock's
didactic novel, 'The Veil of the Temple' (1904), is afflicted
strongly with a fearful sense of his own inauthenticity: 'In my
public life I felt myself an actor before a painted canvas, and behind this canvas was nothing but death and darkness.'(28) Even
that most prosaic of realist writers, John Galsworthy, was affected
by a profound sense of the 'falseness' of British culture, with the
unexpected consequence that in an early novel, 'The Island Pharisees', he wrote a complex, suspended narrative in which values
and categories become indistinct and puzzling. 'The Island Pharisees' (1904), as the title may suggest, is about the hypocrisy and
self-righteousness of the British middle class at the end of the
nineteenth century, the Pharisees of 'this fog-smitten land'. The
book is really little more than a series of meetings and incidents
which become vehicles for Galsworthy's various criticisms of English attitudes and institutions. But Shelton, the young hero, is
far from being sure enough of his own bearings to denounce what
he sees as simply sham. 'If I thought as you do,' his friend
Crocker tells him, 'I should be all adrift.' The book begins with
his engagement to a beautiful young girl of 'good' family, who has
all the conceit of good breeding and the perfect propriety which
her class demands. The novel appears set for the type of romantic
match which ended most Victorian novels. But something goes
gradually wrong as Shelton finds himself ineluctably alienated from
the class to which he belongs and to which his impending marriage
will only bind him more tightly.

In the ensuing, tentative disagreements which he has with people
from his own upper-middle class, he discovers that they are all
consciously defending what they each know to be a falsehood. His
uncle refuses to allow that feelings and passions should ever find
their way into words, and gently but firmly (he is a consummate
paternalist) advises self-repression: ' "Truth's the very devil!
No, my dear", he said, handing a sixpence to the crossing-sweeper,
"feelings are feelings, not words. Like snakes, by Jove! Only fit
to be kept in bottles with tight corks".'(29) And on meeting a Major

at a party some time later, he is greeted with the same relaxed
and brazen defence of deception when the Major says, 'If you
come to that ... the world lives by illusions. I mean, if you look
at history, you'll see that the creation of illusions has always
been her business, don't you know.' Further encounters only
thrust Shelton more into a mood of self-doubt and discontent, his
relation with his fiancée becomes impossibly strained as he discovers himself less and less able to subscribe to the conventions
of her social class. Yet it is never clear on what grounds he feels
such disgust with his class and former friends. Conrad was absolutely accurate when he reviewed the book: 'It is as if he
[Galsworthy] were championing against all these "good" people
some intangible lost cause, some altruism, some higher truth that
for ever seems to soar out of his grasp.'(30)

The novel ends inconclusively, even rather lamely, and it leaves
the reader suspended amongst the false illusions, the deceptions
and the calculated bonhomie with a feeling of awkwardness and
hesitation. Shelton writes to his fiancée after having offended her
once too often and the novel's final paragraph describes his sense
of relief that the bond has been severed. It is a muted ending in
a minor key, and there is little indication that Shelton will take up
political action or, indeed, will know where to go on from there.
The lingering mood is negative, an indictment of 'Life the Impos-
ter': 'Pity we use such fine words - "Society, Religion, Morality."
Humbug!'

It is a novel which precisely confirms the main thesis in John
Lester's book 'Journey Through Despair 1880-1914' which although
centred upon the Decadent Movement may be widened to the period as a whole:(31)

> To know that there is an eternal truth consonant to man's
> being, and to know that man is gifted with a faculty capable
> of perceiving at least a glimmer of that truth - these were
> the necessary axioms, and both were, or appeared to be,
> substantially demolished in the years between 1880-1914.

The lie, the secret and the mystery moved in where confidence in
realism and truth faltered, so that lies and mysteries took on
special narrative responsibility. The problem which afflicted all
three novelists was to remain in good faith with oneself whilst
surviving the manifold twists of social and psychological evasion.
The ideal would be to follow the narrow line between truth and
mendacity, like Peter Brench in James's story The Tree of Knowledge, for whom 'it was nowhere on record that he had, in the
connection, on any occasion, and in any embarrassment, either
lied or spoken the truth.'(32)

The deeper integrity of Brench's relationship with his friends
and with himself can only be preserved by its surface evasions -
'eine Untreue kann in einer tieferen Innenzone eine Vereinigung
sein.'(33) Yet if this almost impossible narrow line between lie and
truth cannot be kept to, certain kinds of mendacity present themselves as being 'truer' than sincere utterance.

Henry James's outstanding short story The Liar (published six

years after R. L. Stevenson's short story The Story of a Lie)(34)
has considerable psychological subtlety in the exploration of a
compulsive liar, quite unable to stop himself 'making up tales'.
Every endeavour which Oliver Lyon makes to break through the
lies and get Capadose to admit that he is a liar fails utterly. Lyon
knows, as all the other indulgent guests know, that Colonel Capadose compulsively lies and that his wife out of love for her husband protects and covers for him. And yet Lyon's attempts to
provoke a confession from the liar, attempts motivated more by
Lyon's lingering affection for the wife who used to be an intimate
friend, are always somehow deflected, negotiated and ignored.
The story is significant for the tenacity with which Colonel Capadose and his wife protect his lying and defy the indignation of
the people to whom they lie. Quite simply, Capadose goes on lying
right to the end of the story just as his wife, without one glimmer
of shame or appeal, goes on protecting him.

A distinction has to be made between the various types of knowledge in the story, something which is always subtly balanced in
James and became increasingly complex in the later novels. The
reader knows that Colonel Capadose is a liar, and he soon discovers that Oliver Lyon also knows, along with all the other
people who meet Capadose. Capadose's wife also knows, of course,
but will never admit it. Capadose himself, however, does not recognize himself as a liar, even when he sees the portrait of himself which Lyon has painted for the Academy, and which reveals
in its every line the physiognomy of a liar. Capadose cannot tell
the difference between truth and falsehood and his lack of self-
consciousness when he lies resides in his non-recognition of his
stories as stories. His fictions weave themselves into reality without his being conscious of any difference. James leaves us in no
doubt in the story that Capadose is a liar and totally without the
integrity and honesty which he ought to have, and thus to this
extent the story resolves itself clearly at the end when Lyon turns
his back on Capadose and his wife: 'He would never go back - he
couldn't.' But in the figure of Capadose, James delineates a
psychological condition which overrides simple moral rejection,
and the passionate loyalty of the wife to the compulsive charlatan-
ism of her husband is a kind of corruption which nevertheless
commands some degree of awe, similar to that which we must feel
at Jimmy Wait's loyalty to illusion in 'The Nigger of The "Narcissus" '. Lyon is considerably piqued that Mrs Capadose never
gives herself away, and his pride is hurt that she does not confess to him how painfully shaming it is to be married to a liar. And
when he turns his back on them in self-congratulatory scorn, the
reader cannot altogether share his sense of righteousness. The
complexity of the relation between Colonel and Mrs Capadose, a
pair made pathetic in the public eye, undermines the smugness of
the artist who wished merely to use them to gratify his artistic
skill at the Academy. Indeed it is Capadose the liar, unable to
prevent himself spinning stories and painting fictions, who in his
fantastic, compulsive generation of lies may more nearly be said to

resemble the artist than Lyon. Indeed Capadose is very like that
image of the artist given by Paulhan in his influential book 'Le
Mensonge de l'art' (published in 1907) in which the fictional nature of art, religion, and society are described as 'directive
deceptions' for mankind:(35)

> La vie de l'humanité est assurée ou rendue possible par de
> grandes fonctions sociales, l'art, la religion ou la science,
> *qui dirigent l'homme en le trompant.* Ces fonctions sont ni
> éternelles, ni invariables, elles se transforment et peuvent
> mourir. Mais tout qu'elles s'accomplissent, *l'homme se méprend
> constamment, d'une façon normale et obligatoire, sur leur
> nature et sur leur portée,* et surtout il se méprend, grace à
> elles, sur les sujets qu'elles lui montrent. Il se méprend en
> diverses façons, et l'illusion artistique, à demi-consciente, à
> demi-voulue, n'a point les mêmes caractères que l'illusion
> scientifique ou l'illusion religieuse .... [My italics]

It is difficult to gauge the influence of contemporary foreign literature which had taken lying as a generalized metaphor for the
intrinsic artificiality of representations and social codes, but in
the work of Nietzsche, Ibsen, Strindberg, Paulhan, Souriau, Mallarmé and Metterlinck one can find an extraordinarily consistent
linkage between 'necessary' deceptions, unconscious drives and
social convention - what Nietzsche called 'lying in the extra-moral
sense'.(36) The direct influences of Nietzsche on Conrad and
Ibsen on James have been documented in this respect,(37) but
cultural transformations of this kind do not require direct personal links for their transmission: by 1912 the relation between
obscurity and 'the public lie' had become sufficiently general and
visible for Vernon Lee to write an extensive two-volume work on
its contemporary form. In 'Vital Lies: Studies of Some Varieties of
Recent Obscurantism'(38) she writes:

> It is to both these groups, [those who maintain that the
> truth of their ideas depends upon them being partially false
> and those who redefine truth in such a way as to include
> edifying and efficacious fallacy and falsehood] and any
> cross-groups derived from them, that I venture to apply the
> name of obscurantists, because they employ, they increase,
> and, for emotional and sometimes aesthetic reasons, they
> prefer, a certain amount of darkness, or at all events a con-
> venient, a reposeful, a suggestive intellectual penumbra.

Conrad's polemical cry in 'Under Western Eyes', 'Obscurantism
is better than the light of incendiary torches,' is a political expression of that 'suggestive intellectual penumbra' which Lee
found a pervasive feature of Edwardian culture. Conrad's directive to 'seek discourse with the shades' is to this extent not a
unique expression of his notorious pessimism or his slide into
'anomie', but something recognized as one general theme of the
period:(39)

> I don't know why, listening to him, I should have noted so
> distinctly the gradual darkening of the river, of the air;
> the irresistible slow work of the night settling on all the

visible forms, effacing the outlines, burying the shapes
deeper and deeper, like a steady fall of impalpable black
dust.

Lee took the title of her study from a dialogue in Ibsen's 'The
Wild Duck':(40)

Relling: I'm fostering the vital lie in him.

Gregers: Vital lie? Is that what you said?

Relling: Yes - I said vital lie - for illusion,
              you know, is *the* stimulating principle.

Ibsen and Lee positively embrace the historical irony of illusion
as a force for good - that, upon premises which may be false,
confused or only partially true, men may act with courage and
dignity. Indeed Ibsen expresses a stronger form of this in asser-
ting that illusion is the stimulating principle - that an unremitting
drive for truth is less likely to produce social good than work
upon the basis of a certain blindness to the real foundations of
its own ideas and values. This is a crucial idea in Conrad. In his
story An Outpost of Progress, Kayerts and Carlier are progres-
sively stripped of the security which society had bestowed upon
them, and the loss of arbitrary social belief and convention leads
to their deaths. Conrad writes:(41)

> They believed their words. Everybody shows a respectful
> deference to certain sounds that he and his fellows can
> make. But about feelings people really know nothing. We
> talk with indignation or enthusiasm; we talk about oppres-
> sion, cruelty, crime, devotion, self-sacrifice, virtue, and
> we know nothing real beyond the words. Nobody knows
> what suffering or sacrifice mean - except, perhaps the
> victims of the mysterious purpose of these illusions.

It is above all the artificiality of civilized values which enable
the individual to survive. Left to himself, there is only the 'dis-
composing intrusion' of 'things vague, uncontrollable, and repulsive....' Much of Conrad's portentous obscurity arises from his
fascination for, and fear of, the unsocialized and inarticulate self
submerged beneath language. His own experience of 'practical
anthropology' during his time as a sailor led him to conceive of
civilization as essentially hollow, as mere words, and yet indispensable to human dignity:(42)

> Few men realize that their life, the very essence of their
> character, their capabilities and their audacities, are only
> the expression of their belief in the safety of their sur-
> roundings. The courage, the composure, the confidence;
> the emotions and the principles; every great and every
> significant thought belongs not to the individual but to the
> crowd: to the crowd that believes blindly in the irresistible
> force of its institutions and of its morals, in the power of
> its police and of its opinion.

Whilst endorsing the value of this social artificiality Conrad was
perpetually pushing at its edges, fascinated by how fragile or
tough, how enduring or transient it might be. His propensity for
creating fantasies in which men are placed in terrifying isolation

(Decoud, Kurtz, Jim, Marlow, Almayer, Razumov) becomes both
a testing of, and a quest for, the degree of individual authenticity outside the pale of society and language. All three elements
- the isolation, the 'extra-territorial' self which is intrinsically
indefinite and the nature of social being as a blind belief in the
authority of institutions - all these contribute to the way in which
Conrad's writing is continually forced to encounter the 'unspeakable', the fundamentally asocial and non-lucid self 'beyond the
words'. In The Return we can find Ibsen's notion of the vital lie,
intoned with bitter irony, advocated in relation to the saving
grace of cultivated falsehood. Clearly, Alvan Harvey is a prototypical modernist figure in his inability to bear very much reality:
(43)

He was a simple human being removed from the delightful
world of crescents and squares. He stood alone, naked and
afraid, like the first man on the first day of evil. There
are in life events, contacts, glimpses, that seem brutally to
bring all the past to a close.... Go and seek another para-
dise, fool or sage. There is a moment of dumb dismay, and
the wandering must begin again; *the painful explaining
away of facts, the feverish raking up of illusions, the cul-
tivation of a fresh crop of lies in the sweat of one's brow,*
to sustain life, to make it supportable, to make it fair, so as
to hand intact to another generation of blind wanderers the
charming legend of a heartless country, of a promised land,
all flowers and blessings... [My italics]

Though the emphasis falls with a different weight and the tone
is less strained or urgent, Meredith also frequently wrote on the
dissimulations of social form and the associated idea that 'truth',
from that perspective, is an intrusive and alien force - not constitutive of human interests but destructive of them. In a passage
from 'The Egoist' where the traditional metaphor of illumination
has been systematically inverted, 'truth' is figured as a shadow,
and its movement an eclipse:(44)

Strange eclipse, when the hue of truth comes shadowing
over our bright, ideal, planet. It will not seem the planet's
fault, but truth's. Reality is the offender.

In James, too, 'reality is the offender.' Contentment in James
is almost always contingent upon the permanent suppression of
compromising facts and the denial of dangerous truths. The balance in James is more refined, the principles more delicately
poised than in the prosaic or bland assertion found in Ibsen of
the 'value of illusion'. They are, however, substantially similar in
their exploration of the idea that fictions are essential to the satisfaction of desire: 'Falsehood is essential to humanity. It plays
as large a part perhaps as the quest for pleasure and is moreover
commanded by that quest.'(45)

The whole of 'The Golden Bowl' is built upon the careful avoidance of a central 'fact' (the affair between Amerigo and Charlotte),
and the 'willed blindness' of which Conrad spoke is what Maggie
Verver most needs:(46)

> If she could have gone on with bandaged eyes she would
> have liked that best; if it were a question of saying what
> she now, apparently, should have to, and of taking from
> him what he would say, any blindness that might wrap it
> would be the nearest approach to a boon.

This is not a temporary withholding of information so that the
'éclatement' of its revelation might be all the more affirmative and
pleasurable (such that one expects from a resolved Victorian narrative), but, rather, a belief that permanent evasion, the stren-
uous effort of constant, self-doubting avoidance, remains a
fundamental task of survival. Maggie turns obfuscation into the
very source of her effort to maintain her marriage and her social
group. 'The Golden Bowl' is important in this respect for the
'verve' with which it subverts the normal romance association of
shared revelation and happy marriage. Maggie's marriage is saved
by her systematic duplicity, by her frustration of the desperate
endeavours of Amerigo and Charlotte to know where they stand.
Her vigilant obscurities are likened to the problems of textual
interpretation: 'she, Maggie, had so shuffled away every link
between consequence and cause, that the intention remained, like
some famous poetic line in a dead language, subject to varieties
of interpretation.'(47)

Hermeneutic complexity, with its multiplied choice of terms and
significance, appears the perfect analogue of these relations
between people. Meredith constantly figured his characters as
obscure texts to be deciphered, and the interconnection between
difficult writing and the growing resistance to self-revelation
becomes apparent in his idea of 'readable people'.(48) At both
levels, textual resistance affords at least a provisional security
between intention and interpretation. The offending reality is
mediated out between subjective choices of meaning so that significance is always falling between subjects, never coinciding
with them. Narrative logic, too, is necessarily weakened by the
extension of hermeneutics into social relationship: the links between consequence and cause are 'shuffled away' in the prolifer-
ation of potential readings. Thus, in the early modernist ideology
of the 'vital lie', one can detect a series of interconnected transformations which point the way towards the 'hermeneutic' fiction
of the twentieth century – the reading of social and private worlds
as tissues of partially indecipherable texts. When Heyst looks at
Lena in 'Victory', 'His mental attitude was that of a man looking
on a piece of writing which he is unable to decipher.'(49)

Heyst's inability to 'figure out' Lena recalls Schomberg's obfus-
cations (described by Conrad in a way which is remarkably close
to James's description of Maggie, interposing words between her
intention and her friends). Conrad writes that Schomberg 'multiplied words, as if to keep as many of them as possible between
himself and the murderous aspect of his purpose.'(50)

The field of language between people appears more and more
like a 'corrupt' text, what Malcolm Lowry was to call 'wrecked
entablature', with slips, lapses, omissions, falsehoods and

indecipherable moments. Obscure language is one refuge of damaged souls from the wounds inflicted by the direct, the specific
and the immediate. Maggie Verver felt (51)

the more sharply how the specific, in almost any direction,
was utterly forbidden her - how the use of it would be, for
all the world, like undoing the leash of a dog eager to follow
up a scent. It would come out, the specific, where the dog
would come out; would run to earth, somehow, the truth -
for she was believing herself in relation to the truth! - at
which she mustn't so much as indirectly point.

Under such pressures language is compromised by the energies
of concealment, and the narrator becomes an 'accomplice'. The
fictions of Meredith, Conrad and James are full of implicated and
reluctant accomplices, people who feel that narrating events will
inevitably compromise someone. The principal narrator in 'The
Sacred Fount' remarks: 'I hadn't in the least had it in mind to
"compromise" an individual; but an individual would be compromised if I didn't now take care.'(52)

Strether, Densher, the Assinghams, Susie Stringham, Hyacinth
Robinson - James fills his novels and stories with people who are
entangled in, and compromised by, what they say, and who, like
Strether, become the reluctant accomplices of discredited or rejected characters. In a sense the narrative role of the reluctant
accomplice - for the novelist as well as for his storytellers - is
determined by the gamut of problems and doubts about the place of
truth among social fictions, private uncertainty, and unconscious
disruptions. There is a moment in Marlow's narrative of 'Lord Jim'
when all these things are suddenly and brilliantly united. The
passage condenses so many of the complex issues discussed here
and which combined to produce literary obscurity in the period
that it is worth giving in full. In it, Marlow describes the risks of
a narrator placed precisely in the difficult and ambiguous role of
mediator between 'conventional' public judgment and an indicted
soul. Neither the society nor the individual give him security of
complete identification, and he has to remain awkwardly suspended
between the two (somewhat like Strether who feels lost between
Woollett and Paris). Marlow goes on to combine this role of reluctant accomplice with an intelligent understanding of the hetero-
geneity of elements deployed in Jim's case, the 'mixed nature of
his feelings', 'the convention that lurks in all truth', and 'the
essential sincerity of falsehood'. His own attitude and that of Jim
make Marlow feel that something distinctively new and important is
being revealed in their interrelation, and it does point to a fascinating moment of complex self-consciousness in the fiction of the
period:(53)

'He [Jim] was not speaking to me, he was only speaking
before me, in a dispute with an invisible personality, an
antagonistic and inseparable partner of his existence -
another possessor of his soul. These were issues beyond
the competency of a court of inquiry: it was a subtle and
momentous quarrel as to the true essence of life, and did

not want a judge. He wanted an ally, a helper, an accomplice. I felt the risk I ran of being circumvented, blinded,
decoyed, bullied perhaps, into taking a definite part in a
dispute impossible of decision if one had to be fair to all
the phantoms in possession – to the reputable that had its
claims and the disreputable that had its exigences. I can't
explain to you who haven't seen him and who hear his words
only at second hand the mixed nature of my feelings... I
know of nothing to compare with the discomfort of such a
sensation. I was made to look at the convention that lurks
in all truth and on the essential sincerity of falsehood. He
appealed to all sides at once – to the side turned perpetually
to the light of day, and to that side of us which, like the
other hemisphere of the moon, exists stealthily in perpetual
darkness, with only a fearful ashy light falling at times on
the edge. He swayed me. I own to it, I own up. The occasion
was obscure, insignificant – what you will: a lost youngster,
one in a million – but then he was one of us; an incident as
completely devoid of importance as the flooding of an ant-
heap, and yet the mystery of his attitude got hold of me as
though he had been an individual in the forefront of his
kind, as if the obscure truth involved were momentous
enough to affect mankind's conception of itself....'
It shows an impressive comprehension of the factors behind the
feeling of obscure compromise so often found in the act of narration in these writers. Marlow is divided in his identification with
Jim and with the society that has condemned Jim. As a narrator,
he feels needed as 'an ally, a helper, an accomplice', but at the
same time this will involve the deep risk of being duped – 'blinded,
decoyed' because Jim's case is fraught with ambiguity and paradox,
the conventionality of truth and the sincerity of falsehood. Compounded with this division is a further split in Marlow between
his healthy, humanist, social self 'perpetually turned to the light
of day,' and that other side which exists stealthily in perpetual
darkness, 'with only a fearful ashy light falling at times on the
edge' (the similarity to Meredith's lunar imagery is striking: the
cloud-discoloured moon expressing the very similar idea of a
reasonable soul obscurely marked by unknown forces). It is above
all the insecurity of narrative position that emerges from the divisions: 'I felt the risk I ran.... I can't explain.... I was made to
look at the convention that lurks in all truth.... He swayed me.
I own to it, I own up....' Marlow is coerced into self-doubt and
reluctant confession by the story he is telling, he is unable to
separate himself from the narrative. The same applies in his
relation to Kurtz in 'Heart of Darkness' and even more in the
relation between the captain and his criminal double in 'The Secret Sharer'. In all these cases the 'place' of the narrative voice is
in the no man's land between social convention (law, communication,
judgment) and 'phantoms in possession' of the subject beyond convention. This 'place' is fraught with compromise, conflict, moral
doubts, extreme difficulties of judgment and action. Marlow (and

it might be Dudley Sowerby or Strether) expresses the anxious
realization that such a point is 'impossible of decision', the truth
is necessarily impure 'if one had to be fair to all the phantoms in
possession - to the reputable that had its claims and the disreputable that had its exigences.'

Many of the major fictions of Meredith, Conrad and James seem
to be written upon these divided and compromised grounds. In
every direction the narrative self is forced to cross some threshold of indecision; and yet even the precise whereabouts of these
thresholds is not certain. The three writers shared, at a basic
level, a common position for narrative utterance which was formed
under the diverse pressures and conditions explored in the last
chapters of this book. The word I have had to force into use most
frequently is 'compromised'. Neither within nor beyond the conventional frameworks of value and judgment, not rebels yet not
comfortably at home in the culture, drawn towards the dark and
disreputable (or the 'vulgar' in Henry James's parlance), and set
adrift from the values of the mass public, their language and narrative perspectives tended to get caught between contradictory
claims and exigences.

They thus found themselves classed together and compared in
terms of their obscurities: they shared certain problems and concerns which afforded, in a general and somewhat abstract way,
common areas of experience in which lucidity and revelation were
difficult. However, upon this basis the particularity of obscurity
for each writer was quite distinct. Each had his own specific
pathway through the network of divergent problems and areas of
indecision. The 'yellow spot' for each writer formed itself differ-
ently, even though some of the forces of contradiction, the
pressures working against clear speech, were shared. Each
writer appropriated what his culture and background delivered
in a distinctive way. The remaining chapters therefore explore
in turn the uses of obscurity specific to each of the three writers.

Part II

4 'GODIVA TO THE GOSSIPS': MEREDITH AND THE LANGUAGE OF SHAME

Speak, and I see the side-lie of a truth

'Modern Love'

... tricked, netted, convulsive, all writhen caught?

Alsace-Lorraine

No one has written more extensively nor more feelingly about shame than George Meredith. Shame is that 'painful emotion arising from the consciousness of something dishonouring, ridiculous, or indecorous in one's own conduct or circumstances... or of being in a situation which offends one's sense of modesty or decency,'(1) and it is absolutely central to Meredith's writing. As Georgina remarks in 'Sandra Belloni':(2) 'I am sure that no man has stood in such a position as he did. To see a man publicly ashamed, and bearing it. I have never had to endure so painful a sight.'

Shame is inscribed in Meredith's novels both as theme and as process. He articulates, out of that painful emotion, a deeply moving and morally intelligent discourse about the most subtly cankering forms of shame in a way which fairly matches Keats's poetic understanding of 'embarrassment'.(3) Shame is a more pervasively and more seriously debilitating state than embarrassment, and in Meredith it attacks his sense of decency. His composure as a man and writer is perpetually convulsed by the vivid remembrance - written over and over again in his novels - of some burning moment of shameful exposure.

Although I agree with Sartre that the relation of literary work to biographical incident is always an uncertain process of inference for the critic ('Mais il faut savoir aussi que l'oeuvre ne révèle jamais les secrets de la biographie')(4) there is nevertheless a single incident which stands out in Meredith's life as appalling - catastrophic - for such a sensitive and proud man. Together with his first wife, Mary Ellen (daughter of Thomas Love Peacock), he became friends with the young painter Henry Wallis, and at some time in 1855 Wallis and Meredith went together to the rooms where the poet Chatterton was said to have killed himself. Wallis painted the scene of Chatterton's death with Meredith posed as the dead poet, lying exposed across a sofa before an open window, the torn fragments of his verse upon the floor and the phial of poison nearby. The painting was an immense success, hung at the Royal Academy Exhibition of 1856 and bought by Augustus Egg. Egg had engravings made of the picture which were distributed and sold in London and the picture became one of the most famous mid-century story-portraits.

But some time between August 1856 and July 1857, Mary Ellen and Wallis began an adulterous affair.(5) It was precisely at this period that the picture was being exhibited, and the prints must have been circulated in the artistic and intellectual groups of London at the same time as the gossip. Wallis and Mary Ellen went off to Wales together, and Meredith was left to look after his young son Arthur whilst the picture of himself, painted by the man who had cuckolded him, continued to attract whispers, insinuations and knowing smiles. What letters exist from this period betray not a flicker of what was really going on in Meredith's wrecked life at this time.(6) Whilst his wife was bearing Wallis a child in Clifton, Meredith writes in a letter to his friend Eyre Crowe in a tone of jolly bravado about Christmas cheer ('Roast Beef, Punch and Mince Pies').(7) It was only later, in 'Modern Love' ('come shame, burn to my soul') and in his novels, that Meredith relived this endless moment of shameful revelation. In his recent biographical work on Meredith, David Williams has written:(8)

It was a scene that marked Meredith, for life. It added that hint of desperation to the high-spirited heartiness which became his outward manner. It implanted in him a need to make people close to him, people dependent upon him, feel small. He had been cuckolded, and he was being deserted: for a Victorian man of his stamp, high-spirited, assertive, consciously and exultantly the possessor of great gifts, the experience must have been shattering indeed.

But even Williams in his excellent study does not dwell sufficiently upon the painful symbolic importance of the double narrative in the portrait (Meredith-as-Chatterton/Meredith-as-cuckold).

In that picture, Meredith is posed and exposed as the fake poet, the marvellous boy who was himself exposed to the world as forger and mad imitator, part inspired and part fraud. The picture must have been an agony for Meredith. Desperately struggling for artistic fame himself, he saw this picture become a source of fame and recognition for the friend who had stolen his wife - 'Faultless and wonderful,' Ruskin said of it, 'a most noble example of the great school.' A picture of horrible and humiliating ironies, it was simultaneously an attack upon himself as an artist and as a man. In every sense the picture mortifies Meredith. His cuckold's body displayed in its deathly stupor, the languorous romantic pose transformed, by the ulterior story, into the ridiculous, indecent body of a man lying and pretending at the feet of his wife's seducer.

Such an episode is not necessarily the 'origin' of shame in Meredith but the iconography freezes the endless moment of shame into a tableau of horrid petrification. It reveals the way in which shame is not only an attack upon one's sense of dignity and

The Death of Chatterton by Wallis

integrity, but upon the body.(9) It is inseparable from the convulsive visceral leap, the 'writhe' of humiliation, which it engenders, both the body's petrifaction and its desperate sideways
twist to escape. And as if intimate relation of the symbolic to the
physical were not insistent enough, Meredith is portrayed (displayed) without his customary beard. Chatterton of course was
too young to be bearded, and Meredith would have had to shave
off his by now customary beard for Wallis. The symbolism of
castration is mockingly apparent (10) and from that time on Meredith sported a full and handsome beard. He was not insensible to
the symbolism of such things. In 'The Shaving of Shagpat' (1855)
the whole allegory turns upon the long and arduous struggle of
the little barber Shibli to shave Shagpat, master of deceit. It is
the eventual shaving of Shagpat which releases the world from its
domination by illusion: once made bald, Shagpat finds his power
melts away. Published in the same year that the picture of Chatterton was painted, the irony of the comparison would not have
been lost on Meredith.

Shibli is not only a barber, despised and beaten by almost
everyone he meets, but also a tailor. His name Bagarag ('Bag of
rag') deliberately recalls that his trade and his family origins in
tailoring are despised in the story. Indeed the tale begins with
him being publicly 'thwacked' for simply being one of the despised race of tailors and barbers. Yet the ignominy of his trade,
which gives him cause to blush and hide so often, is eventually
evoked by the author as the major instrument of his success.
Coming to terms with humiliation brings its own reward:(11)

> The blush, with which their folly they confess,
> Is the first prize of his supreme success.

The Wallis incident only compounded a problem of identity and
insecurity which Meredith also had with respect to his class
origins - for he, like his first fictional hero, was from a family of
failed provincial tailors. The semi-biographical novel 'Evan Harrington' (1860) explores at length the potential embarrassments
and difficulties of being both a sensitive young 'gentleman' and
the son of a tailor, having to endure the cruel jibes of the name
'Mr Snips' as he tries to make a good impression with the local
squire.

Ashamed of his tailoring family, Evan Harrington is placed by
his author in the midst of the landed aristocracy; a petty bourgeois, he is forced to dissemble and battle against innuendo and
suspicion at the risk of being laughed out of the park gates. The
whole of this early Meredith novel is constructed along a fine edge
of concealment and equivocation, it is a book which poses the
choice between open contest and concealment in a repeated and
challenging way. Here the thing to be concealed is class-origin,
and it is the same word, 'impostor', which burns in his ears as
in Nataly's some thirty years later in 'One of Our Conquerors'
('in the recollection of two years' back, the word "Impostor" had
smacked her on both cheeks from her own mouth'). I think that
there can hardly be another novel which is so full of secrets and

deceptions as 'Evan Harrington', nor one which so obsessively
riddles the society it constructs with hollows and deceits. The
types and variety of deceiver are numerous - 'lies! lies and
deceits everywhere!' - and the story has as its origin the Great
Mel, 'that efflorescence of sublime imposture'. Mel was in fact
Meredith's own grandfather and he did not even bother to change
the name for his novel. As Williams remarks of this extraordinary,
larger-than-life character:(12)

> Mel, who on marrying set up in business as a tailor, liked
> cutting a dash more than cutting breeches. He went to balls
> and routs, rode to hounds, womanised, got frequently drunk,
> and allowed naval grandees to go off to sea with their new
> dress uniforms unpaid for. He became known in the town as
> the Great Mel. He rejoiced in being - in both senses - pat-
> ronised by the gentry, and he let his business drift towards
> insolvency.

The fundamental ambiguity of attitude to the Great Mel marks the
story itself. On the one hand this tailor parading as a gentleman
is a ridiculous fraud, 'a snob, an impostor', but on the other he
is such a massive figure, a man of exceptional bravado and, in a
peculiar sense, of honesty (he never appeared self-conscious or
ashamed of his origins, despite his easy adaption to the life-style
of the provincial aristocracy), that the ambiguous attitudes to the
Great Mel reflect the ambiguities of deception and self-defence
which run through the novel itself. This 'singular man' was,
according to Lady Jocelyn,(13)

> The light of his age. The embodied protest against our
> social prejudice. Combine - say, Mirabeau and Alcibiades,
> and the result is the Lymport Tailor: - he measures your
> husband in the morning: in the evening he makes love to
> you, through a series of pantomimic transformations. He
> was a colossal Adonis, and I'm sorry he's dead!

Ironic though this eulogy be, it ends sincerely enough, for Mel
was at once clown and hero, a figure of fun and of bravery. The
matched respect and amusement which he provoked expresses
very near the outset of Meredith's work an ambivalence which is
crucially to mark the rest of it, a dialectic of heroism and imposture which becomes inscribed in Meredith's writing as both a style
and a language. It is the Great Mel, absent from 'Evan Harrington'
(it is his death at the outset which begins the story) but endlessly
reintroduced into it as example, anecdote and narrative, whom
Meredith uses as a signifier in exordium of a double preoccupation
in the fiction.

Mel's ability to win respect ('he could still make himself res-
pected by his betters,' remarks Lady Jocelyn, herself ironized at
the moment of irony by her unconscious use of the word 'betters')
is due to his having no shame. Unlike his offspring, he found
tailoring uncongenial but not humiliating. The other characters in
'Evan Harrington', with the exception of Tom Cogglesby who man-
ipulates his curious plots in the background, are all marked by
the effects of shame. 'The whole house, from garret to kitchen

[was] full of whispers,' and even the minor figures are not ex-
cepted. The disreputable Raikes finds himself continually snubbed
whilst himself adding to Evan's embarrassments, and the terrible
skin blemish or infection which Miss Carrington has to keep concealed from George Uploft, the man she is endeavouring to capture,
is used as subtle blackmail against her by the Countess. The
Countess, Evan's sister, is herself remarkable in equivocating,
lying, concealing, deceiving, hinting and masking her way through
the accumulating embarrassments at Beckley Court. She is an
appalling triumph of the counterfeit – to be ruefully admired for
her brilliance and daring and deplored for her attitude to others,
cynical, careless and vituperative by turns: 'The Countess was
quite aware of the efficacy of a little bit of burlesque lying to
cover her retreat from any petty exposure.'(14)

The treatment of Rose and Evan, still exploring the problem of
honesty and humiliation, subtly centres the moral dilemma involved, 'the fine degrees of pain in public shame weighed against
the sin of deceits,' though the Squire's wife, Lady Jocelyn, nevertheless decides that 'As far as he's concerned, I think he has been
tolerably honest, Tom, for a man and a lover.' Evan's movement
throughout the story from deceit to openness, whilst replicating a
laudable and expected trajectory for a young Victorian hero, is
actually thrown into question by the development of Rose in the
contrary direction. Rose has a tiny black 'L' branded on the palm
of her hand by her mother for telling lies when small (her mother
expressly loathes deceivers and this makes Evan's position all the
more agonizing), and her honesty throughout most of the book is
unflinching: 'Do they think that I am going to put on a mask to
please them?.... Remember, Evan, I conceal nothing.... concealment is never of any service.'(15) But by the close of the story
Rose has changed. The catalogue of humiliations and complexities
has destroyed her youthful bravery, and she has been forced to
adopt strategy:(16)

> Rose had got a mask at last: her colour, voice, expression,
> were perfectly at command. She knew it to be a cowardice
> to wear any mask: but she had been burnt, horribly burnt:
> how much so you may guess from the supple dissimulation
> of such a bold, clear-visaged girl.

This is a singular and highly significant state for a nineteenth-
century heroine at the end (as opposed to the beginning) of a
novel. Rose has achieved a mask. It is a matter, from Meredith's
point of view, for reluctant congratulation, despite the enduring
imperatives of the Victorian convention about heroes and heroines:
that they achieve truth, that they embody truth. In Meredith
truth, in the sense of total openness of thought and word, is not
necessarily an unquestionable precondition for heroic status: Rose
is not Becky Sharp, she is far from being immoral, she has suffered, but the lesson she learns is dissimulation, the truth she
embodies is the truth of the protective mask, even though that
mask appears to remain the face of 'such a bold clear-visaged girl'.
It is only in this way that she 'conquered the sneers of the world

in her soul.' It is an abhorrent truth for Meredith – it is he who
branded her with the 'L' for liar – and it would be easy to sim-
plify his fiction as an untroubled vindication of the white lie. It
is never that: it is rather the painful struggle, marked in the
twists and writhes of his characters, his plots and his prose, to
come to terms with the agony of self-revelation in the fear of
snubs and sneers. What is in question is more than simple self-
defence. In congratulating Rose for 'getting a mask at last' Meredith poses the radical question which Trilling saw as dividing
earlier Victorian sincerity from modernism: 'What practical, moral,
intellectual advantage is there in forcibly bringing to light what
is hidden, that which lies concealed beneath the surface?'(17)
Meredith remarks of 'Evan Harrington' that 'if you have done me
the favour to read it aright [it] has been a chronicle of desperate heroism on the part of almost all the principal personages
represented.' Many Meredith heroes are so afflicted by the curse
of shame that they are driven to break the taboo on dissimulation
and defend themselves however they can. This vulnerability
('Since in our modern days every hero must have his weak heel')
produces a 'desperate' heroism, sincere in its suffering but less
than straightforward in its dealings with the world.

A desperate heroism, but also an exaggerated heroism, and
both driven on by a sense of disgrace and public humiliation. As
time went on Meredith produced more and more 'heroes' and
'heroines' in a very old-fashioned sense, people who are constantly fighting, often physically and with immense courage,
people who seek solutions in combat. In discussing 'Beauchamp's
Career', Gillian Beer writes:(18)

> Beauchamp's Career (1875) is a novel about heroism.... It
> tests a variety of possible heroic attitudes and, while never
> finally repudiating the concept of heroism it demonstrates
> the near impossibility of finding a significant function for
> the hero within English Victorian society. Indeed the novel
> suggests that heroism can now find useful expression only
> by engaging in the corporate struggle to change society
> radically. The individualistic quality of heroism may simply
> be an anachronism.

But Meredith was neither as rational nor as studied about heroism as this suggests. If the 'individualistic quality of heroism may
simply be an anachronism,' then it is hard to know what to make
of the many individualistic warriors who people Meredith's novels
after 'Beauchamp's Career'. If Mrs Beer were correct then it would
be impossible to understand Meredith's near-Amazonian women in
the later fiction: Aminta, wishing to swim the channel and who
'held herself gallantly' and tried no 'female feignings either,
affected misapprehensions, gapy ignorances, and snaky subter-
fuges, and the like'; the martial figure of Lady Charlotte hacking
down the fir-trees in her dispute with Mr Addicote; Diana Warwick
struggling against the innuendo of public opinion; and of course
Carinthia, Meredith's last heroine, the 'woman who protected her
whole sex,' the warrior-woman who escapes the shame of her

treatment from Lord Fleetwood by going to Spain to fight in the
Carlist wars where she 'acquits herself with extraordinary valour.'
   Acts of physical courage in Meredith are the compulsive enact-
ment of a victory over shame, they are the defence – particularly
for women – against the scorn of the world: in 'The Amazing
Marriage' Meredith asserts 'Women should walk in armour as if
they were born to it: for these cold sneerers will never waste
their darts on cuirasses.' The Old Buccaneer, the warrior Lord
Ormont, Chillon, Carinthia, Aminta, Nesta and Vittoria are var-
iations of an heroic composition, each compensating for some guilt
or humiliation in an extravagant, larger-than-life heroism be it
the blast of war or the conquest of nature. Like Meredith strid-
ing his thirty miles a day through the Alps after Mary Ellen had
left him for Wallis, like Skepsey's shameful wife-beating sublimated
into a passion for boxing, extreme physical exertion, often moving over into violence, seems to offer some sort of solution to the
problem of shame. When Lord Fleetwood completes the mortifying
marriage ceremony with Carinthia, it is not simple chance which
makes him take his new wife to a particularly bloody and violent
boxing competition. The humiliation of the woman who has hum-
iliated him appears in the vicarious brutality of 'the noble art'.
Fleetwood admires the boxing for what he calls its 'brute honesty',
and in this phrase we have the precise juxtaposition of the
terms in question, an association of physical violence with honesty
in a way which offers a way out of the cowardly dishonesty of
hiding one's shame.(19) Yet it remains brutality, and the 'double-
bind'(20) in Meredith's prose is that his violent self-assertion
quickly turns to excess, to savage ellipsis and brutal twisting of
phrase and clause. Yet his withdrawal into secrecy and deception
is abominable to him, he hates its insidiousness. Under these conditions, nothing in Meredith can come out 'straight' (his poetry
and prose are full of oblique movement, of 'spin', 'twist', 'turn',
'side-glance', 'side-lie', 'writhe', 'convulse'). The tension is not
only between the opposed acts of signification (to speak out or
retire behind the surfaces of language) but within these acts
there is the further tension that each is marred or compromised
in itself. For Meredith, to represent the things which burned him
and burned within him, required a violent coercion of words and
phrases which clash and jar like the confusions of battle. His long
poem 'Napoleon', for example, is an over-charged riot of energy
and erratic motion. When France accepts Napoleon's domination,
she exchanges liberty won by the revolution for his tyran-
nous yoke:(21)

   Who sprang for Liberty once, found slavery sweet,
   And Tyranny, on alert subservience buoyed,
   Spurred a blood-mare immeasurably fleet
   To shoot the transient leagues in a passing wink,
   Prompt for the glorious bound at the fanged abyss's brink....
                         she bled
   As the bacchante spills his challenging wine
   With whirl o'the cup before the kiss to lip; ....

'Sprang', 'alert', 'prompt', 'spurred', 'shoot', 'wink', 'bound',
'abyss', 'spills', 'whirl' - the verbal motion of the poem gives no
relief from this disjointed, ceaseless leap from phrase to phrase.
Full of shocks and knocks, the nervous energy loses its flow in
the turmoil of the verse: 'his sharp sword/The shower of steel and
lead/Or pastoral sunshine'. Twists of oxymoron like this allow no
respite to the reader already struggling with the poem's savage
ellipses.

The importance of this violence in Meredith's novels, particularly 'The Amazing Marriage' ought not to be underestimated. In
'The Readable People of George Meredith' Judith Wilt writes:(22)

Lionel Stevenson has compared *The Amazing Marriage* to The
Tempest for its 'rich, sunset glow', calling it Meredith's
'tenderest, his least worldly, his most poetic novel' (p. 332).
This seems to me a very 'rose-pink' view indeed of a novel
whose central plot offers one character blowing his brains
out with a pistol, another done to death by the gunpowder
explosion of half his estate, another permanently scarred on
the face by her veil catching fire, another falling halfway
down a mountainside, not to mention a bloody prizefight, an
encounter with a rabid dog, one kidnapping of a pregnant
woman, several private duels, one pitched battle of lower
and upper classes in the streets of London, and the First
Carlist War.

Judith Wilt explains this plethora of violent incidents as Meredith's
attempt to 'confront and humanize a world of extreme violence and
chaos both inside and outside the head'. But a closer look at these
incidents shows that they are endeavours by one party or another
to cope with humiliation. Even Gower Woodseer's fall, though not
coping with humiliation, is explicitly associated with it, like Victor Radnor's slip on London Bridge at the opening of 'One of Our
Conquerors'. The pressure of the rocks where he ends up require to be *'humiliatingly* coaxed' for the sake of comfort. The
battle, which continues throughout the whole novel bringing
together these other violent incidents, is the battle of pride between Fleetwood and Carinthia, each fighting to avoid the public
defeat threatened from the other. Ambrose Mallard's suicide is to
avoid shame, so are the kidnapping of Carinthia, the private
duels, and Carinthia's bold confrontation with the rabid dog
whilst Fleetwood looks on, which leads to Fleetwood's reappraisal
of his wife and the shameful memory of his treatment of her. He
compares their valour in a fantasy of competition:(23)

She stood him in the white ray of the primal vital heat, to
bear unwithering beside her the test of light. They flew,
they chased, battled, embraced, disjoined, adventured
apart, brought back the count of their deeds, compared
them, - and name the one crushed! It was the one weighted
to shame, thrust into the cellar-corner of his own disgust,
by his having asked whether that starry warrior spirit in
the woman's frame would 'take polish a little'.

There is no refuge from this degree of agonized self-consciousness. Outside there is the heat and light which burns and embarrasses him, within there is only private self-accusation whereby he is 'thrust into the cellar-corner of his own disgust.' Fleetwood is finally broken by this exhausting mental rush between public and private self which never gives him rest. His attitude to Carinthia changes and changes again: from rejecting her he rushes to accept her only to become distant once more. The novel charts his gradual disintegration as he compounds his errors and difficulties. He is mortally ashamed to have married Carinthia, yet, acting upon this shame, treats her 'shamefully'. Realizing this he tries to cover it up and make restitution, and this only leads him further into public humiliation. His 'amazing marriage' becomes a public farce and he becomes a laughing-stock – he never escapes the humiliation he dreads and he loses Carinthia as well. His pride and his suffering intertwine to choke him. In Meredith, ignominy such as this – the thing most feared – produces such a degree of self-consciousness that it is the direct equivalent of mental breakdown. Fleetwood's shame is an excess of self, an overwhelming self-presence of body and mind which destroys both. Shame hurts most by producing an excess of self-awareness, and in this respect Fleetwood is like Emilia in 'Sandra Belloni', whose self-control and sense of internal coherence suddenly fracture under the pressure of excessive consciousness in the face of humiliation:(24)

Not only did she know herself now a face of many faces; but the life within her likewise as a soul of many souls. The one Emilia, so unquestioning, so sure, lay dead; and a dozen new spirits, with but a dim likeness to her, were fighting for possession of her frame, now occupying it alone, now in couples; and each casting grim reflection on the other. Which is only a way of telling you that the great result of mortal suffering – consciousness – had fully set in; to ripen, perhaps to debase; at any rate, to prove her.

Meredith's work is everywhere marked by the pressure of an excessive presence such as Emilia experiences, as though everything had to be revealed all at once and narrative time were merely a series of total, arresting revelations. The pressure of exposure is intense, and it reveals itself as a condensed consciousness of the moment at the expense of continuity. Both at the general level of narrative sequence and at the level of syntax, Meredith compresses things so intensely that continuous movement is often lost in the flash of vivid and discrete sparks of consciousness. Here, Meredith is suggesting Victor Radnor's defiance of the weather which might spoil the huge fête he has arranged at Lakelands to drown out the increasing gossip about his past:(25)

Fine tomorrow, to a certainty! he had been heard to say. The doubt weighed for something; the balance inclined with the gentleman who had become so popular: for he had done the trick so suddenly, like a stroke of the wizard; and was a real man, not one of your spangled zodiacs selling for sixpence and hopping to a lucky hit, laughed at nine times out of ten.

Behind the abrupt discontinuity of utterance we can detect the same fear, the same twist of panic that recurs incessantly with Meredith's characters. Here, even the weather is turned into a wager against wagging tongues, a Canute-like gesture of defiance by Victor to prove himself 'a real man' not 'one of your spangled zodiacs'. It recalls Meredith's designation of the malign spirit in 'Modern Love', 'the discord-loving clown':

Used! Used! Hear now the discord-loving clown
Puff his gross spirit in them, worse than death!

These abrupt physical 'cuffs' in the prose appear side by side with obscure and hardly fathomable episodes in Meredith's writing, and there is always strain and ambivalence about what the writing should be - aggressive representation or concealment. It is what makes his discourse so mixed and unpredictable, his narrative oscillates between moments of almost excessive heroic prowess (signs which are clear and bold, which defy injury) and evasive retreat. Meredith is aware that such acute self-consciousness about language blocks it and sends it off in another direction, that shame is specifically a psychological problem of fluency. In chapter XLVI of 'The Amazing Marriage' he writes that 'a block of our speech in the heeded direction drives it storming in another, not the one closely expressing us.' This 'storming' away from concise self-expression seems to me a fundamental aspect of Meredith's obscurity. Both the act of telling and the characters themselves move to and fro between heroic performance and withdrawal.

These alternatives are in the mind of Aminta when faced with the problem of writing to Lord Ormont in Meredith's late novel 'Lord Ormont and his Aminta'. She is bound to him, but he is proud, inflexibly military, and because he is ashamed of her he has unjustly neglected her. She too is ashamed of her neglect, and when forced to write to him the act of writing becomes impossibly fraught. The relation of Aminta and Ormont is close to that of Meredith and his public, and the hesitations of Aminta's pen, always stayed by the anterior problems of writing in a context of shame, express the impossible alternatives:(26)

Aminta's pen declined to run to her lord; and the dipping
it in ink was no acceleration of the process. A sentence,
bearing likeness to an artless infant's trot of the half-
dozen steps to the mother's lap, stumbled upon the full
stop midway. Desperate determination pushed it along, and
there was in consequence a dead stop at the head of the
next sentence. A woman whose nature is insurgent against
the majesty of the man to whom she must, among the singular
injunctions binding her, regularly write, sees no way between
hypocrisy and rebellion. For rebellion, she, with the pen in
her hand, is avowedly not yet ripe; hypocrisy is abominable.
If she abstain from writing, he might travel down to learn
the cause; a similar danger, or worse, haunted the writing
frigidly. She had to be the hypocrite or else - leap.

Hypocrisy or rebellion? The 'achillean roar' or fibbing? The 'whoop of the mountains' or 'dainty rogue falsehoods'? Meredith polarized the choice of strategy into principles of masculine and feminine, and his narratives play out the conflict of these principles upon the formal basis of a shameful story which haunts the narrative with the threat of public revelation and calumny. Each is, in its own way, objectionable. The excessive, public-school masculinity with its crude energy, 'that bestial multiform'(27) as he called it; or the excessively feminine, the strategy of evasive silence and false acquiescence which seemed to Meredith a cowardly kind of duplicity. Either way he was caught in contradiction - the stumbling hesitation and angry rejection evinced by Aminta in her letter. Caught between the two genders she is frightened, and this fear 'haunted the writing frigidly'. In 'Modern Love' Meredith writes:(28)

> 'Tis something to be told, or hidden: - which?
> I get a glimpse of hell in this mild guess.

In his own style and narrative construction, the act of writing confronted him at any moment with Aminta's choice. Framed and exacerbated by the cultural conditions explored in the chapters above, Meredith's 'glimpse of hell' was the choice of 'something to be told, or hidden' at each moment of writing, the violence of confrontation or the retreat into baroque metaphor and devious syntax.

This violence and obscurity come together in what Gillian Beer has brilliantly called 'the savagely gnomic' in Meredith's prose.(29) Together with the 'vindicating eloquence' and 'brute honesty' of Meredith's own stylistic designation, the 'savagely gnomic' appears as obsessively recurrent in the fiction, a third modality of voice both combative and indirect.

In one of the most important and telling metaphors of his own fictional practice, Meredith compares the act of writing an episode of a novel to the act of a government spy opening up private correspondence. In likening his own storytelling to 'violating the post' he writes in a chapter of 'Evan Harrington' called In Which we have to see in The Dark: 'so the history that concerns us wanders out of day for a time, and we must violate the post and open written leaves to mark the turn it takes.'(30) This perfectly indexes the doubleness of Meredith's novel construction. He deliberately obscures the episode - it is he who creates the darkness, who refuses to narrate in a straightforward way - and then he again puts himself in the position of 'a hired government spy' to reveal, in the guilty, shameful way that the metaphor suggests, what was going on. He follows the above passage by quoting from letters written by Mr Goren and others, thus 'dipping further into the secrets of the post'. It is a most curious structure: Meredith is split between guilty revelation and private correspondence, he is both Mr Goren and the suspicious violator of Mr Goren's communication. Meredith seals the episode in an envelope only to put himself (as narrator) immediately into the false position of spy as he intercepts and reopens it. This metaphor of a 'purloined' letter (not dissimilar from that at the end of 'The Wings of the Dove') creates a structure in which Meredith is both sender and

illicit receiver of private communication, setting a scene before
the reader in which he is simultaneously betrayer and betrayed.
The peculiar doubleness of this process is indicative of the specific and complex way in which Meredithian ellipses and omissions
operate as a form of signification. It is to the degree that Meredith interrogates the twinned notions of lucidity and 'truth' even
whilst holding on to their value, that he is important in tracing
the origins of the peculiar difficulties and resistances of modern
English fiction.

In some complex fashion the experience of shame in Meredith's
biography led to a strong identification with women stigmatized
for having a 'history'. This in turn leads to a recurrence, in
both style and narrative structure, of an ever-renewed difficulty
of (self-)presentation. The desire is manifest in the novels to
reveal and replay a female role in which revelation before the
public gaze is an immediate threat, in exactly the way that we go
over and over a moment of burning humiliation, trying to correct
it in our retrospective fantasies. It is a counterposed drive to
expose and deliberately to risk or force exposure which appears
very similar to masochism, and it is significant that in the case of
male masochism there is a strong tendency to put oneself in the
'place' of women. In his essay on masochism Freud wrote: 'if one
has an opportunity of studying cases in which the masochistic
phantasies have been especially richly elaborated, one quickly
discovers that they place the subject in a characteristically female
situation.'(31)

It is not my intention to undermine Meredith's feminism by the
suggestion that it is merely a richly elaborated fantasy of a com
pulsively rewritten masochism. On the contrary, the kind of
fictional self which is projected as one of the combative masks for
a subject tormented by shame is a particular problem for women,
and Meredith identified this with great sensitivity and precision.
The work that Jennie Calder and other critics (32) have done on
Meredith seems to me to have failed to understand this aspect of
his feminism. That peculiar mixture of Amazonian heroism and
multiple deception which is Meredith's heroine is always related
to the problem of shame and exposure. It is related both to his
own problem of exposure/exposition inscribed in the alternating
confrontation and obscurity of his writing, and to his identification with the impossible role-allocation of women in the nineteenth century. Plain speech was extremely difficult for a
Victorian woman: because her role, position and identity were
cast for men, she often felt herself to be living a self-alienated,
double existence. Alienation ('Verfremdung') as defined in the
early writings of Marx is indeed the word – Meredith writes: 'they
soon learn to live out of themselves, and look on themselves as he
looks, almost as little disturbed as he by the undiscovered.' The
image created by men cannot be real, and the woman projects
another self to protect herself, to remain 'the undiscovered' behind the social role created for her.

Many of Meredith's heroines have an interior narrative that can never be told, an area of undisclosed privacy that must not be violated. They have, not exactly an unconscious, but a sub-merged self which appears only to deny itself in equivocation and concealment:(33)

> Nataly could argue her case in her conscience - deep down
> and out of hearing, where women under scourge of the laws
> they have not helped decree may and do deliver their minds.
> She stood in that subterranean recess for Nature against
> the Institutions of Man: a woman little adapted for the post
> of rebel; but to this, by the agency of circumstances, it had
> come.

This 'subterranean recess for Nature against the Institutions of Man' cannot be simply assimilated to the traditional theological commonplace of the 'Eternal Eve'. It is the area of a reserved self, set aside from the social and expected roles of compliant 'Angel in the House' or passive Virgin, it is the place of limited internal freedom from bonds of propriety. In 'Tacita Tacit' (1860) Jane Vaughan Pinkney had written: 'Women are greater dissemblers than men ... by habit, by moral training, and modern education, they are obliged to ... repress their feelings, control their very thoughts.'

It is not surprising, then, that the problem of obscurity and dissimulation should emerge closely associated with those of the heroine and the idea of the feminine in general. In 'Emilia in Eng-land', Emilia is mortified by her treatment when the fickle Wilfred betrays her for someone else. At the moment of humiliating betrayal she loses her wonderful voice, her voice 'breaks' (she is a talented singer) and like Nataly she has to take refuge within herself:(34)

> 'I am unlucky, to-night,' said Emilia. Or, rather, so said
> her surface-self. The submerged self - self in the depths -
> rarely speaks to the occasions, but lies under calamity
> quietly apprehending all; willing that the talker overhead
> should deceive others, and herself likewise, if possible.

What is in question is not hypocrisy, in the old, 'Volpone' sense of the word, but a refusal to identify oneself completely with the social position ascribed by the culture, to displace one's emotional centre outside or inside the required image, which remains a kind of simulacrum. Recent psycho-analytical work has spoken in terms very similar to Meredith's: 'For the woman, as we have seen, the choice of simulation is always open, a choice which must not be conceived as a simple synonym for imposture....'(35) This paral-lels Meredith's description of the demands made upon the Victorian woman in her need to appear 'purity infinite, spotless bloom':(36)

> To keep him in awe and hold him enchained, there are things
> she must never do, dare never say, must not think. She must
> be cloistral. Now, strange and awful though it be to hear,
> women perceive this requirement of them in the spirit of the
> man's ... for in the appeasement of the glutton they have to
> practise much simulation, they are in their way losers like
> their ancient mothers.

Once the heroine can no longer be identified with pure truth,
then ambiguity is introduced into the very heart of the narrative
organization of the novel. It is surely not coincidental that the
love quest and the quest for Truth begin to drift into enigma and
uncertainty at the same moment in the development of the novel,
the moment when Woman as the embodiment of Truth is in question.
This idea has been raised in an interesting general article by
Alexander Welsh, The Allegory of Truth in English Fiction,(37)
which traces the iconic embodiment of Truth as heroine in late-
nineteenth-century literature. Welsh centres upon a most important elision and later separation of the two meanings of 'truth'
(truth-telling, the correspondence of words to facts; loyalty, the
relation between persons). He traces the split between these two
meanings from Thackeray and Trollope, where falsehood is entirely
'bad' and truth necessarily good, to the more complex situation in
Conrad and James, where

> The transformation of the figure of truth is schematically
> very simple. She learns to lie. She overthrows the res-
> trictive rule of Jeanie Deans and Cordelia; she abridges
> the rule about truth-telling in order to exult in the rule
> of loyalty. She becomes, even, an 'actress'.

This seems to me particularly true of Meredith, where the question of truth-telling has a problematic centrality. It is not just
that loyalty ('truth to one another') comes to be more important
and hence overrides veracity ('truth to facts'). It is rather that
both notions of truth become vastly complicated and even over-
turned when the heroine has to be protected from a society less
worthy than she is. The social bond of total truthfulness then
stands against her as the enemy's weapon, and if by evading the
truth she can survive, this appears justifiable.

This is not to say that heroines before Diana Warwick, Nataly
Radnor or Clara Middleton had not occasionally harboured falsehoods, but they were conceived as minor, temporary slips from
goodness, or conscious, mischievous hypocrisies (Moll Flanders),
always recognizable and indexed in the texts, measured against a
female paradigm which was 'pure' and 'whole' (and therefore not
'mixed' and intrinsically obscure).

In Meredith it is precisely the 'common male Egoist ideal of a
waxwork sex' which is criticized and rejected. This version of
woman was so constructed that Meredith felt 'very few women are
able to be straightforwardly sincere in their speech, however
much they may desire to be'. Meredith's women are much closer to
Proust's - to Gisèle, Albertine, Andrée and Odette:(38)

> But at the very moment when she speaks, when she speaks
> of something else beneath which lies hidden the thing that
> she does not mention, the lie is immediately perceived, ...
> since we are conscious of the lie, and cannot succeed in
> discovering the truth.

And in Proust, as in Meredith, we find a recognition of ubiquitous,
necessary fiction woven into the texture of everyday life, fictions
which are associated with a transformed notion of the role of women

and the nature of sexuality. Meredith finds no incongruity (though possibly a little devilment) in congratulating his heroine for her 'parabolic and commendable obscureness'. The novelist is so aware of the widening distance between the authenticity of his women (with their sexual desires, broken marriages, illegitimate children and their vulnerability in a narrowly prurient culture) and the falseness of the image which society endeavours to project upon them (the branding of Mrs Marsett as a 'scarlet woman' in 'One of Our Conquerors' is the appropriate example) that he prefers to protect them by saturating the intervening space with ambiguity and evasion.

Thus, Meredith explores levels of dissimulation constitutive of social reality, neither true nor false, neither clear nor obscure, good nor bad. He explores the haunted middle-ground of psychic and social censorship which is a central site of all social interaction. He had a very strong sense of what was forced and artificial in any important encounter between an ego and its culture, the area of 'cover-up' involved in the defence of the ego and in the social construction of reality.

From this perspective Meredith was, as Gillian Beer has said, the first important English modernist. He wrote in a form distinctively different from his early contemporaries, and it was only in the 1880s that English culture began to catch up with him and appreciation of his art (already widespread in America) suddenly increased. Meredith slightly precedes and then becomes central in a cultural shift - European rather than simply English - which began to prise apart the deep identification of truth with fluency. Shame interacted with writing in Meredith to produce texts which suggested that obscurity and secrecy are constitutive of society, personality and even knowledge itself. Meredith's initial isolation as a writer in the long period of early unpopularity begins to break down at the moment (the 1880s) when 'advanced' groups within the intellectual culture caught up with him and from then until his death he appeared as a prescient and fittingly inscrutable embodiment of the 'modern' novelist. But the argument is complex. Meredith was born in 1828, much of the vocabulary and conceptual material with which he explored the disjunctions of truth and obscurity was that of the mid-nineteenth century. The moral discriminations built into the lexicon of dissimulation were hard set and these Meredith inherited with the words themselves. There is often uncertainty and struggle in his fictions as words deeply complicit with an older ethical and epistemological system are lodged unhappily in new surroundings.

This can be seen most clearly in an episode from 'Diana of the Crossways' (1885) where Diana looks at herself in a mirror and considers exactly what the 'falseness' of a woman's 'false position' in censorious England might really mean:(39)

An odd world, where for the sin we have not participated in we must fib and continue fibbing, she reflected. She did not entirely cheat her clearer mind, for she perceived that her step in flight had been urged both by a weak despondency

and a blind desperation; also that the world of a fluid civilization is perforce artificial. But her mind was in the background of her fevered senses, and when she looked in the
glass and mused on uttering the word 'Liar!' to the lovely
image, her senses were refreshed, her mind somewhat
relieved, the face appeared so sovereignly defiant of
abasement.

Here Meredith is patiently taking apart the traditional conception
of falsehood, and the obvious crucial word is 'fib', which cannot
be assimilated to the hardness and repugnance of 'Liar'. The
word 'fib' here is a traditional term forced to do the work of something far greater and more serious , but no other word in the
1880s is readily available. Here the word does not simply mean a
trivial falsehood, nor is it a euphemism for 'lie'. It is equivalent
to something as modern (and ponderous) as 'ubiquitous social
inauthenticity' in a world where 'for the sin we have *not* participated in we must fib and continue fibbing.' Meredith works hard
in the passage to dissociate Diana's sense of false identity from
the traditional stigma that falsehood bore, and he does it through
the notion of a fib, a white lie, the one concept that transcends
the chromatic identification of lying with darkness (which it
achieves through a kind of domestic oxymoron). Social existence
in Meredith is like a continuous, reluctant, but inescapable white
lie, we must fib and continue fibbing but this does not make us
liars. White lies are the mediation necessary for the defence of a
sensitive ego, not in the encounter with friends but in public, in
the realm of social role (particularly for women), reputation and
identity: 'It is a terrible decree, that all must act who would pre
vail; and the more extended the audience the greater need for the
mask and buskin.'(40)

One of the reasons Diana gives for the existence of these fibs
is that 'the world of a fluid civilization is perforce artificial.' It
is an observation which is quite common from the 1880s, to be
found in Conrad, James and Yeats and which is habitually linked
to the idea of a cultural artificiality which both mitigates and com-
plicates the nature of falsehood. In a later chapter, Meredith
indicts 'the world's clumsy machinery of civilization'. This discom-
fiting, occasionally anguished feeling that culture itself was a
kind of fiction recurs in Meredith as a mistrust of the established
social order and as a viable reason for guarding one's intimate
self from its harmful powers. In 'Lord Ormont and his Aminta' he
wrote:(41)

And if we have the world for the buttress of injustice, then
is Nature the flaring rebel; there is no fixed order possible.
Laws are necessary instruments of the majority; but when
they grind the sane human being to dust for their maintenance, their enthronement is the rule of the savage's old deity,
sniffing blood-sacrifice. There cannot be a society based
upon such conditions.

Time and again in Meredith the world at large is represented
as a vindictive crowd of gossips. Like the word 'fib', the word

'gossip' in Meredith is made the bearer of ideas and judgments quite beyond its normal usage. It is because the world can be discursively figured best as 'gossip' that the individual can find a degree of security, even of honourable self-defence, in the white lie. Beneath the quaint and homely use of fibs and gossip (and also 'wit') Meredith effected an extensive transformation of the received idea of dissimulation. Simultaneously other levels of discourse related to dissimulation and evasion were transformed in the writing so that obscurity of presentation becomes a cor-relative issue of Meredith's fiction. The form of oblique and evasive narration is internally linked to the themes of the later novels in the way that fibs and fiction are forced together across the grain of the later texts. Indeed in 'The Amazing Marriage' (1895), the novelist struggles openly against Dame Gossip for control of the narrative, thus at last making explicit an anxious battle which had been covertly taking place in Meredith's earlier texts for many years.

In chapter XIV of 'The Amazing Marriage', Dame Gossip rushes ahead to tell the story, she constantly pushes aside the novelist with his concern for the inner motives and detailed mental states of the characters, in order to reveal what happened, producing an 'artful pother to rouse excitement at stages of a narrative'. She is not interested in psychology but in the 'frisson' of excite-ment which attaches to events, she is always in a hurry, and in dealing with Lord Fleetwood she dispatches his motives in a series of unresolved contraries:(42)

> Dame Gossip prefers to ejaculate Young men are mysteries and bowl us onward. No one ever did comprehend the Earl of Fleetwood, she says: he was bad, he was good; he was whimsical and steadfast; a splendid figure, a mark for ridicule; romantic and a close arithmetician, often a devil, sometimes the humanest of creatures.

She is an irresponsible, unreliable narrator who wishes to ex-pose the secrets of the characters purely to produce a 'succès de scandale', irrespective of the accuracy of her information and the hurt it will cause to those involved:(43)

> Dame Gossip would recount the tales. She is of the order of persons inclined to suspect the tittle of truth in prodigies of scandal. She is rustling and bustling to us of Carinthia Jane's run up to London to see Sarah Winch's grand new shop,.... [The Dame hears a tavern ballad of Lord Fleet-wood and Carinthia.] The Dame shall expose her confusions. She really would seem to fancy that the ballad verifies the main lines of the story, which is an impossible one. Carinthia had not the means to travel: she was moneyless.

Here the novelist, in a chapter entitled A Further Intrusion Averted, forestalls and corrects the Dame's account of what hap-pened and contradicts her version of the story. The novelist is not interested in the pace of events, the excitement of the action, nor the forward progression of the plot. He frequently halts to explore motive as accurately as he can whilst his co-narrator,

Dame Gossip, is all for the ongoing movement of the action. In chapter XIII, An Irruption of Mistress Gossip in Breach of the Convention, this conflict of interest between the twin voices of the novel is made explicit: Dame Gossip is apprehensive that the novelist is going to hold back the story once again:(44)

it really seems these moderns think [a serious narrative]
designed for a frequent arrest of the actors in the story
and a searching of the internal state of this one or that one
of them: who is laid out stark naked and probed and expounded, like as in the celebrated picture by a great painter:
and we, thirsting for events as we are, are to stop to enjoy
a lecture on Anatomy. And all the while the windows of the
lecture-room are rattling, if not the whole fabric shaking,
with exterior occurrences or impatience for them to come to
pass.

In one sense this is, as Judith Wilt has remarked,(45) a refor-
mulation of an old debate in the novel between narration and
analysis, between romance and intellect. But the dissociation of
plot from character and their opposition in the novel as exclusive,
contradictory viewpoints, is central to Meredith's writing and his
preoccupation with exposure and gossip. Each of the co-narrators
of 'The Amazing Marriage' endeavours to censor the other. The
novelist prevents the Gossip from revealing the actions and from
enjoying the exposition of the hidden histories of the actors.
The Gossip prevents the novelist from stopping to analyse motive
and mental state, and, using a crucial metaphor of nudity which
endlessly recurs in Meredith, she tries to stop the examination of
characters 'laid out stark naked and probed and expounded,'
Meredith divides himself into two narrators who bicker, interrupt
and quarrel, even to the point of cutting off the other's narrative
in mid-sentence.(46) There is a treaty between them, but they
regularly break it to stop the other from telling the novel in their
own way.

The result is a bizarre division of narrative labour in which the
public revelation of events is dislocated from the private revelation of feeling and psychology and each kind of revelation is
unacceptable, each is interrupted and blocked by the other
speaker – though in a bumpy, uneven and curious fashion, the
story does get told. Dame Gossip and Novelist represent two
antagonistic voices in Meredith which conflict perpetually. The
former represents an external voice which sides with society and
the common reader (those 'who intend preserving their taste for
romance') and which hates endeavours to protect characters in the
novel from the gaping exposure to Dame Gossip; whilst the latter,
the Novelist, wishes to understand the characters, to explain
their feelings and fears, to mitigate their secret actions. Dame
Gossip simply loves to tell all, she begins her narrative in a head-
long rush to let the reader in on all that happens:(47)

And first I am going to describe to you the young Earl of
Fleetwood, son of the strange Welsh lady, the richest
nobleman of his time, and how he pursued and shunned

the lady who had fascinated him, Henrietta, the daughter
of Commodore Baldwin Fakenham; and how he met Carinthia
Jane, and concerning that lovely Henrietta and Chillon
Kirby-Levellier, and of....

But halfway through, just as she becomes excited at the prospect
of describing a wedding, the novelist cuts into her speech:(48)

She ceases. According to the terms of the treaty, the
venerable lady's time has passed. An extinguisher descends
on her, giving her the likeness of one under condemnation
of the Most Holy Inquisition, in the ranks of an *auto da fé*;
and singularly resembling that victim at the first sharp bite
of the flames she will be when she hears the version of her
story.

This curious conflict of interrupting voices taking the narrative
in different directions and obscuring some of it completely (the
bizarre omission of Carinthia's conception - her pregnancy comes
as a considerable shock to the reader) lacks the complementarity
of the twin narration in 'Bleak House'. The voices actively oppose
each other; they represent mutually exclusive principles which in
turn reveal a strange double-censorship operative in the novel as
well as a dissociation of levels formerly considered indivisible.

The result is that episodes which burst through this double-
censorship have a demonic energy, the increased resistance to
the narrative process produces an equivalent increase in the force
of language which breaks through, like moments of violent cath-
exis. Carinthia's struggle with the rabid dog and the subsequent
attempt to burn the infected wound of the bitten child; the initial
elopement of Captain Kirby; the boxing match; Diana Cressett
swimming the Shannon and back for a bet; Carinthia going off to
fight an insurrectionist war in Spain - these episodes of physical
endurance are exceptional, capitalized 'Actions', which contrast
strangely with the areas of opaque prose and muted narrative
which are set round them.

Even in the very late novels we hear, besides the reclusive and
elliptical voice, an almost stentorian fellow speaker who advocates
a 'Victorian' set of ideals about manly health in body and mind –
the qualities we find associated with Carlyle's heroism of sincerity
(indeed there is much of Carlyle in Meredith). Young Weyburn in
'Lord Ormont and his Aminta', embodies many of the values which
Meredith wished to teach (there is a constant interest in pedagogy
throughout Meredith's work from 'The Shaving of Shagpat' and
'The Ordeal of Richard Feverel' through to 'Lord Ormont and his
Aminta'). Weyburn, having run off with Aminta (unjustly treated
by her husband Lord Ormont), sets up a foreign school with her
which is so successful in educating the young that Lord Ormont
himself, impressed by its standards, sends his grand-nephew
there as a token of his renewed respect for the runaway couple
and the values they represent. The young schoolmaster's grand
project is 'to bring the nationalities together and teach Old England to the Continent - the Continent to Old England: our healthy
games, our scorn of the lie, manliness; their intellectual valour,

diligence, considerate manners.'(49) His most conspicuous success
in this endeavour is his student Giulio whose story of moral regeneration at the hands of Weyburn and his school is what brings
Lord Ormont to reconcile himself with the man who has run off
with his wife. Giulio's tale is a Meredithian fable of the transformation from evil falsehood to goodness and truth through the
educative power of an excellent school, and recalls his own experience of the Moravian school at Neuwied on the Rhine,(50) as well
as reminding one of 'The Shaving of Shagpat'. Giulio, who has
become a brave, industrious and truth-loving lad, a 'capital fellow'
as his age would call him, tells Ormont:(51)
- I was a sneak and a coward. It follows, I was a liar and
a traitor. Who cured me of that vileness, that scandal? I
will tell you - an Englishman and an Englishwoman.... She
told me no English girl would ever look on a man who was a
coward and lied. From that day I have made Truth my bride.
And what the consequence? I know not fear.
There is no reason to suspect that Meredith's didactic aim in
fostering these robust standards was not sincere; indeed, it is at
the moments when he confidently asserts these manly virtues that
his own strength of purpose seems assured. Yet time after time
they are not only directly contradicted by what is being said elsewhere in the same novels about truthfulness, but they become so
bound up with the form of, and desire for, physical aggression,
that they too become extraordinarily obscure. The question of
intellectual valour in Meredith is inseparable from the idea of
bodily struggle. The moral strenuousness associated with forth-
right honesty becomes contorted into something vertiginous and
exhausting. The acquisition of truth is made inseparable from convulsive physical struggle, a gruff and hearty version of the ideal
education ('I want our fellows to have the habit of speaking from
the chest,' remarks Weyburn, 'they shall have an Achillean roar').
No one has understood this particular kind of excessively mas
culine persona in relation to shame better than Nietzsche. It is
unlikely that Nietzsche knew Meredith's work even though the
following passage of 1886 seems of quite remarkable relevance to
Meredith:(52)
There are events of such delicate nature that one would do
well to bury them in gruffness and make them unrecognizable.
There are deeds of love and extravagant magnanimity after
which nothing is more advisable than to take a stick and beat
up the eye-witness of them, to cloud his memory. There are
people who know how to cloud and abuse their own memories
in order to get revenge on their sole accomplice: modesty is
inventive. The things of which one is most ashamed are by
no means the worst things; not only cunning is found beneath
a mask; there is much goodness in guile. I could imagine that
a man who had something precious and vulnerable to hide
might roll through life rough and round like an old green
heavily hooped wine cask: the subtlety of his modesty would
demand it. The destinies and delicate decisions of a man who

is deeply ashamed, happen to him on paths that few ever
reach and of whose existence his nearest and dearest must
know nothing. The danger to his life is hidden from their
eyes, as is his life-security when he regains it. Such a concealed one, who instinctively uses speech for silence and
withholding, and whose excuses for not communicating are
inexhaustible, wants and encourages a mask of himself to
wander about in the hearts and minds of his friends.
Not only does it capture to perfection Meredith's interest in fights
and pugilism, the burying of feeling in gruffness; it also identifies the 'bon viveur' rolling through life 'rough and round like an
old green heavily hooped wine cask' - all readers of Meredith will
recognize the appositeness of this image, since time and again
Meredith's characters disguise their inner pains with a hearty
indulgence in wine and beer (like Victor Radnor, whose nerves
have been so badly shaken he dare not cross a busy road and who
disguises it perfectly in an expert consumption of champagne with
his friend Fenellan).

David Howard has argued that this division of the fiction into
what he calls the fiction of actions, heroics, 'plain issues' and the
fiction of 'delicate' analysis, is part of Meredith's conscious design.
That 'the preoccupation with action partakes of the general Victorian preoccupation with games, fitness, something to prevent
"morbidity",' and (53)

> Meredith was trying to transform a fiction of delicacy and
> 'morbidity' into a fiction of purpose and action, and in so
> doing providing a model of political and social awareness,
> of the possibilities of a developing consciousness [in the
> England of the 1860s].

But this is to suggest both that Meredith's fiction struggled to
move from the 'delicate' to the 'heroic' and that it was a conscious
political strategy, and yet neither of these things seem true: both
kinds of fiction remain, throughout his work, unpredictable and
uncertainly mixed, and both appear as alternatives in the solution
to the intense problem of self in relation to the act of writing
which afflicted Meredith (an area not far distant from that explored by Erving Goffman in his work on 'embarrassment' and
'interaction ritual').(54) The language Meredith uses is quaintly
defensive ('dainty rogue falsehoods') or overtly aggressive
('Achillean roar'), but it is immensely sensitive to the awkwardness of public interaction. Meredith's logic was to transform the
suffering of public encounter, which he dreaded, into a test of
one's courage and value which, if it was ever to succeed, must
never appear to be a test of courage and value but a 'normal' and
'witty' exchange. It is in contestation against public hostility that
the word and the act receive their baptism of fire, the fire that
burns the 'withering scarlet' on the face and which shows hideous
gleams of 'a body raging with fire behind the veil'.

Meredith always associated this combat with the nightmare of
public nudity. In his 'Maxims for Men', the book of epigrams written by Captain Kirby in 'The Amazing Marriage', we read that 'he

had never failed in an undertaking without stripping bare to ex-
pose to himself where he had been wanting in Intention and
Determination.'(55) Some such agony of embarrassment is implied
in Victor's description of the ordeal that his wife would have to
endure in 'One of Our Conquerors': 'His Nataly might have to go
through a short sharp term of scorching - Godiva to the gossips.'
   'Godiva to the gossips' is the perfect epigrammatic summary of
what is involved, a mixed masochism and expiation, a kind of
terrible thrill in the indulged image of riding naked in public,
Richmond Roy or Nataly nude on their respective steeds, having
'to go through a short sharp term of scorching'. The same image
is recalled later to describe Skepsey, punished after yet another
public scuffle: 'He was a picture of Guilt in the nude, imploring
to be sent into concealment.' Nesta, too, contemplating the possibility of flight from her involvement with the dubious Mrs Marsett, rejects fleeing to the wilderness on the curious grounds that
there, 'to be shorn and naked and shivering is no hardship, for
the solitude clothes.' Even though solitude, escape from public
engagement, is the evident solution, it is rejected by Nesta precisely on the grounds that it will not place her naked before the
public gaze: like Victor, she consciously seeks out the possibility
of painful exposure. Her position after the double revelation of
her illegitimacy and her damaging association with Mrs Marsett is
not unlike Diana Warwick's after separating from her husband,
when Diana declares to herself: 'Wherever I go now, in all weather,
I am perfectly naked!' The pain of being unable to move whilst
naked and in full view comes to signal the utmost depth of
shameful suffering in Meredith. The public (and the readership)
come to seem like some monstrous Polyphemus' eye watching his
characters wither under scrutiny. Like Sir Willoughby in 'The
Egoist', whose whole acquaintance (56)

> had a similarity in the variety of their expressions that made
> up one giant eye for him, perfectly, if awfully, legible. He
> discerned the fact that his demon secret was abroad, uni-
> versal. He ascribed it to fate. He was in the jaws of the
> world, on the world's teeth.... His ears tingled. He and his
> whole story discussed in public. Himself unroofed! And the
> marvel that he of all men should be in such a tangle, naked
> and blown on, condemned to use his cunningest arts to
> unwind and cover himself, struck him as though the lord of
> his kind were running the gauntlet of a legion of imps. He
> felt their lashes.

   The evident way of covering himself in language is in metaphor.
Even more than the savage ellipsis, the syntactic writhing and the
modal oscillation between representation and withdrawal, metaphor
appears as the major obscuring factor in Meredith. The link between naked prose and the clothing of metaphor is a natural one
for a man whose family associations with tailoring and the clothes
trade had been the source of such acute shame in 'Evan Harrington': to reject clothes and yet to fear being without them has more
than ordinary force for a novelist who fought to be free from a

family bondage to clothes manufacture and the humiliating sobri-
quet of 'Mr Snips'. Meredith occasionally uses the literal disguise
of clothing (as in 'Evan Harrington' when Louise 'entered the
house where she was born, unsuspected and unseen, under cover
of a profusion of lace and veil and mantilla'), and there are one
or two puns to the same effect in that novel, about tailors 'liking
to preserve appearances'.

But it is the 'tissue' of metaphor that produces most of the
obscurity in Meredith. He has often been compared to Carlyle in
respect of his views on heroism and for certain strident stylistic
apostrophes, but it is also in the philosophy of clothes that the
two can be fruitfully compared. No one could be better described
as a Sartor Resartus than George Meredith, and it was with dense-
packed, witty and elaborate metaphors that he clothed himself.
Carlyle writes:(57)

> all Emblematic things are properly Clothes, thought-woven
> or hand-woven.... Language is called the Garment of
> Thought: however, it should rather be, Language is the
> Flesh-Garment, the Body, of thought. I said that Imagination
> wove this Flesh-Garment; and does not she? Metaphors are
> her stuff: examine Language.... Moreover, there are sham
> Metaphors, which overhang that same Thought's-Body (best
> naked), and deceptively bedizening, or bolstering it out,
> may be called its false stuffings, superfluous show-cloaks
> (Putz-Mäntel), and tawdry woollen rags.

But Carlyle is being too simple in separating metaphors that represent from those that conceal, even if the attraction of the
clothing metaphor in itself suggests this is so. Metaphors do both
simultaneously, and as Ortega y Gasset remarks in 'The Dehumanization of Art': 'The metaphor disposes of an object by having it
masquerade as something else. Such a procedure would make no
sense if we did not discern beneath it an instinctive avoidance of
certain realities.'(58)

Faced with a crisis which may be humiliating or shameful, Meredith's characters conceal themselves and express themselves in
metaphor. Nesta Victoria in 'One of Our Conquerors' is reflecting
upon the one scourge of her sex, 'a subject thickly veiled, one
which struck at her through her sex, and must, she thought,
ever be unnamed.... It signified shame.' Unable to name it, she
immediately resorts to metaphor:(59)

> There was a torment of earth and a writhing of lurid dust-
> clouds about it at a glimpse. But if the new crusading Hero
> were to come attacking *that* - if some born prince nobly man
> would head the world to take away the withered scarlet from
> the face of women, she felt she could kiss the print of his
> feet upon the ground. Meanwhile she had enjoyment of her
> plunge into the inmost forest-well of medieval imaginative-
> ness, where youthful minds of good aspiration through their
> obscurities find much akin to them.

The 'plunge into the inmost forest-well of medieval imaginativeness' is not only Nesta's but Meredith's leap. There is an

associative spring from the pain of humiliation to the enjoyment
of metaphor which has a parallel in a similar movement in Henry
James. He too submerges a fear (of being compromised) into the
pleasure of language, though in his case it is refined and oblique
dialogue which furnishes him with the displaced and enjoyable
form of discourse which both conceals the difficulty of writing
and provides real gratification.

This kind of inversion seems to me particularly important in
literary production (I have written about it in more general terms
elsewhere),(60) and constitutes a special kind of sublimation into
language. It is precisely because language can function to with-
hold information at the same time as remaining rich in significance
that this process can operate. In Meredith, the moment of shame
finds its representation, though 'not communicably', in discrete
flashes of symbol and metaphor. Aminta suddenly sees Weyburn
walking before her in conversation with Lord Ormont, the husband from whom she has fled in order to live with Weyburn:(61)

> She tried, in shame of the inanimate creature she had
> become, to force herself to think: and had, for a chasten-
> ing result, a series of geometrical figures shooting across
> her brain, mystically expressive of the situation, not com-
> municably.

I suppose the appropriate term for these elaborate metaphors
which act to save one's pride would be 'conceit', and it is the
conceits in Meredith which combine with syntactic compressions
to produce very obscure writing indeed. In the following passage
from 'The Amazing Marriage', Gower Woodseer sees gambling-
tables for the first time and I rather doubt that this would have
been apparent to the reader without a gloss: the prose seems to
combine Lyly's fondness for elaborate conceit with John Barth's
ability to drift a scene into baroque fantasy which takes over
completely:(62)

> Philosophy withdrew him from his temporary interest in the
> tricks of a circling white marble ball. The chuck-farthing
> of street urchins has quite as much dignity. He compared
> the creatures dabbling over the board to summer flies on
> butcher's meat, periodically scared by a cloth. More in the
> abstract, they were snatching at a snap-dragon bowl. It
> struck him that the gamblers had thronged on an invitation
> to drink the round of seed-time and harvest in a gulp.
> Again, they were desperate gleaners, hopping, skipping,
> bleeding, amid a whizz of scythe-blades, for small wisps of
> booty. Nor was it long before the presidency of an ancient
> hoary Goat-Satan might be perceived, with skew-eyes and
> pucker-mouth, nursing a hoof on a knee.

This passage presents very real problems of reading. Is it mere
Gongorism, a crazy riot of ornament obscuring the narrative line,
or a precursor of modernist fantasy, in which the writing becomes
so foregrounded that the episode is devoured by its own words?
For me, these sudden fantastic trips into metaphor are a genuine
pleasure in Meredith's writing, all the more so because they follow

the arcs and curves of his overall literary impetus, which is to escape from literal revelation into the enjoyment of 'the inmost forest-well of medieval imaginativeness'. Events in Meredith are almost always smaller or larger links in a syntax of shame, and even the above passage envisages the gamblers as derisory, absurd beings. A part of Meredith longs to abandon this painful story of shame told over and over in his novels and simply take pleasure in the energy of language which it engenders. As Gillian Beer remarks about 'One of Our Conquerors',(63) the novel

is, self-consciously, a novel *about* language and the limits
of language. At times it inadvertently oversteps those limits.
At other times, it deliberately explores the territory beyond
them. Morally, the novel reveals the responsibilities imposed
by language and by the articulated consciousness. Decor-
atively, it allows Meredith to try out stylistic effects which
ignore his readers. There is a paradox here which strikes to
the very heart of his artistic dilemma. In his late novels
Meredith often seems to have lost faith in language as communication.

At certain moments and in certain novels, he combines the pathos of his narrative of shame with a quite new order of vigorous difficulty. 'One of Our Conquerors' (serialized 1890, first published in three volumes in 1891) seems to me the very best of Meredith in this respect. In her excellent book 'On Shame and the Search for Identity' Helen Lynd writes:(64)

The characteristics that have been suggested as central in
experiences of shame - the sudden exposure of unanticipated
incongruity, the seemingly trivial incident that arouses overwhelming and almost unbearably painful emotion, the threat
to the core of identity, the loss of trust in expectations of
oneself, of other persons, of one's society, and a reluctant
recognized questioning of meaning in the world - all these
things continue to make experiences of shame almost impossible to communicate.

In 'One of Our Conquerors', Meredith overcomes these 'almost impossible' difficulties to write an outstanding fiction about the sufferings of ashamed people. In the process, the experience of shame gives him a penetrating awareness that his society - England of the 1880s - stands uncovered as well as he. The novel is an ambitious critique of Victorian England, its oppression of women, the hardening of sensibility and sympathy required for success in business, its imperialist intentions, and its harrying pursuit of anyone standing against its prurient codes (in the destruction of the Radnor family there is presciently reflected the humiliating destruction of Oscar Wilde and the socially endorsed assaults upon Vizetelly, Zola, Hardy, even Dreyfus).

The ultimate equation in the novel is between shame and petrifaction. From the cruel embarrassment of Victor's banana-skin fall in the first chapter to Nataly's death and his own mental breakdown at the end of the book, an insidious, persistent shame has eaten out the health and peace of mind of the Radnors. Victor

and Nataly represent the two usual ways of coping with shame –
he fronts it out with opulent parties and large houses, she retires
in upon herself. But since they present themselves as man and
wife to protect their illegitimate daughter, Nesta, their strategies
and needs are in constant tension – just as in Meredith himself.
In the end Nataly can only find refuge in death ('Death is our
common cloak') and Victor in madness, 'chattering a mixture of
the rational and the monstrous'. These two represent the opposed
figures of the fundamental equivocation in Meredith, whose split
between them is ultimately schizoid.(65) Throughout his work, the
pressure of shame (as the frozen tableau, the pressure of 'mortification') has been towards a horrible stasis, and this is compounded by the struggle of schizoid principles (aggressive male/
retiring female) within him. There seems to me little doubt that
the endless contests in his books between hard, inflexible characters like Victor and vulnerable, self-obscuring ones like Nataly
express the internal struggle of the two sides split by shame. In
a recent review David Holbrook has written:(66)

> The schizoid person is ontologically insecure, and feels 'an
> ego structure which is metaphorically, a living core sur-
> rounded by a hard dead shell'.... The inner core is
> associated with emotional vulnerability, emptiness and need:
> and the female element which embodies the need for love and
> meaning. The outer defensive shield tends to be pseudo-
> male, tough and unresponsive in a defensive way.

The most common fears of the schizoid are that the hard dead
shell will petrify into an impenetrable casing from which he will
never escape, or that suddenly, in full view, it will crack, to
reveal the vulnerable self within. In Meredith, both these fears
are played out in vivid, horrible narrative moments. We may recall
the episode in 'The Adventures of Harry Richmond' in which
Harry's madcap father has had himself coated in plaster and
painted to look like the bronze statue which he was supposed to
produce and could not. There is a great unveiling ceremony before hundreds of people, Harry is in the crowd, and suddenly his
father catches a glimpse of him:(67)

> The eyes, from being an instant ago dull carved balls,
> were animated. They were fixed on me. I was unable to give
> out a breath. Its chest heaved; both bronze hands struck
> against the bosom.
> 'Richmond! my son! Richie! Harry Richmond! Richmond
> Roy!'
> That was what the statue gave forth. My head was like
> a ringing pan. I knew it was my father, but my father with
> death and strangeness, earth, metal, about him; and his
> voice was like a human cry contending with earth and metal –
> mine was stifled. I saw him descend. I dismounted. We met
> at the ropes and embraced. All his figure was stiff, smooth,
> cold. My arms slid on him. Each time he spoke I thought it
> an unnatural thing: I myself had not spoken once.... I looked
> up at the sky, thinking that it had fallen dark.

To be petrified thus is as great a fear as the cracking of the outer shell. Harry Richmond's father almost destroys his son in his farcical, ignominious covering worn to avoid humiliation, but making humiliation many times worse when cracked open. Again, the immediate effect is an attack upon the ability to speak - 'Each time he spoke I thought it an unnatural thing: I myself had not spoken once.' The manic energy in Meredith often seems to arise from the desperate drive to overcome this petrifaction-in-shame, the fear of being turned into an object devoid of life by the very carapace one uses as a defence. Victor Radnor fights against this with all his immense resources in 'One of Our Conquerors' but eventually succumbs: 'For a while he hung, then fell, like an icicle.' Victor Radnor has made his skin thicker and tougher in order to survive the gossip and insinuation, but he ends as trapped inside it, 'hugged fast in iron muscles, the unhappy creature raved of his being a caged lion.'

Nataly does not have the strength for this contestation and her weakness is simply that. Inwardly bruised and wincing in an 'atmosphere of hints and revealings', Nataly does not 'belong to the party of the readily heroical':(68)

> She scourged her weakness: and the intimation of the truth
> stood over her, more than ever manifest, that the deficiency
> affecting her character lay in her want of language. A tongue
> to speak and contend, would have helped her to carve a
> clearer way.

I know of no other writer who conceived so readily of language as a weapon for the defence of a sensitive soul. 'A tongue to speak and contend', not in the sense of an offensive use of rhetoric or argument, but an instrument of finely self-conscious protection: language fashioned for the purpose of saving oneself from the insinuations and contempt of the outer world. The tongue that could defend in this way 'must be one which could reproach, and strike at errors, fence, and continually summon resources.' This use of language is the articulate defence against the withering power of whatever be shameful even in the knowledge that it is precisely language that shame drives back into silence and stammering vulnerability. Meredith's major achievement was to write more sensitively and extensively of shame than any other English writer despite this intense pressure which shame exerts to remain unarticulated. Difficulty of utterance (in both senses of the word 'difficulty') was a major aspect of this endeavour. It was only in the 'twisting' displacements of metaphor, in discontinuous leaps and ellipsis, in the modal conflict of attack against retreat and stasis against energetic movement - it was only through these obscurities, producing and produced by the encounter of shame and language, that the achievement became possible. Narrative movement is symbolized in the greedy, overpowering figure of Dame Gossip, whilst not telling stories, avoiding the issue, becomes a kind of heroic refusal. Meredith's prose moves back and forth between these two like a pendulum, hiding, telling, hiding, and it is this image which he invokes to describe Victor's distress after the interview with

Mrs Burman, one of the most moving scenes of ritualized humiliation in his work. Shortly afterwards Victor breaks down into
madness, haunted by the gilt pendulum which had swung to and
fro remorselessly as he was forced to kneel in expiation by the
bed of his dying wife:(69)

> Mention of the clock swung that silly gilt figure. Victor
> entered into it, condemned to swing, and be a thrall. His
> intensity of sensation launched him on an eternity of the
> swinging in ridiculous nakedness to the measure of Time
> gone crazy.

This above all was Meredith's nightmare, and the image condenses within itself all the terrifying force, the visceral and mental
affliction, which drives through the novels - the reification,
nudity and vertiginous oscillation. However accidental that pun
on 'gilt',(70) it identifies not only Victor Radnor but the compulsive rhythm and return of both a figure and a metaphor working
backwards and forwards through these texts. It produces the
desperate need to clothe in formal obscurity their author's strange
and touching fear of their 'ridiculous nakedness'.

5 CONRAD AND THE RHETORIC OF ENIGMA

> *Tell all the Truth but tell it slant -*
> *Success in Circuit lies*
>
> Emily Dickinson

> *Here all is clear. No, all is not clear. But the discourse*
> *must go on. So one invents obscurities. Rhetoric.*
>
> Samuel Beckett

Unlike the late novels of Meredith and Henry James, the fiction of
Joseph Conrad is not 'difficult'. That is to say, there is not the
syntactic difficulty of deciphering the 'grammar' of the story commonly encountered in the other two writers. The obscurity in
Conrad is generally semantic and not syntactic. Frequent shifts
in chronological order generate problems of reading in 'Nostromo',
(1) but for the most part the indecipherable aspects of his fiction
relate to lexicon and register rather than to syntagmatic sequence.

Indeed Conrad has been praised for his simplicity of utterance,
and M. C. Bradbrook has remarked that one of his triumphs consists in 'reducing the complex to the simple'.(2) There is often a
clarity of moral purpose and of episodic description in Conrad
which, by all the criteria adopted so far, could never be judged
'obscure'. Conrad does not have the fastidious social adjustments
of tone or phrase which are constantly redressed in James's prose;
nor does he compress and condense his writing into the knotty
ellipses found in Meredith. Often Conrad's fiction appears exemplary in its clarity. We have no reason to believe him ironic when
he writes: 'Those who read me know my conviction that the world,
the temporal world, rests on a few very simple ideas; so simple
that they must be as old as the hills.'(3) Fidelity, Duty, Courage,
Honest Work, these are a few of the solid virtues which often act
as anchors to his characters and to his own writing. The day to
day work of the sailor offers a 'point de repère' at moments when
pressures of disorientation are greatest.

But if Conrad's writing appears simple, its meaning is by no
means fixed. It continually gestures beyond itself to some anterior region (interior? - the geography and topography in Conrad
are never as clear as they seem), some hinterland of reference
which cannot be clearly mapped out. His fiction, especially 'Heart
of Darkness' which is the focus of my concern here, solicits a
hermeneutic approach, it defies the reader to remain at the literal

level of the story. This means that the fiction opens to a wide
range of interpretative possibilities. The obscurity arises from
this fact, that the narrative often disclaims that it is 'just a story'
and suggests insistently that its true meaning is elsewhere: yet
this 'elsewhere' is never located, it is a lost domain of symbolic
resonance and enigmatic suggestion always glimpsed just beyond
knowledge. This domain is the 'interpretative field' of the fiction
as suggested by the fiction itself, it is a metatextual realm which,
if we could only locate it, would appear to solve the mystery of
the text.

Thus the fiction (especially 'Heart of Darkness', 'Lord Jim',
'Under Western Eyes', The Return, 'The Nigger of the "Narcissus" ' and The Secret Sharer) deploys a variety of figures which
combine to imply that the narrative is only a hint or a clue to
some immense secret enclosed within it. The tragic gloom which
hangs listlessly over so many of the stories can be related both
to the threatening proximity of this transcendent symbolic realm,
and the lack of any possibility of locating it. The area of sunlight
always seems pale and transient when hemmed in by so much
shadow,(4) and yet Conrad constantly affirms that the one only
has any meaning when understood in the 'dark' terms of the other.
The obscurity is a kind of shadow text cast by the actual text in
such a way that its projection is somehow more 'true' than its
original. Even walking over a hill can be suddenly defined in
relation to this secret symbolic domain. In The Planter of Malata,
Geoffrey Renouard returns home after being rejected by Felicia:
(5)

Slowly a complete darkness enveloped Geoffrey Renouard...
This walk up the hill and down again was like the supreme
effort of an explorer trying to penetrate the interior of an
unknown country, the secret of which is too well defended
by its cruel and barren nature.

In this respect, F. R. Leavis's criticism of 'Heart of Darkness'
still seems to me the central problem with respect to Conrad's
work. In 'The Great Tradition' Leavis writes: 'He [Conrad] is
intent on making a virtue out of not knowing what he means. The
vague and unrealizable, he asserts with a strained impressiveness,
is the profound and tremendously significant.'(6) He remarks
further that in 'Heart of Darkness' there are places 'where we
become aware of comment as an interposition, and worse, as an
intrusion, at times an exasperating one. Hadn't he, we find ourselves asking, overworked "inscrutable", "inconceivable", "unspeakable", and that kind of word already? - yet still they recur.'(7)

Several subsequent critics have endeavoured to counter Leavis's
remarks but none very successfully. Robert Secor defends Conrad
by insisting that these inflated and repetitious phrases are to be
ascribed to Marlow alone, not the author, but this is surely
vitiated by the frequency with which they occur in other Conrad
works where Marlow is not the narrator.(8) David Thorburn in
'Conrad's Romanticism' seems to me partly correct in suggesting
that the 'adjectival insistence' of which F. R. Leavis complained

is intrinsic to the meaning of both 'Heart of Darkness' and 'Lord
Jim',(9) but even so he fails to explain the presence of so many
repeated phrases which border on banal mystification. In his
recent book on language and self-consciousness in Conrad, Jeremy Hawthorn surely avoids the central problem by saying that
'Where something is too deep for words then you leave them out..
.. It is not too outrageous to suggest that Conrad is using a com-
parable technique in his "adjectival insistence".'(10) But the
adjectival insistence is not simply the equivalent to words which
we omit because the feelings experienced are too profound. The
adjectives deployed in 'Victory', 'hinting at some awful mystery,'
form an identifiable rhetoric in the novels, the very insistence of
which sometimes seems mere pretentious repetition. What is the
status and function of this blatant obscurity in Conrad, and is
there more to the rhetoric of enigma than Leavis suggests? Is the
'immense secret' of the narrative merely a bluff?

In Conrad, mystery is everywhere and nowhere. The narratives
constantly dissolve into 'the opal mystery of great distances'.
The sea, the land, women, religion, nature, life, the unconscious,
language itself, all present themselves to Conrad as radically unknowable. One's own personality 'is only a ridiculous and aimless
masquerade of something hopelessly unknown,'(11) and absolute
Truth is 'like Beauty itself' and 'floats elusive, obscure, half
submerged, in the silent still waters of mystery.'(12) It is not
difficult to be cynical about this kind of language, and suggest
that it is used self-consciously to disguise ignorance or to give a
vague mystical glow to otherwise mundane material. Indeed there
is evidence in Conrad's letters to support this view. In a letter
to R. B. Cunninghame Graham he wrote: 'Straight vision is a bad
form... as you know. The proper thing is to look round the corner, because if Truth is not there, there is at any rate a something that distributes shekels.'(13)
    This direct equation of commercial profit with obliqueness of
vision and fictional technique can be compared to a remark made
by Conrad in an essay on Guy de Maupassant: 'Nobody has ever
gained the vast applause of a crowd by the simple and clear
exposition of vital facts....'(14) On the basis of these remarks
one wonders how far Conrad himself possessed the 'Russian simplicity' of which he wrote in 'Under Western Eyes':(15)
    That propensity of lifting every problem from the plane of
    the understandable by means of some sort of mystic ex-
    pression... I suppose one must be a Russian to understand
    Russian simplicity, a terrible corroding simplicity in which
    mystic phrases clothe a naive and hopeless cynicism.
    Even with these fairly explicit remarks in mind, it is impossible
to measure if, and how far, Conrad cynically deploys a code of
enigma in his more oracular works simply to create a profitable
mystical glow: if the phrases clothe cynicism, they do it successfully enough. When he writes in 'Heart of Darkness' that 'the air
of mystery would deepen a little over the muddle of the station,'

or when he ends The Planter of Malata under a mysterious cloud
(a favourite narrative termination in Conrad which he also uses
in 'Nostromo' and 'Heart of Darkness') it is impossible to read a
disguised cynical intention into the words:(16)

> A black cloud hung listlessly over the high rock on the
> middle hill; and under the mysterious silence of that shadow
> Malata lay mournful with an air of anguish in the wild sun-
> set, as if remembering the heart that was broken there.

This is magazine sentimentalism - Conrad at his worst - but it does
not sound hollow or cynical. It is only by analysing the extensive
network of figures and ciphers in his work which relate the narrative to an obscure interpretative domain supposedly hidden
within, that the uses of the enigmatic code may be judged.

In a series of brilliant essays Walter Benjamin describes a process of change in the period from Baudelaire to Proust which he
called the elimination of the 'aura' of the work of art.(17) That
which withers in the age of mechanical reproduction, he says, is
the aura of the work of art. It is clearly related to secularization
but not reducible to it. Benjamin writes:(18)

> The definition of the aura as a 'unique phenomenon of a
> distance however close it may be' represents nothing but
> the cult value of the work of art in categories of space and
> time perception. Distance is the opposite of closeness. The
> essentially distant object is the unapproachable one. Un-
> approachability is indeed a major quality of the cult image.
> True to its nature, it remains 'distant, however close it may
> be'. The closeness which one may gain from its subject mat-
> ter does not impair the distance which it retains in its
> appearance.

It seems to me a primary function of the rhetoric of enigma in
Conrad to preserve - indeed to intensify - the 'aura' of the art
work. Benjamin's description of the aura in terms of a distance
preserved even in closeness is fundamental to Conrad's fiction.
He constructs narratives in which 'impenetrability', literal and
metaphorical, is profoundly important. There is a certain epistemological threshold which he refuses to cross, always with the dis-
claimer that a near approach to the matter is beyond his power:
'The essentials of this affair lay deep under the surface, beyond
my reach, and beyond my power of meddling.'(19) His stories are
full of boundaries, limits and thresholds which, like horizons,
recede as one approaches. With characteristic insistence, the
journey up river into the heart of darkness is into an 'impenetrable'
realm, and Marlow remarks:(20)

> I looked around, and I don't know why, but I assure you
> that never, never before, did this land, this river, this
> jungle, the very arch of this blazing sky, appear to me so
> hopeless and so dark, so impenetrable to human thought, so
> pitiless to human weakness.

Geoffrey Renouard is exemplary of the Conradian hero in this
respect, feeling like an explorer 'trying to penetrate the interior
of an unknown country, the secret of which is too well defended

by its cruel and barren nature.' The opposed tensions in the
narratives are perfectly indexed in this simile, for his characters
are often poised on the outer border of some physical or mental
territory which simultaneously fascinates and repels. This unknown domain marks the limit to the narrative in that its boundaries define the ultimate horizon of expectation, the 'non plus
ultra' of desire and fear in the story. Within the territory we are
assured that there resides something immensely precious and
immensely corrupting, but also, inevitably, just beyond our comprehension. And this is as much a matter of subjective interiority
as physical extension. Almayer's 'treasure', the Gould Concession,
the ivory, the 'mystery of Samburan' all have their analogues in
the psychic 'treasure' buried deep in the personality of his characters. Indeed the 'mystery' of earth and of mind are given as a
unity, and Conrad's stories often write the one in terms of the
other through a symbolic coalescence of nature and psyche. Heyst,
pushed to his limits by Mr Jones, says to Lena: (21)

> That's it. I don't know how to talk. I have managed to
> refine everything away. I've said to the Earth that bore me:
> 'I am I and you are a shadow' and, by Jove, it is so. But it
> appears that such words cannot be uttered with impunity.
> Here I am on a Shadow inhabited by Shades. How helpless a
> man is against the Shades! How is one to intimidate, persuade,
> resist, assert oneself against them?

Dissolution into shades of intangibility places the active force of
his narrative in the noumenal margins of something approached
but never reached. This preserved distance which creates the
aura of the work is necessarily an external relationship between
the 'impenetrable' core of the narrative (personality/territory)
and the outer zone of conjecture and uncertainty which envelops
it. The narrator in 'Heart of Darkness' describes Marlow's story
in terms which precisely confirm Benjamin's description of aura:
(22)

> The yarns of seamen have a direct simplicity, the whole
> meaning of which lies within the shell of a cracked nut.
> But Marlow was not typical ... and to him the meaning of
> an episode was not inside like a kernel but outside, envel-
> oping the tale which brought it out only as a glow brings
> out a haze, in the likeness of one of these misty halos that
> sometimes are made visible by the spectral illumination of
> moonshine.

In terms of the literary signs and symbols used in these stories,
this external 'haze' is the primary region of interpretative obscurity. There are obscurities of extension as well as of compression,
and Conrad creates obscurity by simplification and extension. By
contrast, Meredith's obscurity results from compression, the need
to reduce self-exposure by condensation into ellipses and dense
tissues of metaphor. Meredith writes as though subjectivity had
to be squeezed into a single point of energy – as though the self
were only secure when refined to a rapid, discontinuous movement. As he writes in The Empty Purse: (23)

> The plural swarm round us; ourself in the thick,
> A dot or a stop: that is our task;

But it is important to note that the multiplication of potential
interpretations or signs is not to be confused with the multiplication of the number of signs themselves. A surplus of meaning
is most often due, not to a concentration of signs as in Meredith,
but to a lack of information, and it is the absence of a sufficient
context of signs, of framing, which leaves a message open. Communication theory has convincingly shown that the relation between information and signification is in inverse ratio, and the
greater the information (redundancy) the less the chance of multiple readings.

This principle is a foundation of obscurity in Conrad. It is not
a density of signification which produces the sense of mystery
here, but an attenuation of form and feature. Conrad effaces
boundary limits so that distinctions dissolve into distances. This
'tensile' obscurity is presented as much by the topography of
Conrad's fiction as by its symbolic resonance. Walter Benjamin
remarks that 'Experience of the aura [thus] rests on the transposition of a response common in human relationships to the
relationship between the inanimate or natural object and man.'(24)

This is amply demonstrated with respect to Conrad by a close
analysis of the rhetoric of enigma in 'Heart of Darkness'. Unlike
James, Conrad does not obscure things by involution or the multiplication of subtle distinctions. He tends instead to remove the
categorical divisions between different areas so that his prose
aspires to the universalism of 'nature' represented as mute,
primeval and illimitable. As Walter Benjamin suggests, a mysterious aura is generated by a transposition of interpersonal response
(in this case, that of 'guarding secrets') into a relationship between men and nature. In 'Heart of Darkness', Conrad writes as if
the words on the page were only 'surface markers' of some vast
secret, and the following pages trace through this enigmatic code
of secrecy as it appears in some of these surface markers.

'Heart of Darkness' opens with an image of 'maintained distance'.
At the very outset of the story the reader learns that the narrative position, the place from which the story will be told, is in
a suspended off-shore zone:(25)

> The *Nellie*, a cruising yawl, swung to her anchor without
> a flutter of the sails, and was at rest. The flood had made,
> the wind was nearly calm, and being bound down the river,
> the only thing for it was to come to and wait for the turn
> of the tide.

The position of the 'Nellie' (deceptively innocuous name!) introduces us immediately to two of the five physical parameters which
are to define the spatial organization of secrecy in the text. In
contrast to many of Conrad's other stories, 'Heart of Darkness' is
curiously static, even though it deals with a journey. The moral
disintegration associated with a closed and secret universe is
counterposed with the open world of work and production: 'Heart
of Darkness' is a story of continually frustrated work, of enforced

inactivity and stillness. This first marker inaugurates both of
these semantic unities, stillness and frustrated activity. Stillness
applies to both noise and movement, denoting their combined
stasis, and it is used henceforth to cover both silence (a
crucial term in the story) and lack of motion.

Another aspect of the spatial organization of secrecy introduced
from the outset is the confusion of limits and boundaries. Analogous to figures of equivocation, physical barriers throughout
the story will become vague, disordered, concealed or muddled.
The very basis of knowledge - the clear perception of differences
between things - will gradually disintegrate as land, water and
sky melt untidily into each other. In this first 'marker' the changing tide holds the sailors off from finishing their journey, and
initiates a spatial sequence of uncertain boundaries which will
continue throughout the book. Both stillness and vagueness are
thus presented in exordium as preliminary signifiers of the dominant code: 'The sea-reach of the Thames stretched before us like
the beginning of an *interminable waterway*.'(26)

The fictional world we are about to enter is not only very still,
it is also vast. Sheer physical size, as it increases towards the
infinite, becomes ungraspable and hence mysterious (literally
beyond knowledge). Endless space has always been associated
with silence, the absence of language, a suspension of communication: 'L'espace m'a toujours rendu silencieux.'(27) Much of the
power of the Sphinx, the essential and eternal symbol of secrecy
and enigma, comes not from the Sphinx at all, but from the desert
which surrounds it. There, too, we find a space organized along
the parameters of those in 'Heart of Darkness', a space in which
silence, immensity and stillness, the uncertainty of boundaries
and limits, the frustration of human endeavour, close round the
Sphinx to form a secret geography, a terrain in which each of its
qualities is a connotation of mystery. In 'Heart of Darkness' the
various spaces in which Marlow finds himself will be endless,
immense, defying knowledge and the symbolic dominion of language,
not by labyrinthine involution (Dickens's London), but by extend-
ing itself beyond measure:(28)

A *haze* rested on the low shores and ran out to sea in
vanishing flatness. The air was *dark* above Gravesend,
and farther back still seemed condensed into a *mournful
gloom*, brooding *motionless* over the *biggest*, and the
greatest town on earth. [My italics]

'Haze' and 'vanishing flatness' recapitulate the spatial anxiety
of uncertain boundaries, just as 'motionless' reinforces the signifier stillness, and 'biggest' and 'greatest' reinforce the
immensity. The fourth parameter introduced here is darkness,
already signified in the title of the story and condensing both evil
and secrecy into a single quality. It is repeated in the phrase
'brooding gloom' in the next paragraph, and is much more directly
signifying than the other terms - we can be in little doubt of the
tone (providing it is not a trap) after the 'darkness' and 'gloom'
of this paragraph. Here, at the beginning, the darkness is only

gloomy: it will intensify to total blackness as the narrative un-
folds.

The sombre lyricism of this and many similar markers in the
story uses language and space in a way which recalls the early
symbolist aesthetic of Gauthier and Baudelaire. The obscurity is,
significantly, not that of gothic fantasy but of symbolist 'brume'.
Conrad occasionally derives his semantic shades from the gothic
tradition (as in The Inn of the Two Witches) but the dominant
inter-textual (29) form is undoubtedly symbolist. His procedure
here matches almost word for word the aesthetic prescription
which emanated from the famous 1867 salon:(30)

la clarté, de quelque manière qu'on l'entende, nuit à
l'enthousiasme. Poète, parler sans cesse d'éternité, d'infini,
d'immensité, du temps, de l'éspace, de la Divinité, des tom-
beaux, des manes, des enfers, d'un ciel obscur, des mers
profondes, des forêts obscures, du tonnerre, des éclairs
qui déchirent la nue. Soyez ténébreux.

'Soyez ténébreux' perfectly matches Conrad's own description
for writing, 'seek discourse with the Shades'. (In 'Heart of Darkness' he uses *all* the symbolist elements listed above which the
salon recommends!) In an excellent article,(31) Ian Watt has
argued that Conrad's achievement in the story is to have combined
the techniques of Impressionism and Symbolism by having given 'a
larger symbolic meaning to an Impressionist recording of particular experience'. Despite the strictures of Eloise Knapp Hay that
Conrad's Impressionism was quite limited,(32) Watt's article seems
to me very persuasive. Impressionism, with its attention to the
subjectively received blurring or misting of clarity, is surely very
close to Conrad's technique in 'Heart of Darkness'. (Monet wrote
of the critics who ridiculed his obscurity: 'poor blind idiots. They
want us to see everything clearly, even through the fog.')(33)
Watt goes on to remark that with both Monet and Conrad, 'the difficulty and obscurity are essential parts of what the artist is
trying to say.' By combining the interpretative openness of symbolism with the maintained distance and misty vision of Impressionism, Conrad achieves the perspective imprecision which is
fundamental to aura:(34)

The water shone pacifically; the sky without a speck, was a
benign immensity of unstained light; the very mist on the
Essex marshes was like a gauzy and radiant fabric, hung
from the wooded rises inland, and draping the low shores
in diaphanous folds. Only the gloom to the west, brooding
over the upper reaches became more sombre every minute....

This sentence resumes all the previous spatial parameters, and
brings them together between the silence on board the yacht
(where the phrase 'we felt meditative, and fit for nothing except
placid staring' once more takes up the notion of inactivity) and
the setting sun, the disappearance of light and all the shades of
'Götterdämmerung' which this suggests. Once again, the boundary
of sea and shore is obscured, this time by mists, which anticipate
two further 'misty passages' later in the narrative which also 'blur

distinctions'. Edges become fluid and intangible 'like a [...] line, far, far away along a blue sea whose glitter was blurred by a creeping mist.' Marlow continues: 'What greatness had not floated on the ebb of that river into the mystery of an unknown earth!.. ..'(35)

This is the first time that secrecy is openly introduced under the metaphysical form of mystery. The spatial image which bears it is once again that of immensity though here, through the references to Sir Francis Drake, Sir John Franklin and to the Roman invaders, the immensity is also historical. The rather inflated rhetoric of this marker indicates secrecy and wonder through the distance of remote time. Historical and cultural remoteness strengthen the connotation of 'cult' (primitive and exotic) which is an important sub-structure of the book. It is the nexus of cult and remoteness which forms a key significance in a story which has 'unspeakable rites' at 'heart' (rites which are always approached but never reached: it is this combination of inapproachability and ritual which is distinctive in the creation of literary aura). If aura is the 'unique manifestation of a distance', this definition 'has the advantage of clarifying the ceremonial character of the phenomenon. The essentially distant is the inapproachable: inapproachability is in fact a primary quality of the ceremonial image.'(36) The 'drone of weird incantations' which Marlow finds in the 'Heart of Darkness' is an interior index of the formal ceremonial structure of language which envelops it, the 'magic current of phrases' which constitute the unapproachable (because radically indeterminate) reference of the tale.

The perpetual transference effected by the text from the secrecy of human relations to the 'inscrutable' and 'infinite' surface of nature is increased by a rhetorical process of 'reciprocation'. Proust has remarked that 'Some people who are fond of secrets flatter themselves that objects retain something of the gaze that has rested upon them.' This enigmatic flattery operates like Borges's story 'The Mirror of Enigmas' in that it makes the enigmatic endlessly reflective (in both senses of this word). The transference from subject to object, inverting the relation of questioned and questioner (which becomes a familiar and pleasurable game amongst schoolchildren, each refusing to answer until his own question has been asked again) is an essential part of the structure in 'Heart of Darkness':(37)

The smell of mud, of primeval mud, by Jove! was in my
nostrils, the high stillness of primeval forest was before
my eyes, ... I wondered whether the stillness on the face
of the immensity looking at us two were meant as an appeal
or as a menace. What were we who had strayed in here?
Could we handle that dumb thing, or would it handle us?

This is not simply the conjuring of anthropomorphic hostility from the inanimate, it is the discursive production of 'mystery' by the mirror-process. Marlow continually grants the forest eyes in a way which duplicates the most ancient act of totemic endowment. But at the same time the simple, unilateral relation of questioner

and questioned, subject and object, becomes a complex process
of reciprocation, an enigmatic movement. Benjamin once again is
remarkably concise on this point:(38)

The person we look at, or who feels he is being looked at,
looks at us in turn. To perceive the aura of an object we
look at means to invest it with the ability to look at us in
return... (the ability, it would seem, of returning the gaze).

This gaze (which, as will become apparent below, is characteristically feminine in Conrad) is the specular equivalent of narrative suspension. Like the Sphinx, the object 'holds' the subject
in its gaze, which is the visual moment of expectation. In 'Heart
of Darkness', the visual and the verbal become entwined in the
following passage as Marlow transfers interrogative priority from
himself to the forest:(39)

There was no sign on the face of nature of this amazing tale
that was not so much told to me as suggested in desolate
exclamations, completed by shrugs, in interrupted phrases,
in hints ending in deep sighs. The woods were unmoved,
like a mask - heavy, like the closed door of a prison - they
looked with their air of hidden knowledge, of patient expectation, of unapproachable silence.

The assimilation of the signs of the tale to the signs of nature
is given in the first sentence of the passage, 'there was no sign
on the face of nature of this amazing tale....' a metonymic identification of the surfaces which indexes their perfect unity. This
reciprocation is used frequently by Marlow. He recounts how, as
a child, he had been fascinated by the blank spaces of unexplored
territory on the map of Africa: 'It [the map] had ceased to be a
blank space of delightful mystery - a white patch for a boy to
dream gloriously over. It had become a place of darkness... one
river... resembling an immense snake uncoiled....'(40) He was
enchanted by the absence of signs which indicated the presence
of secrets. What Conrad gives here, in a vignette, is the perfect
expression of the signifier which I have termed enigma. It is precisely the 'presence of missing signs', the blankness of the paper
where geographical symbols ought to be, that signals the position
of a secret, something quite literally to be discovered. Conrad
uses the habitual associations of the term 'whiteness' to give this
enigma a positive value - it is the innocent mystery of a child's
universe, boyhood dreams of adventure in remote lands. But in a
sudden reversal, Conrad then overthrows this positive valuation
with its opposite, using darkness and the snake. The darkness is
the now familiar physical metaphor of secrecy and evil, and the
snake is the long coils of the Congo drawn on the white patch of
the map. So the enigma of the blank space is 'solved', but only by
replacing it with further symbols of secrecy and deception, of
darkness and the serpent. The antithesis does not develop the
reader's knowledge, but instead blocks that knowledge by leading
from one discursive figure to another in a repertoire of deception.
Blank space, full space, both signify mystery.

The reader is thus made to feel that there is something to be

expressed other than that which objectively offers itself to expression. In that remarkable critical work 'La Poétique de l'Espace',
Gaston Bachelard wrote on the spatial relation of immensity to the
psychological or spiritual state of transcendence as evoked by
romantic poety. Concentrating upon the poetic theme of 'l'immensité de la Forêt', he wrote:(41)

> Ce qu'il faudrait exprimer, c'est la grandeur cachée, une
> profondeur. Loin de se livrer à la prolixité des impressions,
> loin de se perdre dans le détail de la lumière et des ombres,
> on se sent devant une impression 'essentielle' qui cherche
> son expression, bref dans la perspective de ce que nos
> auteurs appellent un 'transcendant psychologique.'

Little enough work has been done on the interconnections between spatial and textual structure, and Bachelard's study is a
suggestive beginning rather than a definitive analysis. The immensity of the forest and of the sea in Conrad is intimately related
to the receding horizon which, as it vanishes towards the infinite,
transforms the merely physical into the metaphysical. 'Facts' melt
into the indeterminancy of blank surfaces:(42)

> But there was the fact facing me - the fact dazzling, to be
> seen, like the foam on the depths of the sea, like a ripple
> on an unfathomable enigma, a mystery greater - when I
> thought of it - than the curious, inexplicable note of des-
> perate grief in this savage clamour that had swept by us
> on the river-bank, behind the blind whiteness of the fog.

Here, most clearly visible in its willed mystification, is the fear
of disenchantment. Conrad will not allow a fact to remain a 'fact',
but instead he sends it into the mediating obscurity of these vast
and 'unfathomable' poetic spaces, the sea-foam and the fog. 'For
a time I would feel I belonged still to a world of straight-forward
facts; but the feeling would not last long,' Marlow remarks earlier
in the story. In the movement from the mundane fact to the 'inexplicable' note of desperate grief behind the 'blind whiteness of the
fog', one can detect a characteristic type of translation in Conrad's fiction, whereby a given fact (here it is the self-restraint
exercised by the cannabalistic crew) is set over into a language
which mystifies it.

The importance of this translation process is not only that it rewrites the facts 'sub specie aeternitatis' thereby tending to push
the specific historical moment of the story towards the mythic and
transcendent. But also it makes the language of enigma a univer-
salizing equivalent between different symbolic aspects of Conrad's
world. His rhetoric of mystery is omnivorous. 'Woman', 'unconscious', 'nature', 'language', these are effectively placed into a
single paradigmatic set by their common designation as 'enigma'.
They are all rewritten 'like a script in an unknown language', and
this has the crucial consequence that they are symbolically interchangeable on the basis of their resistant incomprehensibility.(43)
It is this paradigmatic relation which makes 'Heart of Darkness' a
text which is open to so many different interpretations - indeed it
is one of the most 'interpreted' texts of modern times.(44) The

usual critical activity in this respect is to fix upon one of the
mysterious equivalents in the book (the two women dressed in
black in the Brussels office is a favourite point)(45) and to provide a 'solution' to 'Heart of Darkness' in terms of this single
equivalent. But critics rarely ask why the reader feels almost
obliged to read 'Heart of Darkness' as a question, as though the
whole narrative were an oppressive interrogative. It has produced
over one hundred different 'interpretations' yet what is the basis
of this hermeneutic fecundity? How is it that 'Heart of Darkness'
appears as essentially enigmatic, as coercive in the sense that
André Jolles ascribes to the riddle:(46)

> Dans la forme du Mythe nous sommes questionneurs, dans
> la Devinette nous sommes questionnés - et de telle sorte
> qu'il nous faut répondre. C'est pourquoi le Mythe porte
> les couleurs de la liberté et la Devinette celles de la con-
> trainte.   C'est pourquoi le Mythe soulage quand la
> Devinette oppresse. Et ce n'est pas un hasard si l'équi-
> valent en vieux-haut-allemand de la Devinette était le mot
> *Tunkal*, qui signifie 'la chose ténébreuse'.

'Heart of Darkness' precisely confirms Jolles's etymological
identification of the riddle with 'the thing of shades'. Its rhetoric
of enigma presents the narrative as a dark rebus to which there
must be some 'answer'. Jolles goes on to show that a riddle functions as a form of initiation, and that it exists as a de-coding test
which, if solved, results in the successful 'association' of the
questioned (the reader) with the questioner. Once more, the
structural obscurities of the text point to an hieratic function.
The implicit reader (47) of 'Heart of Darkness' is that ardent
young novice-critic whom James portrayed so well in John Delavoy
and The Figure in the Carpet. Conrad's fiction is full of initiation
ceremonies and rites of passage (The Shadow-Line is the most
obvious example), the crossing of some boundary which divides the
mature and successful from the rest. In the Author's Note to that
dreadful novel 'The Arrow of Gold', Conrad wrote:(48)

> What the story of the *Tremolino* in its anecdotic character
> has in common with the story of 'The Arrow of Gold' is the
> quality of initiation (through an ordeal which required
> some resolution to face) into the life of passion. In the few
> pages at the end of 'The Mirror of the Sea' and in the whole
> volume of 'The Arrow of Gold', *that* and no other is the
> subject offered to the public.

The complexity of 'Heart of Darkness' resides in this double-
structure. It presents itself as an enigma both fascinating and
oppressive, a threshold of initiation; but at the same time it keeps
itself semantically 'unapproachable' and 'impenetrable', pushing
this threshold further and further away so that it becomes impossible to cross. This 'unique maintenance of a distance' preserves
the aura of the work whilst simultaneously tantalizing the reader
with an offer of initiation into mysteries. It is a powerful combination of narrative and semantic form which continuously promises
and defers a moment of revelation (Thomas Pynchon's 'The Crying

of Lot 49' operates in a structurally similar way). There is a
moment when Marlow offers yet another gnomic commentary on the
'mystery of life' which in fact gives a significant clue to the form
of revelation operative within the story: 'Perhaps all the wisdom,
and all truth, and all sincerity, are just compressed into that
inappreciable moment of time in which we step over the threshold
of the invisible.'(49)

I once thought this the most strained and pretentious of all
Marlow's utterances, devoid of any significant content except as
providing another support to the code of enigma. After all, we
are unlikely to know, even metaphorically, when we step over the
threshold of that which cannot be perceived. It remains true that
Conrad's anxiety to express the code in weighty and general
terms puts a burden of strain upon the assent and aesthetic judgment of the reader: he risks the reader seeing this as a 'device'
to increase the density of mystification in the text, which is what
it is. But at the same time it defines very precisely the kind of
'threshold' which the story itself possesses. There is no better
way of describing the way in which 'Heart of Darkness' sets up
its limits of disclosure and then dissolves them into the air than
to call its thresholds 'invisible'. That magical moment of revelation
('*all* the wisdom, and *all* truth and *all* sincerity') is a function of
the textual boundaries which are continually displaced.

The symbolist poet Jules Laforgue coined the neologism 'eternullité' to describe the ultimately mystical, 'negative-and-eternal'
yearning of symbolist verse. 'Eternullité' is the transcendental
'signified'(50) of 'Heart of Darkness'. Marlow tells the whole tale
in 'the pose of a Buddha preaching in European clothes and without a lotus flower' and the discourse he tells is of an immense
darkness ('Eternullité') leading to the uttermost ends of the earth.
That infinite negativity, immense darkness, is the field of interpretation of the story, the 'genotext' within which any particular
critical 'phenotext' must be formed.(51) The end of the tale re-
capitulates the beginning by ending on the word of the title.
There has been movement but no progress (which is true of all
Conrad's writing: he is in this sense 'non-progressive'). The
closing surface marker asserts the same enigmatic code in a cyc-
lical gesture which is an oppressive and hopeless return to its
beginning:(52)

> Marlow ceased, and sat apart, indistinct and silent, in the
> pose of a meditating Buddha. Nobody moved for a time. 'We
> have lost the first of the ebb', said the Director, suddenly.
> I raised my head. The offing was barred by a black bank of
> clouds, and the tranquil waterway leading to the uttermost
> ends of the earth flowed sombre under an overcast sky -
> seemed to lead into the heart of an immense darkness.

Of course, 'Heart of Darkness' is not a Buddhist tale, but it
deploys a considerable variety of quasi-religious references which
(like the 'crucifixion' at the end of An Outpost of Progress) create
a network of possible critical 'interpretations' in terms of specific
systems of religious belief. 'Heart of Darkness' has been read as a

coherent Buddhist story, just as it has been read as a symbolist
rewriting of Dante's descent into Hell and Orpheus' into the
Underworld.(53) The desire to fix the shifting semantic limits of
the text into a certain configuration is given every encouragement
by the transcendental connotations of the enigmatic code in the
story. But there is also little doubt that this is a trap. The
important reference in this respect is a letter Conrad wrote to
Richard Curle in 1922, in which he complains that critical interpretation destroys the deliberately cultivated obscurity of certain
of his works and threatens to make them disappointing;(54)

It is a strange fate that everything that I have, of set
artistic purpose, laboured to leave indefinite, suggestive,
in the penumbra of initial inspiration, should have that
light turned on to it and its insignificance... exposed for
any fool to comment upon or even for average minds to be
disappointed with. Didn't it ever occur to you, my dear
Curle, that I knew what I was doing in leaving the facts of
my life and even of my tales in the background? Explicitness
my dear fellow, is fatal to the glamour of all artistic work,
robbing it of all suggestiveness, destroying all illusion.

Conrad's plaintive cry is expressive of a standard romantic dilemma. As John Bayley has written, the 'obscure thought processes' which make the work (Conrad's 'penumbra of initial inspiration') cannot be paralleled on the level of hypostasis and reason
without the work losing its power:(55)

Once author and reader had been made conscious of how
these processes are presumed to work, it is difficult for
them to do anything else. The novelist's original language
of myth and symbol is thus being continually glossed, or
dubbed - while it is actually in the process of creation by
the writer or of appreciation by the reader - into the more
commonplace language of the interpretative consciousness.

Conrad's letter to Curle makes clear how conscious he was that
his own work was vulnerable to critical interpretation and that
his obscurity was intentional - 'of set artistic purpose'. It confirms the feeling of disillusionment, the fear of a world devoid of
romantic or spiritual enchantment which suddenly floods over the
young narrator in The Shadow-Line:(56)

A great discouragement fell on me. A spiritual drowsiness.
Giles's voice was going on complacently; the very voice of
the universal hollow conceit... There was nothing original,
nothing new, startling, informing to expect from the world:
no opportunities, to find out something about oneself, no
wisdom to acquire, no fun to enjoy. Everything was stupid
and overrated, even as Captain Giles was. So be it.

But Conrad as author could not face this calmly spoken 'So be
it.' Authorship allowed him to make spiritual reparation to the
world, to invest it once more with the glamour which he felt it
was losing or had already lost. It is not accidental that when he
recalled the fateful morning on which he began his novel-writing
career, it was 'an autumn day with an opaline atmosphere, a veiled,

semi-opaque, lustrous day ... one of those London days that have the charm of mysterious amenity.' Conrad has already surrounded the original moment of his career with a semi-translucent aura of mysterious charm. His friend Arthur Symons (who was one of the first English writers to see the way in which symbolist practice confirmed this displacement of religious feeling into art) described literature as 'a kind of religion, with all the duties and the responsibilities of the sacred ritual'. In an important letter back to Symons, Conrad wrote most explicitly of his own 'quasi-religious sentiment' and the importance this had for his fiction:(57)

One thing that I am certain of is that I have approached that object of my task, things human, in a spirit of piety. The earth is a temple where there is going on a mystery play, childish and poignant, ridiculous and awful enough in all conscience. Once in I've tried to behave decently. I have not degraded my quasi-religious sentiment by tears and groans; and if I have been amused or indignant, I have neither grinned nor gnashed my teeth. In other words, I've tried to write with dignity, not out of regard for myself, but for the sake of the spectacle, the play with an obscure beginning and an unfathomable *dénouement*.

The romantic nostalgia of Conrad's letter to Symons betrays the constant risk of any literary endeavour to displace religious mystery into the form of art: indulgence and spiritual overselling are intrinsic threats to a literary project which defines itself as a rewriting of a 'mystery play' under the aegis of fin-de-siècle symbolist practice.

In all these respects Conrad's literary practice appears as conservative rather than modernist. He belongs to what John Bayley has called the 'Romantic survival', and his insistence upon thoughts that do lie too deep for words suggests a very traditional preoccupation with obscurity. He certainly appears less modernist in this aspect of his fiction than Meredith, who could transform the defensive opacity of language into startlingly new forms of signification. In 'Heart of Darkness', 'Lord Jim', The Return, 'Under Western Eyes', The Planter of Malata, and at various moments in other novels and tales, Conrad indulges in indiscriminate, sham universalism, created by making everything into an aspect of some sinister, cosmic mystery. The worst aspect of Conrad's fiction resides in this use of enigma as a way of artificially generating value. In the end it is an inflationary procedure and by qualifying so many things as intrinsically unknowable it devalues them. The impalpable obscure becomes visible as an inflated textual effect:(58)

the patient wilderness, that closed upon it as a sea closes over a diver.... An empty stream, a great silence, an impenetrable forest... cut off for ever from everything you had known once.... *It was the stillness of an implacable force brooding over an inscrutable intention.* [My italics]

However, it would not give a just understanding of the way obscurity functions in Conrad's work to consider it solely in this way. Despite its tendency to excess and to repetition, Conrad's preoccupation with what he called the 'mystic nature of material things' had two very positive consequences. It made him sensitive to the fluidity of language and interpretation to an extent unmatched by any other writer in English at the end of the nineteenth century. It is not accidental that 'Heart of Darkness' has produced, and is still producing, such a remarkable stream of different (if frequently overlapping) interpretations. Conrad no more believed in the fixed text than he did in the last word: he thought language could never definitively capture either that which is beyond itself or even its own form, and as such it could never end its quest for that elusive, final meaning just beyond the threshold of expression. Midway through 'Lord Jim' Marlow remarks:(59)

the last word is not said - probably shall never be said. Are not our lives too short for that full utterance which through all our stammerings is of course our only and abiding intention? I have given up expecting those last words, whose ring, if they could only be pronounced, would shake both heaven and earth.

This is the 'positive' obscurity in Conrad's work, the internal link which exists between its 'openness' to further linguistic translation or interpretation and its realization that the writer never has the last word. A fundamental and terrifying kind of obscurity arises from this loss of 'finality' in human affairs - which is perhaps only another way of saying a loss in the power of narrative termination to convince us of its truth. Marlow's 'inconclusive experiences' have their logical counterpart in the interminable nature of exegesis and textual enigma. In 'A Personal Record' Conrad wrote: 'The part of the inexplicable should be allowed for in appraising the conduct of men in a world where no explanation is final.'(60)

Where 'no explanation is final' no authority dictates a precise and unalterable form to the work or the world. It is not only that Conrad wrote obscurely simply out of a desire for romantic or quasi religious effect. He felt that the gap between reference and signification was so great - a kind of abyss - that language itself could only provide a provisional and inadequate staging post on a quest for meanings which had no final destination. The wanderers and drifters in his fiction are both image and bearer of what he called 'an unrelated existence, following faithfully, too, the traced way of an inexplicable impulse'. Language is thus less monolithic and less powerful for Conrad than for most other writers. The important things are beyond language, neither terror nor pleasure can be satisfactorily accommodated by it. A key ambiguity in Conrad is that his pessimistic belief that there can be no referential fixity in language leads to the creation of fictions which are rich in hermeneutic potential precisely on account of this fact. In The Author's Note to 'Within The Tides' he wrote: 'To render a crucial point of feelings in terms of human speech is really an impossible task. Written words can only form a sort of translation.'(61)

On the one hand this is still not far removed from a traditional romantic doctrine, but on the other it leads him to conceive of all forms of rational clarity as constituting a small, constructed shelter within a world 'that seemed to wear a vast and dismal aspect of disorder.' In 'The Nigger of the "Narcissus" ' Conrad talks of the 'narrow limits of human speech' and our incapacity to resolve the problems of life within their confines. Thus, any attempt to articulate the truth must take account of this relation between the two domains - the relation between known order (work, civilization, the male shipboard community) and the obscure forces of disorder (anarchy, the unconscious, the sea, 'untameable' women, savagery). Conrad's narratives play out the conflict between these two domains, the latter always threatening to engulf the former. The problem is clearly that the forces of disorder are not subject to linguistic control, and in this Conrad's 'descriptions' of them - like any 'description' of the unconscious - can only ever be an obscure intimation. In particular, the threshold of language marks the barrier to rational penetration of the enigmatic demands of the unconscious, and Conrad's grappling with this is frequently intelligent and convincing: 'enigma', which is the central linguistic structure of 'Heart of Darkness', is the form in which unconscious desire presents itself. Jacques Lacan has described it in 'Le Discours de Rome' in the following way:(62)

The unconscious is that chapter of my history which is marked by a blank or occupied by a falsehood: it is the censored chapter. But the Truth can be found again; it is most often already written down elsewhere.

The enigma in Conrad is close to what classic psycho-analysis has called the 'omphalos' of the dream, the point at which the question which the unconscious demands, insists upon a representation. Marlow's phrase about 'hints for nightmares' is a perfect analogue of this. It was termed 'omphalos', not simply to indicate the umbilical cord between desire and the body of language, but because 'omphalos' was at Delphi, the navel of the earth, the place where the enigmatic voice could speak.

Conrad's use of obscurity thus leads on from his intuitive feeling that the dark forces of the unconscious enter language as pure enigma, that the enigmatic as such is its form of representation. It is impossible to penetrate directly into the domain of the unconscious, and most of the time we inhabit language as a refuge from its demands. Marlow says:(63)

For a moment I had a view of a world that seemed to wear a vast and dismal aspect of disorder, while, in truth, thanks to our unwearied efforts, it is as sunny an arrangement of small conveniences as the mind of man can conceive. But still - it was only a moment: I went back into my shell directly. One *must* - don't you know? - though I seemed to have lost all my words in the chaos of dark thoughts I had contemplated for a second or two beyond the pale. These came back, too, very soon, for words also belong to the sheltering conception of light and order which is our refuge.

This is part of Conrad's deep suspicion of language in general
and eloquence in particular. As Jeremy Hawthorn remarks:
' "Eloquent" is a word he hardly ever uses innocently: by it he
nearly always implies a morally suspect facility with words, an
ability to build beautiful verbal structures which are at variance
with what is really the case.'(64)

In 'Heart of Darkness' the most notable of Mr Kurtz's many
abilities and skills is his rhetoric. His pamphlet, which like the
seaman's manual has a strange and contradictory subscript appen-
ded to it ('exterminate all the brutes!') is nevertheless a 'beautiful piece of writing'. It was 'the unbounded power of eloquence -
of words - of burning noble words'. And later, when Kurtz is
dying, Marlow is fascinated by his voice - 'A voice! A voice! It
was grave, profound, vibrating, while the man did not seem
capable of a whisper.' Yet Kurtz was hollow. The eloquence was
an elegant lie, the rhetoric false, and above all the charisma which
Kurtz had generated was insubstantial. It was all a brilliant, linguistic surface, a chain mail of words which had charmed even the
savages of the jungle. Beneath it was not simply 'nothing', but an
existence which, in its abandonment to primitive violence and
sexuality, never corresponded to the charismatic image Kurtz had
woven around himself. This web of words is a lie, in the strict
sense in which it has been defined above, which suppresses a
secret beneath a false narrative. In this case, a narrative of
civilization (Kurtz's qualities are emphatically those of western
civilization) which remains only just beyond the cliché of the
'civilized veneer'. Yet what saves Kurtz from being a banal and
anachronistic symbol is the way in which the opposition of savagery and civilization is coded: it is not simply false surface
disguising true interior, but a relation which is perfectly consonant with post-Freudian knowledge of dream, fantasy and
representation, and sociological notions of ideology.(65) In Kurtz,
the relation of savagery to language is mediated by the codes of
secrecy which operate in the dream and in political ideology, a
relation which is in no sense 'straight', but always ambiguous and
unclear, like Marlow's attitude to Kurtz himself. Fascination and
repulsion play subtly back and forth through the representations
of violence (the severed heads) and of eloquence (the voice) which,
in their intrinsically obscure relation, are both 'Kurtz'.

It is between this degraded violence and this rhetoric that
enigma - the hint of lies, pretence, evasion, secrecy - acts to
transfix the two, holding them in place in a structure, a mechanism, which is as much that of the nightmare as of Fascism
('exterminate all the brutes!'). The power of Kurtz, his power to
both attract and repel, resides in this 'coded space' between the
exterior and the interior, a space which exists between the rhetoric and the unspeakable rites, between the 'magnificent folds of
eloquence', and the 'hints for nightmares'. The reader never hears
this eloquence and he never sees the violence, they are effects of
the code of enigma, its dark hints and ambiguous markers. Thus
Kurtz is not simply hollow (morally degenerate, vice personified),(66)

nor simply great (urbane, civilized, cultured), but the two held together at once by a set of signs which fascinate, which captivate the attention in the same way as another voice did in Weimar, and as the voices do in our dreams.

In one sense, we know all about Kurtz. We know his history, that he was worshipped by savage tribes whose orgies and sacrifices were often instigated at his word, that he almost certainly lived with a 'barbarous and superb woman' despite having a fiancée at home, we know what he did and how he died. We know all this in the same way that we 'know' that dreams are the distorted expressions of fears and desires. In another sense, we know nothing of Kurtz at all, just as we know nothing of our dreams, for both are not properly graspable by the cool and rational faculties of analysis and intellection. The closest we can come is to a tantalization of the intellect in its essential desire to know, to frustrate it through enigma and ambiguity, as Conrad does throught Kurtz's famous cry 'The horror! The horror!' It is only as we experience the fascination and frustration of the code of enigma (the empty excess of 'The horror! The horror!' for example) that we begin to 'know' the inner darkness of Mr Kurtz, 'a shadow darker than the shadow of the night, and draped nobly in the folds of a gorgeous eloquence.'

But the triumph of the story is that we cannot simply 'read off' the unconscious as Kurtz, just as we cannot fix one total, all-embracing interpretation that will account for every element in the narrative. In his recent book 'The Genesis of Secrecy', Frank Kermode writes:(67)

> It is... a paradox applying to all narrative that although its function is mnemonic it always recalls different things. The mode of recall will depend in some measure on the fashion of a period - what it seems natural or reasonable to expect a text to say. This is another way of affirming that all narratives possess 'hermeneutic potential', which is another way of saying that they must be obscure... the narrative inhibits its proper dark, in which the interpreter traces its lineaments as best he can.

One should, of course, beware of the consequences of equating obscurity with hermeneutic potential, thereby defining all narrative as obscure. Nevertheless, if ever a narrative inhabited 'its proper dark' as the metaphor of its own textual obscurity, it is Conrad's tale of the Congo. It is a story which perpetually 'recalls different things', and its power resides in its capacity to produce entirely different, resonant interpretations in a range of distinct domains - religious, psychological, anthropological, aesthetic or moral. The story even appears generically protean - sailor's yarn, novella, myth, riddle, parable, adventure story - all flow into each other to merge the structural features of their own form with those of the others. Yet it is not banal to insist that, despite generic fusion and plethoric interpretation, at the heart of darkness there is always ('always', because excessive to any given reading) semantic darkness, something further to localize, accommodate or 'resolve'. It is only by acknowledging this as essentially constitutive of the sign system of the narrative that one can begin to account for the vast range of readings which it has convincingly produced. It is a matter of looking at the darkness rather than through it to some single discursive outline (even though one can never escape from the paradox of interpretation, that even by trying to account for the 'dark forms' which allow for a wide range of reading, one is always producing yet another reading. In this respect interpretation is subject to Russell's paradox of classes.)(68)

Thus, whilst it would be wrong to say that 'Heart of Darkness' is 'about' secrecy and enigma, it is true enough to say that what takes over and becomes determining is not a secret but secrecy, the forms of language which are the coded indicators or markers of concealed meaning independent of any specific, hidden content. The story is to that extent completely bi-functional, it writes about the code of secrecy, exploring the problems of guilt, lies, betrayal and mystery, but it also writes that code itself, is the expression and figuration of secrecy, its form as fiction. The obfuscation is frequently caused because, if anything is being revealed, it is the nature of enigmatic concealment. The whole journey was, says Marlow, (69)

> the farthest point of navigation and the culminating point
> of my experience. It seemed somehow to throw a kind of
> light on everything about me - and into my thoughts. It
> was sombre enough, too - and pitiful - not extraordinary
> in any way - not very clear either. No, not very clear.
> And yet it seemed to throw a kind of light.

The usual source of clarity and refuge in Conrad is physical work, but when it is embodied in 'An Enquiry into some Points of Seamanship'(70) it is subverted by its exotic, indecipherable Russian marginalia and its bizarre context in a heap of rubbish at the 'dark corner' of a jungle hut. Conrad grants his story a 'gefühlter Eindruckspunkt',(71) a felt, central point of impression in the discovery of Kurtz and the phrase 'The horror! The horror!', but this does not provide an interpretative solution to the work, only a repulsive centre of interrogative force. What is the horror? Kurtz's own depraved behaviour, or his death, or even his fiancée, who has been interpreted as a figure of destiny and whose name is equated with Kurtz's last words? By decontextualizing the utterance, and by qualifying every aspect of his story as enigmatic, Conrad simultaneously demands a solution and refuses, not only to give an answer, but the whereabouts of an answer, so that all the enigmatic elements of the tale become a source of hermeneutic suspicion. The fiancée, heavily draped in black, is assimilated to the superb African woman who was with Kurtz at the heart of the forest, and both women, like the sinister pair of women in Brussels 'introducing continuously to the unknown', are powers of darkness. Marlow says of the fiancée:(72)

> I shall see her too, a tragic and familiar Shade, resembling
> in this gesture another one, tragic also, and bedecked with

powerless charms, stretching bare brown arms over the
glitter of the infernal stream, the stream of darkness.
Conrad always associated these exotic 'feral' women with the
Sphinx. In 'Victory', Lena appears to Schomberg 'like a script in
an unknown language, or even more simply mysterious; like any
writing to the illiterate.' When Miss Haldin speaks in 'Under Western Eyes', 'the most precise of her sayings seemed always to me
to have enigmatical prolongations vanishing somewhere beyond my
reach.' The captain in The Shadow-Line becomes infatuated by 'a
professional sorceress from the slums', and Renouard conceives
of Miss Moorsom as 'some sinister riddle of a beautiful sphinx met
on the wild road of his life.' This traditional association of woman
and enigma which is used in 'Heart of Darkness' to some effect is
simply inflated and pretentious in The Return. The narrator's
wife is about to abandon him:(73)

> and when he stood up he was penetrated by an irresistible
> belief in an enigma, by the conviction that within his reach
> and passing away from him was the very secret of existence -
> its certitude, immaterial and precious! She moved to the
> door, and he followed at her elbow, casting about for a magic
> word that would compel the surrender of the gift. And there
> is no such word! The enigma is only made clear by sacrifice,
> and the gift of heaven is in the hands of every man.

Conrad's fantasy woman is an embarrassing mixture of Mata Hari
and the Eternal Eve and it is precisely to the degree that she is a
purely inaccessible romantic enigma - 'impenetrable' - that she
remains coincident with the disposition of his own writing. Despite its tendency to excess, the grand invocation of enigma by a
man in extremis is symptomatic of the form in which all writing
makes its demand felt: my first chapter discusses the way in which
the mediation of desire into the language of fiction is necessarily
enigmatic to the writer. If the process becomes transparent then
the fiction itself becomes superfluous, the enigma no longer needs
to be answered as a text. In 'A Personal Record', Conrad expresses this perfectly when he acknowledges that:(74)

> I dare say I am compelled, unconsciously compelled, now to
> write volume after volume, as in past years I was compelled
> to go to sea voyage after voyage... I do not know which of
> the two impulses appeared more mysterious and more won-
> derful to me.

The precise form of this compelling need to write is 'demand' -
that specific form of insistence which moves between the imperative
('command') and the interrogative ('question'). In Conrad the
demand reinscribes itself as the fiction, with perilously little mediation: his particular combination of pessimism and romanticism
leads him to acknowledge this compelling enigma but to despair of
any solution to it, and his writing is frequently the compulsive
restatement of the demand as mystery. The search for 'a magic
word that would make the enigma clear' is pre-empted from the
outset by the fact that 'there is no such word.' Conrad is singular
in creating a fiction which is fixed in place by the question which

marks its own field of reference: correct in its intimation that the unconscious re-presents itself as beyond discursive control, as pure demand. Conrad's narratives can only occasionally go 'beyond the pale', and when they do they find a realm beyond words: 'a heart of darkness', 'unspeakable rites' or 'a great enigma'. It produces a haunting and solipsistic discourse uncomfortably aware that in touching upon the nature of enigma it erodes its own foundations. The problem is clear: by discovering a solution to its own enigmatic code, the fiction would destroy itself.

Having ventured 'beyond the pale', Marlow scuttles back into the familiarity of language, for 'words also belong to the sheltering conception of light and order which is our refuge.' And this is to say no more than was asserted at the outset: that a penetration to the enigmatic demand behind the words betokens the internal disintegration of the fiction.

6 'THE DETERRENT FACT': VULGARITY AND OBSCURITY IN JAMES

There is no crudity here, no sudden kisses.

V. Woolf

Of the three authors considered here Henry James was the most self-consciously obscure. James cultivated obscurity. There is an elaborate, refined quality to his indirection which contrasts both with the great bounds and sudden ellipses of Meredith and the metaphysical enigmas of Conrad. If there is something nervy and tense in Meredith's difficult style which is to be distinguished from Conrad's stoical confrontation with a dark and treacherous obscure, then James presents a third and different kind of occluded text. His late novels have a rare, civilized chiaroscuro, qualities of oblique delineation and sophisticated control which always appear precise, mannered and urbane.

This obscurity in Henry James has been discussed far more fully than it has in Conrad or Meredith (1) but always under the critical aegis of formal 'ambiguity'. The evaluative debate which has grown up around the term 'ambiguity' is an august and continuing tradition, and so in a very recent book on the theory of ambiguity (2) Henry James was once more taken as the exemplary case. The choice becomes simple. One either finds the ambiguity 'confused' and 'unreadably dense' in which case the work is poor; or one finds the ambiguity a 'rich texture of meanings', in which case the work is good. As Wayne Booth put it:(3)

It is so much easier to 'dislike James' for his obscurities – without troubling very much to say what we mean – or to idolize him for his subtle ambiguities. Both positions are wholly safe, backed by troops in rank on rank, with traditions of honourable battle going back several decades.

Thus in his well-known book 'The Ambiguity of Henry James',(4) C. T. Samuels arranges the works in order of merit, beginning 'with James's confused novels, moving through his ambiguous ones, and end[ing] with his examples of achieved complexity'. And J. F. Blackall in 'Jamesian Ambiguity and "The Sacred Fount"'(5) comes to the conclusion that 'no book which has so consistently failed to reveal itself even to the most patient and practiced of readers is wholly successful.'

I have argued in chapter 1 that the term 'ambiguity', when applied to prose fiction, ought to be reserved for a very specific set of (modified Empsonian) types, and whenever it is used to blanket the field of obscurity, carries within it a number of ideo-

logical presuppositions and undiscriminated differences which
always take the critical discourse in a certain predictable direction.
The discovery of ambiguities satisfies a hermeneutic desire to pro-
liferate interpretations, but thereby fails to account for the specific textual function of the form of obscurity involved. Furthermore, to say that this or that novel is 'ambiguous' leads almost
inevitably into an anachronistic debate about intention and self-
consciousness - 'Did he mean it or was he just muddled up?' Thus
Samuels in 'The Ambiguity of Henry James':(6)

> But a multifaceted character or theme differs from one that
> invites and supports incompatible or contradictory responses.
> The former is a sign of control/and profundity; the latter a
> sign of confusion and deviousness.

It is precisely this debate which gets Edmund Wilson's otherwise
brilliant essay, The Ambiguity of Henry James,(7) into trouble
about intentionality, and forces him to 'recant' in his 1959 post-
script ('Since writing the above, I have become convinced that
James knew exactly what he was doing and that he intended the
governess to be suffering from delusions.') But no novelist 'knows
exactly what he is doing' when writing a fiction and the act of
fictional production is a dialectical interplay of conscious control,
unconscious compulsions, and the available range of cultural
forms.(8) Ambiguity signifies certain things by the very nature
of its ambiguity and it is not always necessary or even desirable
to refer back to some notion of authorial intention as to which of
the possible meanings was 'really' meant. In The Turn of the
Screw, analysed by Edmund Wilson, the important thing is surely
the difficulty of ever knowing whether the governess is deluded,
not that she is or is not deluded - it is the 'undecidability' of the
text which operates powerfully to make it so unsettling.(9)

This is not to say that James is not often ambiguous, but that
ambiguity is only one rather restricted kind of obscurity alongside others, and that the function of ambiguity in James is precisely its resistance to any clarification of the author's narrative
position. Here are several simple examples:(10)

(i)   her weakness, her desire ... flowered in her
      face like a light or darkness.
(ii) the warmth of his [Amerigo's] face - frowning,
      smiling, she mightn't know which.
(iii) 'I alone was magnificently and absurdly aware....'
(iv) The two wearers of the waistcoat, either with
      sincerity or hypocrisy, professed in the matter
      an equal expertness.
(v)   And he turned away as if there were either too
      much or too little to say about her.
(vi) I felt on her part, precisely as much and precisely
      as little of an invitation as it had constituted at
      the moment... of my first seeing them linked.

These are not subtle or complex Jamesian ambiguities, but their
narrative offerings of opposed and often mutually exclusive quali-
fiers to a single referent hold the reader in a moment of indecision,

he is held at the level of surface signs and ambivalent gestures, refused immediate entrance to the inner life of the character. Ambiguity in these examples has nothing to do with 'richness' or 'paucity' of narrative texture. It is a linguistic structure deployed within the novels' range of obscuring processes to produce mild, localized perplexity (the ambiguity in James is never aggressively arresting, it simply gives pause). It is the habit of a narrator hovering on the threshold, outside in the corridor, held in the external hiatus of indecision. The ambiguities produce a textual encounter with a narrator who at significant moments refuses to enter the mind and body of the person discussed, who refuses to be 'at one' with the subject of his own discourse, and who therefore holds off identification. And again it must be emphasized that this has nothing to do with 'reliable versus unreliable' narrators. Amerigo, in the second example given above, is neither frowning nor smiling - it is not a case of the reader attempting to decide which - Amerigo is held in a certain position from which neither Maggie nor the reader may decide: and the perspective from which the frozen narrative frame is taken fixes the reader in the place of the narrator. In other words the ambiguity operates at a primary (and almost invisible) level. It communicates doubt, hesitation, dubious identification, unresolved indication from a place always outside amongst the signs and representations, never inside passion or the body's energy.

From this we can begin to see that Jamesian ambiguity is but one revelatory instance of a wider narrative concern. It indexes a narrative position, a point of 'view' from which passion might be 'like a light or a darkness' but which, only available as external evidence, is never clear and never identified by or with the narrator. A facial expression might be a smile or a frown but he is just unable to make out which; he may have said too much or too little, been too subtle or too vulgar, but where, since no immediate, loving, impassioned response confirms or denies, he is left to wonder and peer: the ambiguities reveal the solitude of a narrative position which is a silent analogue to that of Strether's, a place outside, where passionate identification with the other sublimates itself into the pathos of eternal, patient observation.

Thus ambiguity in James is only one indication of a much broader issue, related to a narrator's position whose exteriority to the expressed centres of desire in the novels is productive of a whole range of mediating obscurities. I therefore do not wish the following analysis of the function of obscurity in Henry James to be assimilated to the comfortable tradition of 'ambiguity' hunting.

My alternative starting-point is an unlikely and coerced juxtaposition of iconoclasts taken from the 1930s and the 1960s, Stephen Spender placed 'coude à coude' with Jacques Lacan. In 'The Destructive Element', Spender located what I take to be an essential - perhaps the essential - category in James, the category of 'vulgarity':(11)

The vulgarity is not explained by his superficial snobbishness or by any ethical failing. The key to it is, in the earlier

novels, in his attitude to the body and the sexual act. It
is not that he ignores the sexual act; on the contrary it
plays a very important part in many of his novels. 'The
Wings of the Dove' and 'The Golden Bowl' and even, to a
large extent, 'The Ambassadors', are novels about sexual
subjects. The vulgarity consists at first in the sexual act
being regarded as the merest formality; and secondly, in
the later novels, in its being nearly always presented as
if it were base.
I wish to relate this to Lacan's simple proposition that 'Il y a une
affinité des énigmaes de la sexualité avec le jeu du signifiant.'
The affinity between the enigmas of sexuality and the 'play' of
signification in James seems to me a crucial generating complex of
obscurity in the later novels. In order to analyse this affinity, I
have used what S. Kappeler in her thesis on Writing and Reading
in James (12) has called a 'secondary hermeneutics of form':
But with the Jamesian game, 'the events' do not furnish a
singular level of reference and are suspended in the structural ambiguity of their presentation.... Since plot
hermeneutics fails to solve a mystery of plot, the necessity
of another hermeneutics, exploring this enigma of form,
becomes imperative.
In a 'secondary hermeneutics' I take it that one is not so much
reading through an obscure passage to its 'underlying' meanings,
as attempting to relate the obscure forms themselves to their contexts. In this analysis of James various kinds of equivocation
and ellipsis relate to the sublimation and foreclosure of sexual
enigma. All the novels and stories examined contain two 'actants'
(13) around whom obscurities are woven with particular density;
one actant is the Jamesian observer and the other the 'liaising
couple' (obviously two characters but forming a single actantial
unit on the basis of the liaison), and the relation between these
actants is caught between obscurity and vulgarity; the vulgarity,
precisely, that Spender saw as rooted in James's 'attitude to the
body and the sexual act' and which Geismar in 'Henry James and
his Cult' considered essentially voyeuristic:(14)
His vision of sex was essentially voyeuristic. A whole series
of infantile Jamesian 'observers' - some of them, as in 'What
Maisie Knew', actually being children - stand outside of a
mysterious realm of adult 'intimacy', which always turns out,
however, to be coarse and vulgar, if not actually sinful.
Sexuality as 'base', 'coarse', 'sinful', 'vulgar'; and yet the
fascinating kernel of numerous Jamesian stories, attracting and
repelling, covered and discovered, sexuality in James is never an
experience, it is an enigma - the sign of the existence of a secret.
And that secret in James is always both 'cheap' (often indeed it is
ultimately related to the relative poverty of the character(s))
and 'rich', endlessly attracting a sideways glance or surreptitious
nod. In his criticism, art reviews, stories and novels, the word
'vulgar' occurs more than 160 times, and I would go so far as to
say that the term 'vulgar' is a central organizing category in

James, all other kinds of moral, social and aesthetic judgment
being located with reference to this one. It comes to have extraordinary power in the narrative disposition of characters and
actions according to what may or may not be said or seen. This
is particularly because, especially in the later fiction, James
extends the term so that anything which announces itself directly
and immediately appears somehow 'vulgar'. But it is also that the
word itself elides, in a specifically ideological fashion, aesthetic
failure with social class. James moves through this word across
its four main areas of application: 'vulgarism' as language, the
common, ordinary use of the vernacular for public communication
(James reacts against the democratic idea of the vulgate); 'vulgar'
as a designation of class, referring to people belonging to the
middle class and below, the ignorant commonality; 'vulgar' as
describing a lack of taste, the uncultured, unrefined, cheap and
tawdry; and fourth, 'vulgarity' as sexual blatancy, the indelicate
obtrusiveness of sexual desire and sexual appetite in public. It is
clearer to see in this analytical separation the different meanings
of the term 'vulgar' bound up in James's fiction. In the realms of
language, class, taste and sexuality the active, evaluative restraint is the fear of vulgarity. In The Art of Fiction James
remarks of the novel as a form that 'It has been vulgarized, like
all other kinds of literature, like everything else to-day, and it
has proved more than some kinds accessible to vulgarization.'(15)

This is not to say that we can locate the pure origin of Jamesian
obscurity in snobbery, in his desire to get away from the common
into the rarefied as soon as possible - obscurity as a direct out-
come of 'odi profanum vulgus'. There is snobbery in James, and
one part of my argument at least concerns itself with the relation
of obscurity to the class embarrassments of the 'arriviste', the
cultivated esotericism of the coterie and the division of the reading public into 'common' and 'elite'. Cultivated obscurity often
functions quite simply in this respect as a stylistic barricade
against the mob, a disdainful rejection of the common reader. In
an essay of art criticism of 1875 James wrote:(16)

Art, at the present day, is being steadily and rapidly
vulgarized (we do not here use the word in the invidious
sense); it appeals to greater numbers of people than
formerly, and the gate of communication has had to be
widened, perhaps in a rather barbarous fashion.

Vulgarized 'in the invidious sense' or not, the disdain is evident
enough, as indeed is the polarity of barbarism and civilization
which is the binary opposition sustaining the notion itself. James
is not only (or not narrowly) concerned with class position, and
the extent of his obscurity is not simply a measure of his distance
from the lower-middle class. It is rather that 'vulgarity' in all its
aesthetic, social and sexual senses comes to be a source of powerful attraction and simultaneous repulsion in James. It becomes
what Stephen Ullmann in his book 'Semantics' has called a 'pathological' sign: 'With regard to polysemy, then, a pathological
situation arises whenever two or more incompatible senses capable

of figuring meaningfully in the same context develop round the
same name.'(17)

Fastidious and sensitive to the least intimation of crudity,
James's fiction is haunted by the anxiety that its narrative preoccupations may be seen as vulgar. The author is caught in a
position where his desire to comprehend 'intimacy' and all its close
associations of act and feeling can never be given full expression.
Particularly in the late fiction, the centre of my concern here,
this anxiety finds a natural resolution in a kind of writing at once
as far removed from intimacy and earthy materiality as possible.
The danger (which is in fact the danger of being disgusted with
oneself) is that afflicting the narrator in 'The Sacred Fount':
'For what had so suddenly overtaken me was the consciousness of
this anomaly: that I was at the same time as disgusted as if I had
exposed Mrs Server and absolutely convinced that I had yet *not*
exposed her.'(18)

The fascinating thing in James is the complex interpenetration
of social and sexual censorship against a felt desire to 'know'
things which he could not reveal without indicting himself by his
own standards. The representation of sexual desire is paramount
in this.

James's most central and extended discussion of the place of sex
in the novel is in his essay on D'Annunzio.(19) There he heavily
criticizes D'Annunzio for spoiling 'the effect of distinction so art-
fully and so copiously produced.... by a positive element of the
vulgar'.(20) We can see in this statement the way James sets up
an opposition of sexual vulgarity to distinction, artfulness and
copiousness, and these three elements re-emerge in his own work
as a complex cover to the appearance of sex. But the crucial
paragraph in the D'Annunzio essay needs quoting in full:(21)

> That sexual passion from which he extracts with admirable
> detached pictures insists on remaining for him *only* the act
> of a moment, beginning and ending in itself and disowning
> any representative character. From the moment it depends
> on itself alone for its beauty it endangers extremely its
> distinction, so precarious at the best. For what it represents,
> precisely, it is poetically interesting; it finds its extension
> and consummation only in the rest of life. Shut out from the
> rest of life, shut out from all fruition and assimilation, it has
> no more dignity than – to use a homely image – the boots and
> shoes that we see, in the corridors of promiscuous hotels,
> standing, often in double pairs, at the doors of rooms. De-
> tached and unassociated these clusters of objects present,
> however obtruded, no importance.

In substance, James is complaining that D'Annunzio spoils his
work by treating sex as separate from the rest of life, as a moment 'beginning and ending in itself', and this is wrong for James
because in itself, sex is vulgar – it has to be mitigated by its
extension into 'the rest of life'. The passage is remarkable for its
striking image, the idea of James in the corridor of a 'promiscuous
hotel', staring with fascinated disgust at the pairs of boots and

shoes ('often in double pairs') confirms not only the tendency for
James to be compromised by images of voyeurism but to image sex
as something from which he is shut out, he is left hovering 'at
the doors of rooms'. Yet he has the very strongest aversion to
vulgarity, to what is tasteless, undignified and obtrusive. We can
thus begin to trace through this passage a tension in James's
attitude towards sexuality: a feeling that the moment of encounter
only becomes dignified and important if it is mediated out into
representation and relationship, which is opposed to a position
(given literally in the hotel-corridor image) of an excluded observer left outside amongst tawdry hints and clues. This means that
the felt vulgarity of sexuality can be lost by embedding it in a
form of mediating complexity ('it finds its extension and consum-
mation only in the rest of life.')

Significantly, the single sentence which Richard Ohmann takes
as his example in his now celebrated article on James's style does
precisely this: it 'loses' the intimation of a 'horrid, brutal, *vulgar*'
menace by embedding it in a syntactical structure so complex that
'the strain on attention and memory required to follow the progress of the main sentence over and around so many obstacles is
considerable.'(22) The sentence thus reproduces in its form the
solution to the intimation of vulgarity which had afflicted James
in the essay on D'Annunzio:(23)

She had practically, he believed, conveyed the intimation,
the horrid, brutal, vulgar menace, in the course of their
last dreadful conversation, when, for whatever was left him
of pluck or confidence - confidence in what he would fain
have called a little more aggressively the strength of his
position - he had judged best not to take it up.

The D'Annunzio passage thus indicates the two dominant obscuring processes which James himself is to use: 'sublimation' of the
positive, elemental and self-contained 'act of a moment' into a form
which generates complexity, interrelatedness, negativity and
extension until it has lost its 'baseness'; and 'foreclosure' of sexuality by remaining 'outside' the scene of seduction among the
hints and clues - by the process of omission and exclusion which
we call ellipsis.(24) Buried beneath the obliquity, the equivocation
and refined talk, there is a common story of seduction and sexual
intrigue. As a reader of later James, I occasionally halt at points
in the text where relative clarity of narration suddenly afflicts me
with a sense of what is almost bathos. What on earth did Strether
imagine was going on between Chad and Mme de Vionnet? Why,
after all, couldn't Maggie just come straight out with a direct
challenge to Amerigo and Charlotte, accuse them of having an
affair, produce a good row, and sort things out 'sur place'? And
at times it troubles me deeply that 'The Wings of the Dove' is one
of the most sordid and miserable tales - a failed confidence trick
on a dying woman. Yet drawn once more into the arch subtleties
of those salon dialogues, captivated by the allusive delicacy of
glance and gesture and the 'finesse' of evasiveness, the commonness of what is behind it all soon drops out of sight. It is only at

Mr Henry James by Max Beerbohm

rare moments of directness that we see with a feeling of unease
and perhaps even shock, that the central events of these novels
are low, minor sexual intrigues, stories endeavouring to distance
themselves from a certain 'vague moral dinginess'. Again and again,
James returned to the story of a compromised and compromising
seduction, a passion forced into deviousness. The passion is central to the story, it is the energy which drives the narrative, but
it is unacknowledged as such and 'the scene of seduction'
('Verführungsszene' in Freud's terminology)(25) which is the
pivotal moment of this narrative, remains as concealed as possible.
Indeed the 'scene of seduction' in James constitutes a fundamental
moment of obscurity and fascination and is characterized by a
strange doubleness. It constitutes what Pierre Macherey has
termed a 'determining absent centre' to the fiction (26) and relates
closely to Todorov's now celebrated analysis of James's tales.(27)
The doubleness is not only the simultaneous attraction and repulsion of seduction in James (the apparent contradiction of it being
continuously present but ever-deferred and removed) but it is
also a doubleness of representation, a tracing-back in the evasiveness and ellipsis – in the blatancy of avoidance – a reference to
that which is so evidently and consciously not said. It is this
which enables R. B. Yeazell to write in 'Language and Knowledge
in the Late Novels of Henry James':(28)

> [But] the sexual reticence of his late fiction is in direct
> proportion to the felt presence of sexuality as a force at
> the very centre of human life. Beginning with the fiction
> of the late nineties – 'What Maisie Knew', The Turn of the
> Screw, 'The Awkward Age' – and continuing through 'The
> Sacred Fount' and the novels of the major phase, sexual
> passion becomes the major mystery, the hidden knowledge
> which the Jamesian innocent must at last confront.

The reticence gives an index of the centrality of sexuality in
James where sexuality is less a 'mystery' than a dubiously concealed
threat: it is less a case of the innocent confronting sexuality than
of sexuality occasionally escaping from the restraining nets of
equivocation and horrifying those it confronts. It is in this respect that obscurity in James often functions as a kind of extensive,
complicated euphemism. Euphemism operates by substituting polite and vague expression in place of direct statement of fact,
particularly in matters concerning sexuality and death. In the
analysis of 'The Wings of the Dove' which follows, a euphemistic
substitution of obscure and mannered expression for direct statement is clearly a central type of obscurity in the novel.

In fact, euphemistic substitution is one of several forms of indirect reference which suggests that in James *any* direct, unmediated presentation is flagrant. So much is never allowed 'simply'
to appear. Full of discrimination against the obvious (like Fanny
Assingham), James backs further and further away from generous, public kinds of mimesis to a realm of 'hauteur' where any
immediacy appears as shockingly precipitant and where direct
representation appears ostentatious and 'showy'. The obscurity is

deeply rooted in an equation of self-representation with a too
obvious purchasing or parading of self, and this James strives to
avoid through the (celebrated and detested) forms of his indirection. In the earlier novels it is rare that the narrator is
endangered by the kinds of defective sophistication which he
portrays, and there is a trimness and clarity to the narratives as
a result. When his spirited 'ingénues' fall victim to the gracious
villany which they mistake for culture, the sharpness of injury is
clearly felt by the reader: there is no difficulty in identifying the
'bad form' involved. The freshness (of Daisy, Isabel, Milly) is so
fresh that the kinds of refined nastiness which tarnish them become clearly visible. There is always a spectator to the drama
whose uncorrupted discretion keeps him safe from the disingen-
uous urbanity of the villains and the bright-eyed vulnerability of
the victims. It is this spectator position which offers the reader
enough security in James's earlier fiction to be able to exercise
his sympathy and displeasure with confidence. It is one reason
why F. R. Leavis enjoyed them so much more than the late fiction.
(29) Winterbourne, Mr Acton, Doctor Sloper, Basil Ransome,
Ralph Touchett – these concerned observers are usually mildly
blemished by the privileges of consciousness, taste and vision
ascribed to them, but this only serves to strengthen our faith in
their 'real' value. With this spectator at hand, there are really
only two kinds of obscurity in the early fiction, and neither
impinges deeply into the texture of the novels. James 'knows' the
limits to sophistication with a sureness of touch which strengthens
itself in the pleasure of revealing vulgar and flawed behaviour.

Thus one kind of obscurity is a discreet forbearance to indict
more than is necessary, and in this lightness of touch we have an
indication of the underlying sureness of response. The author
can align himself with the polite reticence (superior precisely
because it is reticent) of the careful observer. In 'The Europeans',
it is Mr Acton who, reflecting upon some new proof of the Baron-
ess's 'lively disposition', is identified with the general authorial
voice: 'At any rate, Acton, with his characteristic discretion for-
bore to give expression to whatever else it might imply, and the
narrator of these incidents is not obliged to be more definite.'(30)

The refusal of the narrator/observer to identify completely with
the exquisite but ensnared victim points up the degree to which
James's earlier fiction is founded upon an aesthetics of discretion.
The distance which observers (such as Ralph Touchett or Acton)
maintain from the subject of their caring scrutiny keeps them from
the passionate involvement which they wistfully desire and never
get. But even quite late into the 1880s this abnegation of desire
appeared as the necessary price to be paid for the artistic privilege of discreet attachment. Even Basil's engagement at the end
of 'The Bostonians' intimates a loss of privileged integrity rather
than the winning of a wife.

It is the inherent danger posed by engagement which creates
the second kind of obscurity in James's earlier* fiction. Indeed,

* By 'earlier' I generally refer to the novels and tales written
  before 1895.

'The Princess Casamassima' is a novel which thoroughly explores
the elision of 'engagement' and vulgarity, that 'forwardness' in
both women and public movements which James found difficult to
cope with. It is James's evident distaste for the vulgarities of
'active' women and the working and lower-middle classes - who
nevertheless occupy the centre stage in the novel - which is
surely what makes 'The Princess Casamassima' such an uneven,
unsatisfactory work. The categories of engagement and vulgarity
are fundamentally important within it, but they are elided so
easily that the tone becomes almost didactic. Here, the terms are
being openly debated between Lady Aurora, the shy, philan-
thropic aristocrat, and that preposterous creation, Hyacinth
Robinson:(31)

Lady Aurora went on anxiously, eagerly: 'Don't you consider
him [Captain Sholto] decidedly vulgar?'
'How can I know?'
'You know perfectly - as well as anyone!' Then she added:
'I think it's a pity they should form relations with any one
of that kind.'
'They' of course meant Paul Muniment and his sister. 'With
a person who may be vulgar?' - Hyacinth regarded this sol-
icitude as exquisite. 'But think of the people they know -
think of those they're surrounded with - think of all Audley
Court!'
'The poor, the unhappy, the labouring classes? Oh, I
don't call *them* vulgar!' cried her ladyship with radiant eyes.
The young man, lying awake a good deal that night, laughed
to himself, on his pillow, not unkindly, at her fear that he
and his friends would be contaminated by the familiar of a
princess. He even wondered if she wouldn't find the Princess
herself a bit vulgar.

The point being of course that the Princess is vulgar, and her
obtrusive, undignified enthusiasm for 'the lower orders' does contaminate Robinson. But the extract is chiefly interesting for the
way it moves across two different aspects of the vulgar - across
class and taste. From the outset, Hyacinth Robinson is caught
between these two (the opposition is given by his parents and
hence in his own ludicrous name) and often the novel seems very
similar to Meredith's 'Evan Harrington'. Both the young tailor at
Beckley Court and the young bookbinder at Medley suffer the
embarrassment of feeling themselves to be gentlemen in terms of
taste and understanding but disqualified unjustly from being
gentlemen by the class structure.(32) Hyacinth's resentment of
the material advantages of the 'upper' class gradually changes,
after his visit to Paris, into a resentment of the lack of taste and
cultural refinement of his own class. Unlike Lady Aurora he is
unable to dissociate the two forms and his waning political activism and death result from this identification of 'plebeian' with
'tasteless'. Vulgarity in James never loses its class dimension, and
in removing himself even further from the contamination of a put-
ative vulgarity, his stories move towards a rarefied world of

princes and princesses, palaces and millionaires. It is here that
the divergences between 'Evan Harrington' and 'The Princess
Casamassima' become apparent. In Meredith, concealment and
evasion spring directly from the endeavour to hide Evan's class
origin in a hostile milieu so that he may marry a girl in a 'higher'
class. In 'The Princess Casamassima' there is also obscurity, but
it is not motivated in the same way. In his preface to the novel,
James calls attention to its 'abyss of ambiguities', to Hyacinth's
'subterraneous politics and occult affiliations' and to the mysteries
of London itself, what James terms in a memorable phrase the
'dense categories of dark arcana'. But here the obscurity has
none of the constitutive importance that it has in the late novels,
it appears as superficial embellishment, as a willed attempt to
suggest a world inimical to James's own and closed off from him,
the 'shady underworld of militant socialism', the 'revolutionary
politics of a hole-and-corner sort'. The attempt is perfectly self-
conscious:(33)

> the value I wished most to render and the effect I wished
> most to produce were precisely those of our not knowing,
> but only guessing and suspecting and trying to ignore,
> what 'goes on' irreconcileably, subversively, beneath the
> vast smug surface.

This does not mean of course that James endeavoured to reveal
any real secrets about anarchist activity in the 1880s, but that in
the novel he attempts to reproduce the public's uneasy sense of
incomplete knowledge, the feeling of a shadowy threat beneath
the 'vast smug surface'. The reader, like one of James's touch-
stones of moral and political 'restraint' in the novel, Mr Vetch, is
made to feel 'worried by the absence of full knowledge'.

This deliberate, tactical use of obscurity is confined almost
entirely to the central political characters of the novel - Paul
Muniment, Diedrich Hoffendahl the revolutionary leader, and the
Princess herself. James also uses the common device of displacing
the fear of urban,working-class political activity into the topography of the city itself. 'Hyacinth Robinson', wrote James,
'sprang up for me out of the London pavement', and indeed, London in the novel becomes the exoteric cloak, the external, enigmatical form of hidden political subversion. It is a kind of political
synecdoche familiar in Dickens, Balzac and Zola, and in this, the
most 'Victorian' of James's novels, London is 'vague and blurred,
inarticulate, blunt and dim', its streets nothing but a 'vast vague
murmur':(34)

> The puddles glittered round about and the silent vista of the
> street, bordered with low black houses, stretched away in
> the wintry drizzle to right and left, losing itself in the huge
> tragic city where unmeasured misery lurked beneath the
> dirty night, ominously, monstrously still, ...

But if this invocation of the ominous urban streets is a function
of naturalism and Dickensian social criticism, the novel as a whole
lacks both the indignation and the intimate knowledge of the urban
proletariat possessed by Zola and Dickens. James keeps Hoffendahl

just off-stage and keeps Muniment as a charismatic enigma - the 'inscrutable Paul' - whose knowledge, power and precise political position we never learn. It seems to me a book written in bad faith: only Anastasius Vetch and Lady Aurora - the helpless observers - escape the insecurities and betrayals engendered by the author's basic antipathy to the anarchists at the centre of his plot. As such it contrasts unfavourably with Meredith's treatment of Lassalle in 'The Tragic Comedians' and appears much like Conrad's 'The Secret Agent', engendering from its political obscurantism a world without trust. It uses the paraphernalia of the secret society, the forms of obscurity pointed up and emphasized by James in the preface, simply to suggest and discredit the incompletely known world of counter-cultural political activism.(35) From the outset, despite flirtation with Dickensian engagement in the description of Pinny's visit to the grim prison, and the smoky backroom of the 'Sun and Moon', James is only really threatened by vulgarity (a vulgarity 'from below') which effectively vitiates the social conscience he might otherwise have had. As such, the forms of obscurity and shadiness in the novel to which James draws our attention do not seem to be of the same kind, nor as centrally important, as those in the late novels: James positively wants to reveal the vulgarity of what he calls 'The British Philistia', the world of Madeira Crescent,(36) and in this novel he has no investment at all in keeping this 'philistinism' concealed; indeed, by showing it he demonstrated its supposed hostility to the high cultural values he held precious. In the later novels and stories, however, the obscurities and vulgarities are of a different sort.

Here gross unrefinement serves to designate not only social commonness, but the emergence of a threatening sexual obtrusiveness. Vulgarity becomes most unsettling in James when it is meretricious. It is not just that the democratizing of art is a vulgarizing process, but that anyone (and specifically in James, any woman) who blatantly reveals sexual desire or sexual experience becomes an object of suspicion and anxiety.(37) James will rarely allow passion to manifest itself in a direct way. Any sign indicating the existence of sexuality is like a gash or a wound and has to be avoided or covered up, and this is not simply a shrinking from sexuality, but part of a structured relation between the obvious voyeurism in James (which Maxwell Geismar makes so much of in 'Henry James and the Jacobites') and a counterposed desire to obscure the visible, public signification of desire. It is when sexual desire or experience is actively and immediately represented that it becomes intimidating, shocking and 'vulgar'.

But at the same time and with countervailing pressure the Jamesian narrator wants to know. James sets up narratives which centre on the indices (signs, scenes, hints and traces) of sexual intrigue, and these indices are placed between an observer who attempts to decipher them and a subject who attempts to conceal them. By the time of the late novels this basic narrative kernel has become diffuse and complexly mediated but still holds. The principal change from the earlier novels, after James's mental

crisis of 1895,(38) is that the distance maintained by the earlier
narrative observers like Mr Acton no longer provides a position
secure from the combined forces of vulgarity and desire. The
later observers like Strether and Fanny Assingham are deeply
troubled by their exclusion from the scene of intimacy and yet
more than ever in danger of proving themselves to be spotted by
their wish to see it and to be part of it. The contradiction between
the desire to 'know' the intimate scene and the fear that this will
appear an indelicate, even obscene interest, increases the pressure to blur the central narrative focus. Strether feels stranded
in a curious no man's land, at once exhilarating and depressing,
between Woollett and Paris. But, above all, he feels a lonely
vulnerability to precisely the improper scenes he has come to
witness:(39)

> It was exactly as if they [Woollett] had imputed to him
> [Chad] a vulgarity which he had by a mere gesture caused
> to fall from him. The devil of the case was that Strether
> felt it, by the same stroke, as falling straight upon himself.

The transference of this imputed impropriety from the observed
to the observer is immensely important in the growth of obscure
representations in the late James. The moral and aesthetic tension
between intimacy and indelicacy had always been present, but in
the later work the fear of self-indictment is greater and the need
to codify elaborately the material interest in the narrative correspondingly increased. James constructs a large number of his later
narratives upon this drama of decipherment, the 'cryptadion' of
which is an active sexuality, an 'affair' which must exist without
overt signification. Obscurity is intimately drawn round this
cryptadion which becomes the intriguing source of narrative
interest, over-signified as meretricious or half-concealed within
refined innuendo.

This is nowhere more apparent than in the decadent sophistication of 'The Sacred Fount' (1901), that 'mystifying, even
maddening' novel as Edmund Wilson called it in his essay on the
ambiguity of James.(40) Just preceding the three major novels of
the last phase, and published within a year of that other 'mystifying and maddening' fiction 'Heart of Darkness', 'The Sacred
Fount' is as obscure in terms of local narrative episode, style,
and significance as any of James's work. As Edel remarks in his
introduction:(41)

> we are left at the end of the novel with a house of cards in
> collapse, a series of speculations indulged in feverishly and
> obsessively by the narrator and with such an accumulation
> of theories and introspections that we can never be sure of
> the purity of our 'facts'.

The story concerns the attempt of a narrator to verify the
existence of a liaison at a country-house week-end party, and
despite the formidable complexities of narration, the centre of
intrigue and investigation in the novel is as simple as that.
Although it has been quoted many times before, Rebecca West's
judgment is worth repeating. She called it a 'small, mean story'

that 'worries one like a rat nibbling at a wainscot', and she sum-
marizes it thus:(42)

- how a week-end visitor spends more intellectual force
than Kant can have used on *The Critique of Pure Reason*,
in an unsuccessful attempt to discover whether there exists
between certain of his fellow-guests a relationship not more
interesting among these vacuous people than it is among
sparrows.

Like The Turn of the Screw, the story centres upon an observer who may be indulging in quite mad, baroque sexual fantasy,
or may be witnessing the effects (it is never the origins in James)
of an unhealthy, dangerous liaison. The narrator has noticed how,
in one couple at the party, the older woman has become mirac-
ulously rejuvenated at the expense of her much younger husband,
who has aged appallingly. Using this exchange as a model, he
notices that Gilbert Long, formerly a rather dull and stupid young
man, has become suddenly witty, intelligent and lively, and the
narrator speculates that he must have formed a liaison with a most
intelligent and sophisticated woman who now, if the hypothesis of
the old-young couple holds, must have become correspondingly
duller, drained of her intellectual life by the vastly improved
Gilbert Long. As James put it in his notebook:(43)

Keep my play on idea: the *liaison* that betrays itself by
the *transfer* of qualities - qualities to be determined - from
one to the other parties to it. They *exchange*. I see two
couples. One is married - this is the *old-young* pair. I
watch *their* process, and it gives me my light for the spectacle of the other (covert, obscure unavowed) pair who are
not married.

James was aware of the absurdity of his story (which on one
level is a kind of amusing anecdote) but also uneasy at its impli-
cations - he wrote to Mrs Humphrey Ward that he 'mortally loathed
it!' and at points, the narrator is afflicted by the sense that the
liaison 'isn't any of one's business' and refers to his obsessive
investigation as 'my private madness' (he compares himself to Mad
King Ludwig and the last words spoken to him in the novel dis-
miss him as crazy). The reader is never sure whether this first-
person narrator is a deluded and obsessed voyeur indulging
baseless fantasies or a brilliantly subtle observer piecing together
the evidence of a liaison as an urbane 'jeu d'esprit' which he
shares with two of the other house guests.

This it seems to me is the central anxiety of the novel: is the
narrative 'I' an obsessed voyeur indulging a vulgar fantasy, or
an urbane observer who skilfully unravels all the minute signals
given out by a group of sensitive and highly intelligent guests?
The novel problematizes a modern hesitation in the process of
reading, between reading fiction as either a modified sexual fantasy of the narrator or as a perceptive, intelligent acount of an
'external reality'. Furthermore, it is a hesitation about which the
narrator is quite self-conscious, for he shows himself caught
between embarrassment and pride in his inquiry. The narrator

discusses his 'story' with another of the guests - who happens to be an artist - and together they wonder whether the endeavour to discover the identity of a woman's lover and the nature of her relationship is not unforgivably vulgar:(44)

'We ought to remember,' I pursued, even at the risk of showing as too sententious, 'that success in such an inquiry may perhaps be more embarrassing than failure. To nose about for a relation that a lady has her reasons for keeping secret - '

'Is made not only quite inoffensive, I hold' - he [the artist Obert] immediately took me up - 'but positively honourable, by being confined to psychologic evidence.'

I wondered a little. 'Honourable to whom?'

'Why, to the investigator. Resting on the *kind* of signs that the game takes account of when fairly played - resting on psychologic signs alone, it's a high application of intelligence. What's ignoble is the detective at the keyhole.'

'I see,' I after a moment admitted. 'I did have, last night, my scruples, but you warm me up. Yet I confess also,' I still added, 'that if I do muster the courage of my curiosity, it's a little because I feel even yet, as I think you also must, altogether destitute of a material clue. If I had a material clue I should feel ashamed: the fact would be a deterrent.'

This is a key passage for understanding not only 'The Sacred Fount' but many obscure moments in James. James has split himself into an unnamed narrator and a practising artist and he sets up a debate between them. The unnamed narrator is anxious lest his observation may be improper, an unseemly and tasteless fascination ('To nose about for a relation that a lady has her reasons for keeping secret - .') The artist on the other hand assures him that if the observation is restricted to 'psychologic signs alone' then the activity is not only respectable but 'a high application of intelligence'. The only thing that separates the one from the other is the materiality of that which is observed, it all rests upon 'the *kind* of signs' and the absence of material fact. If the signs are 'psychologic' and if no material clues are given or discovered, then the narrator is involved in something 'positively honourable'. If, however, a fact is discovered, a graspable, unambiguous registration of the object searched out (the sexual liaison), then the narrative is vulgar and embarrassing. It is worth emphasizing the narrator's peculiar remark, 'the fact would be a deterrent.' It applies as much to Strether, Maggie Verver and Densher as to the nameless speaker in 'The Sacred Fount'. It means that if the narrator should actually come up with a fact it would throw the moral basis of the narrative quest into doubt: if the narrator should really see a clear sign of what he is looking for it would invalidate his project - the fact would be deterrent to the quest. In this respect, as the narrator intimates, the real danger to the quest for knowledge is the success of the quest ('We ought to remember... that success in such an inquiry may perhaps be more embarrassing than failure.') The kind of knowledge in question in

the story is such that its material presentation would be a matter
for 'embarrassment', 'scruple' and shame. The narrator is thus
compromised by his inquiry, and at certain moments decides to
give it up ('I took a lively resolve to get rid of my ridiculous
obsession'), and at others is led to question seriously his mental
state ('What was the matter with *me*? - so much as that I had
ended by asking myself.') Nevertheless he continues to search
out the lover and to prove the existence of the liaison by remaining at the level of 'psychologic signs', a vertiginous inferential
process which loses all but the most tough-minded reader in a
minute and intricate tangle of supposition ('If she knows that I
think she is aware of my theory then....')

Obscurity here is the necessary result of the moral conflict in
which the narrator loses himself. If he succeeds in his quest then
he is indicted as a vulgar keyhole-peeper; if he fails he succeeds
in keeping some integrity. Following the presciptions of the
painter, Obert, the narrator in James must, by an act of will, not
register the obvious material facts but must follow his inquiry at
one remove, at the level of signs and psychological evidence alone.
By its own laws the narrative becomes a quest for the semiological
correlative of a sexual liaison which can never be allowed direct
representation. 'The Golden Bowl' and 'The Ambassadors' both
conform to this narrative interdiction. Furthermore, as the split
between 'narrator' and 'artist' indicates, the status of the story
as a work of art is also implicated in the opposition of obscurity to
vulgarity. The narrator admits that his observation and the story
it produces is a ridiculous obsession which leads him to question
his sanity: this is the psychological 'root' of the narrative process, but if it is mediated into an indirect quest for a certain kind
of sign - sign as verbal and gestural clue - then it repudiates
the stigma of its obsessed psychological origin and becomes a
'high application of intelligence'.

I want to dwell less on the obvious similarity this has to the
Freudian theory of artistic production (with which it is roughly
contemporary) and point to the logic of obscurity which it implies.
(45) The period of transition between the collapse of the moral
censorship imposed by Mudie and the post-war euphoria of the
1920s left the novelist caught between the inhibitions of a strict
past and an emergent sexual candour. A central problem of the
period was the degree to which the felt importance of sexuality
was allowed to trespass on the moral reluctance to treat sexual
themes openly. In James and Meredith the result is a negotiated
narrative written out of a felt uncertainty as to its 'origin' - the
literary observer's fascination with the facts of life or the vulgar
and tasteless prying of the obsessed? In 'The Sacred Fount' this
becomes a manifest and central dilemma.

This is one reason why Jamesian obscurity is not merely an
evasion but is made to constitute a source of value in the fiction.
I want to stress here what was said in the first chapter about the
relation of obscurity and value, blindness and insight, in these
fictions. The obscurities are never 'merely' defensive. In the very

nature of verbal obscurity there is always both signification and
evasion, the simultaneous effacement and creation of meanings.
The value of obscurity is that in the process of effacement a new
range of imaginative and linguistic forms may be created, sometimes forms of outstanding importance. In James, the drive to get
away from the 'material' basis of the recurrent narrative interest
produces an extraordinary range of discriminatory insight into
the difficulties and pleasures of 'fine consciousness'. The obscurity connotes a rare and elevated discourse, and in terms of the
Jamesian narrative economy creates value by making the reader's
purchase of significance difficult and costly. Not only can James
thereby conceal the sexual liaison of the unmarried couple which
his notebook reveals was the focus of his interest ('covert, obscure, unavowed') but at the same time he can generate discursive
value by avoiding 'giving away' anything to the reader which is
common, blatant or cheap. By forcing the level of discrimination
and intellectual observation as high as possible, the narrator (46)
establishes a hierarchy of vision with himself at the top, and this
not in the service of egoism (James comically deflates the narrator's pretentiousness) but to create value, to mark the 'fine
quality' of his state. It is a kind of compensatory exchange (and
as such a clear analogue to the basic exchange structure of the
story) whereby the act of observation is raised to an extreme
pitch only so long as it is not a vision held in common with others
(47) and only so long as its object is never directly seen. As such
it is a wager between insane intensity of perception and superior
moral insight:(48)

> It comes back to me that the sense thus established of my
> superior vision may perfectly have gone a little to my head.
> If it was a frenzied fallacy I was all to blame, but if it was
> anything else whatever it was naturally intoxicating.... I
> think there must fairly have been a pitch at which I was
> not sure that not to partake of that state was, on the part
> of others, the sign of gregarious vulgarity; as if there were
> a positive advantage, an undiluted bliss, in the intensity of
> consciousness that I had reached.

When we look at the kinds of obscurity employed in 'The Sacred
Fount' they can be seen to strengthen the paradoxical bond which
exists in the novel between this intensity of perception and obscurity of narration. Whereas in Conrad the obscurity arises from
a story told by someone overwhelmed by the lack of significant
information (for Marlow in 'Heart of Darkness' it was 'an immense
mystery'), in 'The Sacred Fount' the obscurity arises from the
opposite case - a narrator overwhelmed by an excess of information - as Mrs Brissenden tells the narrator, 'You see too much.'
The reader is overwhelmed by scenes and by language within
which it is almost impossible to extract the significant from the
insignificant. Possibilities multiply, every gesture and word seems
to contain volumes, the tiniest alteration of tone and form in an
otherwise casual remark becomes portentous:(49)

Her look alone did it, for, though it was a look that
partly spoiled her lie, it - by that very fact - sufficed to
my confidence.
　'I've not spoken to a creature.'
　It was beautifully said, but I felt again the abysses that
the mere saying of it covered, and the sense of these wonderful things was not a little, no doubt, in my immediate
cheer.

This technique (50) of supplementing a very commonplace remark in direct speech with a commentary by the narrator which
suggests that the remark contains unspoken volumes is often used
in 'The Sacred Fount', and constantly puts the reader at a singular disadvantage. It requires him to stop and reread the remark,
and possibly the passage that has preceded it, in order to 'see'
what the super-subtle narrator has seen in it. We are enticed
into seaching for the felt 'abysses' and 'wonderful things' beneath
the commonplace words. An extension of this is the positing of an
edgy, probing understanding between speakers such that the
direct speech of their dialogue creates a single ellipsis (often
typographically signalled by a dash) closed off from the reader.

The following characteristic piece of dialogue contains both
techniques and thoroughly deserves Edmund Wilson's cry of 'mystifying, even maddening!' It is a conversation between the narrator and Obert: (51)

'Of course the Brissendens are immense! If they hadn't
been immense they wouldn't have been - nothing would have
been - anything.' Then after a pause. 'Your image* is
splendid,' I went on - 'your being out of the cave. But what
is it exactly,' *I insidiously threw out*, 'that you *call* the
'light of day'?'
　I remained a moment, however, not sure whether I had
been too subtle or too simple. He had another of his cautions.
'What do you - ?'
　But I was determined to make him give it me all himself,
for it was from my not prompting him that its value would
come. 'You tell me,' I accordingly rather crudely pleaded,
'first.'
　It gave us a moment during which he so looked as if I
asked too much, that I had a fear of losing all. He even
spoke with some impatience. 'If you really haven't found it
for yourself, you know, I scarce see what you *can* have
found.'

This may be considered fatuous squirming or urbane amusement
but it also has a clear underlying function which predicates discursive value upon elusiveness. (52) In James this hieratic principle is more in evidence than in Meredith. Crudity of response is

---

* Obert has just said that the narrator has enlightened him so
　much that he now feels he has been guided 'out into the light
　of day'.

measured by the inability to 'follow' the subtlety of thought
through the most tortuous of paths, and this establishes a purely
formal measure of intelligence and sensitivity. The reader, in his
attempt to see exactly what the narrator wishes Obert to divulge,
is forced to switch his attention to the form. It is quite likely that
many readers will never fathom the specific fact which the narrator is coaxing from his adversary and which Obert cleverly
avoids giving, but the passage is not thereby rendered meaningless, its significance is shifted into the forms in which the implied
content is concealed (the narrator tells us as much when he says
that 'it was from my not prompting him that its value would come.')
To a greater or lesser extent obscurity always involves this transference. It seems to me axiomatic that the more obscure a discourse appears, the more its formal features are foregrounded,
and the more significance shifts away from the (ever more remote)
denotation of the discourse to its formal, verbal connotations.
Here, as elsewhere in James, the connotations are of 'civilized wit',
'superior intelligence' and 'sophisticated verbal competition', even
when the denotation of precisely what is said remains vague. This
transference is one of the grounding processes of modernism. It
leads on to the kind of literature which relies more and more upon
the fusion of connotative echo and discursive resonance, the distant, often fragmentary allusion to the infinite repertoire of
'civilization'.

   Here we are made aware that the two speakers, ostensibly in
verbal combat, subscribe to the same ground rule as the text itself. That is to say, their compulsive desire to know is yoked to
an equally strong reluctance to give away or exchange information,
and the competition of these opposed forces is played out in elusive, civilized talk. The form of talk is not simply evasion but the
ever-renewed ground upon which evasion and desire encounter
each other. It is doubly determined because it is so sophisticated
and elliptical that it connotes cultured refinement removed in the
furthest degree from the object of knowledge (a week-end party
liaison); and, at the same time, though the desire to discover
this object haunts the hinterland of the speech, the obscuring
verbal processes produce their own satisfaction. The narrator
remarks to the reader:(53)

   It could *not* but be exciting to talk, as we talked, on the
   basis of those suppressed processes and unavowed references which made the meaning of our meeting so different
   from its form. We knew ourselves - what moved me, that is,
   was that she knew me - to mean, at every point, immensely
   more than I said or than she [Mrs Server] answered: just
   as she saw me, at the same points, measure the space by
   which her answers fell short.

The precise term to describe this process is sublimation (54)
which exactly captures the double function of the transference.
The narrator sublimates his desire to know whether Gilbert Long
and May Server are having an affair and what effects this may
have, into the satisfaction of linguistic creation and intellectual

inquiry (recall Obert's remark that the quest is honourable if
confined to 'psychologic evidence'). But also, sublimation was
chosen by Freud because it evokes the sense of 'sublime' in
artistic or spiritual terms, and it is this which the narrator
attempts to create. He calls his linguistic edifice my 'quite sublime structure', and 'The Sacred Fount' (even the title is a result
of the same process) seems to confirm Freud's suggestion that the
activities described as sublimated in a given culture are those
accorded particularly high social esteem. Further, even the origin
of the metaphor in chemistry seems perfectly adapted for 'The
Sacred Fount': as the procedure whereby a body is caused to pass
directly from the solid to a gaseous state, sublimation nicely captures the narrator's movement away from 'material fact' to his own
narrative which he calls 'all of the finest wind-blown intimations,
woven of silence and secrecy and air'. The 'airy intimations' then
rematerialize into the substance of the composition, they resolid-
ify precisely as the form of the narrative.

'The Sacred Fount' thus works over as its form what is also its
originating procedure, the sublimation into 'artful' discourse of
a quest for sexual information which cannot be directly avowed.
This latter interdiction is made quite explicit in the text: 'Now my
[the narrator's] personal problem, unaltered in the least particular by anything, was for me to have worked to the end without
breathing in another ear that Long had been her [Mrs Server's]
lover.'(55) In so doing he turns obscurity into 'art', and his recognition of the same dilemma and solution for Gilbert Long applies
equally to himself – 'if his excited acuteness was henceforth to
protect itself by dissimulation, what wouldn't perhaps, for one's
diversion, be the new spectacle and wonder?'

'Wonder', 'wonderful', 'immense', 'splendid', 'magnificent' –
sublimation goes a long way to isolate the curious fact that these
elevated words increase in James's work at the same time as it
increases in obscurity.(56) He sometimes reaches out too readily
for the superlative degree. Of course there is always a tendency
for writers who become famous during their own active lifetime to
write about higher and higher social strata as they themselves
gain access to them (George Eliot is an example), but in James
the straining after nobility, grandeur and superior refinement is
accompanied by a noticeable increase in obscurity (even when
measured by usual stylistic means).(57) If, as I suggest here,
sublimation in 'The Sacred Fount' is an almost classic case, the
internal linkage of aspiration towards sublimity and the process
of sublimation into elliptical speech is easily discernible. It is not
just that ellipsis is the prerogative of the leisured but that, with
an economy of structure I find fascinating, 'sublime' obscurity is
exactly the type of sublimation adopted by James. Since it is obviousness of preoccupation which the narrator finds vulgar and
which would give away his own obsessive voyeurism, the exclusion
of the obvious accomplishes both functions simultaneously:(58)

　　Newmarch had always, in our time, carried itself as the
　　great asylum of the finer wit, more or less expressly giving

out that, as invoking hospitality or other countenance, none
of the stupid, *none even of the votaries of the grossly obvious*, need apply; .... [My italics]
Newmarch itself is exemplary of the way location and setting in
James connote leisure, wealth, culture and artistic refinement
whilst also being the covert scene of sexual intrigue. Indeed we
can almost predict that any 'wonderful', 'splendid' or 'magnificent'
setting in James will have, hidden within it, the shadow of some
threatening sexual liaison. As the governess approaches Bly in
The Turn of the Screw, and before she has learned of the violent
affair of Quint and Miss Jessel which haunts it, she remarks that
it is a scene possessing 'greatness':(59)

I remember as a most pleasant impression the broad, clear
front, its open windows and fresh curtains and the pair of
maids looking out, I remember the lawn and the bright
flowers and the crunch of my wheels on the gravel and the
clustered tree-tops over which the rooks circled and cawed
in the golden sky. The scene had a greatness that made it
a different affair from my own scant home, ...

That sexual intrigue makes its gradual appearance in settings
of great beauty and cultural value is not an accident. Paris,
Florence, Venice, Rome, the great country houses of Gardencourt,
Poynton, Fawns and Matcham are all part of the way in which
James sublimates 'vulgar' sexual quests into aesthetic form. These
locations sublimate the sexuality which is allowed to appear
obliquely in the *place* of art - in fine and allusive talk, beautiful
cities and grand houses, painting and documents.(60) As early as
Daisy Miller (1878), James manifests the tendency (which is to
become a reflex of his fiction) to frame and contain a threatening
sexual intimacy with the monuments of European culture. The
Castle of Chillon and the Colosseum,(61) the scenes of both Daisy's
'indiscretions', are the two places where Winterbourne sees Daisy
as most attractive and most 'vulgar'. At Chillon, Winterbourne is
'bewildered' and 'amazed' by Daisy's directness, and at the Colosseum he is afflicted with 'a sort of horror' when he sees Daisy
there alone with Giovanelli, even at the moment when she appears
'lovely in the flattering moonlight'. Stigmatized by everyone
(especially Winterbourne's aunt) as 'being hopelessly vulgar',
Daisy commits the sin which in James is unpardonable: she signifies her attraction and desire in public, she appears as a votary
of the grossly obvious, and it is precisely when such desire fails
to be mediated or contained by its cultural location that trouble
is precipitated. Indeed, once sexual desire has directly broken its
aesthetic containment, the composure and composition of the
Jamesian scene serve to increase the visual shock of a liaison, or
compromising intimate 'rapport', by virtue of the contrast imposed.

This is illustrated most beautifully in the famous scene with
Strether by the river in 'The Ambassadors'. When he decides on
his little excursion into the countryside outside Paris, Strether
has in mind, as his idealization of the scene, a beautiful painting
by Lambinet which he had once wished to purchase in an art

gallery in Boston. His day appears perfect when his hope that
the actuality of the 'paysage' will approximate to the picture, is
realized:(62)

> He hadn't·gone far without the quick confidence that it
> would be quite sufficiently kept. The oblong gilt frame
> disposed its enclosed lines; the poplars and willows, the
> reeds and river – a river of which he didn't know, and
> didn't want to know, the name – fell into a composition,
> full of felicity, within them; the sky was silver and tur-
> quoise and varnish; the village on the left was white and
> the church on the right was grey; it was all there, in short –
> it was what he wanted: it was Tremont Street, it was France,
> it was Lambinet. Moreover he was freely walking about in it.

The perfect, joyful repose of the view, its assimilation to
Strether's aesthetic ideal, make it secure and complete ('He felt
in short a confidence, and it was general, and it was what he
wanted to feel.') The sudden appearance, within this 'oblong gilt
frame', of Chad and Mme de Vionnet is a violently coerced recognition which for Strether is 'a sharp, fantastic crisis that had
popped up as if in a dream,' and he felt it to be 'quite horrible'.
Such visual shocks are most important crises in the novels, and
the horror of this moment is obviously not simply that at last
Strether will be forced to face the fact of Chad's liaison and will
no longer be able to prevaricate between Woollett and Paris. The
horror is much more at the fact of appearance of the liaison right
in the middle of Strether's artistic vision, a vision which had its
enclosed lines, had taken refuge and comfort in a foreclosed
aesthetic space. In view of what has so far been said about the
sublimation of sexual desire into artistic form, Strether's response
may now seem more comprehensible. For it is precisely when desire does reassert itself, despite its concealment and attenuation,
that the whole elaborate process is destroyed. It is as though the
canvas of the Lambinet had been rent to reveal through the tear
'the deep, deep truth of the intimacy revealed'. The art and the
intimacy are hopelessly compromised when the one is seen through
the other. Strether, 'lonely and cold', lies in the dark the even-
ing after the meeting and realizes that 'Verily, verily, his labour
had been lost.' If, as I have suggested, James's fiction continually
transposes and obscures a fascination with the meretricious into
the mystifications of art, beautiful places and elliptical dialogue,
the immediate public registration of sexual intimacy tokens the
collapse of the fiction from within: the narrative, which was
nothing other than the form in which the sublimation appeared, is
gravely threatened by the unmediated representation of desire –
there is nothing else left, and the sense of anticlimax, the emptiness, the obviousness of what was at the root of it all, strikes
Strether with a mixture of shame and desolation:(63)

> That was what, in his vain vigil, he oftenest reverted to:
> intimacy, at such a point, was *like* that – and what in the
> world else would one have wished it to be like? .... he
> almost blushed, in the dark, for the way he had dressed

the possibility in vagueness, as a little girl might have
dressed her doll.

Again and again in James we find 'the possibility of intimacy
dressed in vagueness' at the basis of the fiction, and the obscurities accumulate to delay and deflect its revelation. In 'The Sacred
Fount' the narrator even suggests to Mrs Brissenden that the
degree of concealment is in direct proportion to the degree of
intimacy, the appearance of which 'is inevitably a kind of betrayal,
it's in somebody's interest to conceal it.' Mrs Brissenden immediately grasps the implication of this:(64)

'I see. You call the appearance a kind of betrayal because
it points to the relation behind it.'

'Precisely.'

'And the relation - to do that sort of thing - must be
necessarily so awfully intimate.'

'*Intimissima.*'

'And kept therefore in the background exactly in that
proportion.'

'Exactly in that proportion.'

Nothing is more horrifying in James's fiction than that rare
moment when the obscurity clears to reveal the evidence of some
'awful intimacy'. In a very early tale, The Story of a Masterpiece
(1868), the violent reaction which such a moment unleashes in an
observer shows an extremity of revulsion which borders on the
manic. Lennox, the observer in question, has commissioned a portrait of his bride-to-be from an artist who, unbeknown to Lennox,
was once himself in love with the lady but subsequently found her
to be 'hollow, trivial, vulgar'. The portrait is a subtle horror,
technically excellent and superficially flattering to the sitter, but
none the less a cruel, refined jest in which the discerning will
see that the woman is 'faintly discoloured ... by a certain vague
moral dinginess.'

When it is finally delivered to him on the eve of his wedding,
Lennox is horrified, and the description of him attacking the portrait I find alarmingly sadistic:(65)

He looked about him with angry despair, and his eye fell
on a long, keen poinard, given him by a friend who had
bought it in the East, and which lay as an ornament on his
mantelshelf. He seized it and thrust it, with barbarous glee,
straight into the lovely face of the image. He dragged it
downward, and made a long fissure in the living canvas.
Then, with half a dozen strokes, he wantonly hacked it
across. The act afforded him an immense relief.

The melodramatic energy of the scene reads more like the murder
of a prostitute from a yellowback (66) than an episode from Henry
James. The mixture of sexual pleasure and sadistic violence in
destroying the image of this 'vulgar' woman (who is a kind of
prostitute figure - she had been 'lightly and loosely' involved
with several men whilst abroad) gives us a clear and crude version of the recurrent structure in James's fiction, and the violence
of the response here should give us pause. Modulating with time

from this violent, Zolaesque revulsion to the melancholy sorrow of
Strether, the response of countless Jamesian 'observers' is never
to register directly and immediately the intimacies, liaisons, intrigues and sexual involvements which threaten them: like Lennox
(who is a most acute and sensitive man) they only ever recognize
these relations when mediated through displaced forms of representation (pictures, documents, even ghosts as in The Third
Person (1900), The Turn of the Screw (1898), Sir Edmund Orme
(1892)). This is usually an abstraction (67) or an intellectual-
ization (68) of the basic quest, but also its transposition into an
ineffable appearance or 'apparition'. In these fictions the danger
of vulgar ostentation re-emerges in the comforting literary 'frisson'
of gothic and romance iconography.(69)

Thus far the perspective adopted has been that of the observer,
and there is always the tendency to assimilate the narrator and
the novelist to the point of view adopted by the observer.(70) But
Jamesian stories are structured so as to set up opposed figures
and communities within which the observer is only one element.
His role is crucial, but disappointment and tragedy is not his
alone. Those who are observed and yet who feel passion or desire
and wish to express it are constrained by a contrary but complementary set of inhibitions to those James imposes upon his watch-
ful observers.

Particularly in the late fiction, we can be sure that if someone
makes a direct, unambiguous avowal of love for someone else, then
they are heading for disappointment. Such moments are in any
case rare, but when we find a simple declaration it tends to be
described in terms of punishment or desolation. In 'The Spoils of
Poynton' (1897) Fleda Vetch, after months of evasion and silence,
finally admits her love for Owen:(71)

> What had taken place was that, with the click of a spring,
> he saw. He had cleared the high wall at a bound; they were
> together without a veil. She had not a single shred of a
> secret left; it was as if a whirlwind had come and gone, lay-
> ing low the great false front she had built up stone by stone.
> The strangest thing of all was the momentary sense of deso-
> lation.

Shortly after her remarkably direct declaration of love, Owen
disappears from Fleda's life and marries Mona Brigstock. But the
passage itself reveals clearly that the moment is one of vulnerability and danger for Fleda simply because she has been direct,
and the violence of the 'whirlwind', 'laying low the great false
front she had built up stone by stone', would in other circumstances appear quite excessive. Here it is a fitting part of the
general metaphor, the 'high wall' and stone facade which indicate
the massiveness of her defensive concealment and the commensur-
ate violence required to break through it. The moment of honesty
does not however bring its reward. We are not told for whom there
'was the momentary sense of desolation' - it could be Owen, Fleda,
or the narrator - and the generality of reference is as if sorrow
pervaded the whole scene:(72)

'Ah all the while you *cared?*' Owen read the truth, with
a wonder so great that it was visibly almost a sadness, a
terror caused by his sudden perception of where the impossibility was not. That treacherously placed it perhaps elsewhere.
'I cared, I cared, I cared!' - she wailed it as to confess a
misdeed. 'How couldn't I care? But you mustn't, you must
never, never ask! It isn't for us to talk about,' she pro-
tested. 'Don't speak of it, don't speak!'
The inferred reason for Fleda's injunction is her sense of scruple
about Mona, for after all Owen is engaged to her. But Owen makes
it quite clear in this scene that he does not care much for Mona
and that she in turn will not marry him until the 'spoils' are returned to Poynton. The urgency and sense of terror which Fleda
displays in the above passage would seem, given these circumstances, quite excessive. Her response is almost histrionic with
its repetitions, exclamations and passionate injunctions, Her
sense of having broken some strict rule is given clearly in the
phrase 'she wailed as if to confess a misdeed', and she follows her
open declaration of love for Owen by the immediate articulation of
a fundamental (narrative) interdiction which she realizes she has
broken - 'It isn't for us to talk about.... Don't speak of it, don't
speak.'
As if to emphasize the crucial importance of how wrong it is to
voice their love, she repeats her interdiction a little later, ' "we
mustn't talk, we mustn't talk; we must wait" - she had to make
that clear.' This seems to me of central significance in understanding the Jamesian drive for obscurity, evasion and passivity.
The double injunction, not to talk and to wait, which occurs in
remarkably similar scenes in 'The Golden Bowl', 'The Wings of the
Dove' and 'The Ambassadors', constitutes a root function in the
narratives, and recurs to govern the scene of seduction. It is a
complementary function to that governing the observer's relation
to the same scene explored above in 'The Sacred Fount'.
Thus if a character openly signifies his desire for something
(the 'spoils' of 'The Spoils of Poynton' come into the same category) or someone, they open themselves to betrayal and lose the
object of their desire. Need and desire are only satisfied in James
at the cost of remaining as far away from direct communication as
possible. Fulfilment and satisfaction are predicated upon the suppression, not of the need itself, but of all signs of the existence
of the need. More particularly, the maintenance of value rests
upon the same principle of not 'giving oneself away'. To return
to the quotation by James used at the outset (p. 134), the devaluation of something is directly related to opening 'the gates of
communication'.
This inverse relationship between representation and fulfilment
seems to have existed from the very earliest stories. In A Landscape Painter (1866) the painter Locksley believes that he will
only win Miss Quarterman if he conceals the fact that he is infatuated with her and that he is very rich. During his discreet

wooing of her he keeps a diary (in which he mentions this secret resolve) and it is the private diary which forms the bulk of the story. At the end of the tale, having just married Miss Quarterman, Locksley breaks his rule. He is looking through his diary and realizes how often he had confided to its pages his love for Miss Quarterman, and he adds:(73)

I have been reading over these pages for the first time in – I don't know when. They are filled with *her* – even more in thought than in word. I believe I will show them to her when she comes in. I will give her the book to read, and sit by her, watching her face – watching the great secret dawn upon her.

As well as displaying the characteristic use of a private document as the mediated expression of sexual desire (also used in The Aspern Papers, the telegrams of In the Cage, the 'too frank' unpublished article in John Delavoy, the memoirs in The Abasement of the Northmores, and of course the secret papers in Sir Dominick Ferrand), this passage also contains a characteristic ambiguity, in that it is not quite clear whether 'the great secret' refers to his wealth or his love. His decision to show her the diary seems to come more from the fact that the pages are 'filled with her' than because it reveals his wealth. However, when he does reveal his secret he learns that she had already read the diary whilst he had been ill and he is shocked and upset at her betrayal:(74)

'It was the act of a false woman,' said I.

'A false woman? No, it was the act of any woman – placed as I was placed. You don't believe it?' And she began to smile. 'Come you may abuse me in your diary if you like – I shall never peep into it again!'

This dénouement is strikingly similar to that of 'The Tree of Knowledge' written thirty-four years later near the end of James's active writing career. Again, the central character had kept secret his love only to find when finally forced to reveal it that he is a deceived and disappointed man: his moment of declaration is simultaneously the moment of loss. In The Tree of Knowledge the same interdiction that Fleda Vetch and Locksley impose upon themselves and then break applies to the central character Peter Brench.

Brench at the beginning of the story is in the position of having revealed neither his contempt for his friend Morgan Mallow's lack of artistic ability (Mallow is a sculptor) nor his own love for Mallow's wife. The two secrets – just like Locksley's two secrets concealing his wealth and his love – are given as being somehow connected from the outset. Brench, 'who had been in love with Mrs Mallow for years without breathing it', is, again like Locksley, gradually put into a position where the revelation of the lesser secret (how vulgar and worthless he considers Mallow's art work) simultaneously involves the revelation of the greater, his love for Mrs Mallow. He is caught out by the Mallow's perceptive son, Lancelot:(75)

'Oh, the game for me is only to hold my tongue,' said
placid Peter. 'And I have my reason.'
   'Still my mother?'
   Peter showed, as he had often shown it before - that is
by turning it straight away - a queer face. 'What will you
have? I haven't ceased to like her.' . . . .
   Lance took a turn about the room, but with his eyes still
on his host. 'How awfully - always - you must have liked
her!'
   'Awfully. Always,' said Peter.
'The game for me is only to hold my tongue'; 'We mustn't talk;
we must wait.' By breaking these rules the characters involved
lose the objects of their love. The tendency in the novels (particularly the later ones) is for desire to become satisfaction only
by remaining outside direct signification. And as these stories
show, the secret desire is often yoked to another secret concerning art or money which compromises the concealment of desire.
Thus Fleda Vetch's love for Owen Gereth is compromised by her
involvement in the sordid intrigue to filch the art treasures at
Poynton; Locksley's love for Miss Quarterman is compromised by
the concealment of his own wealth; Peter Brench's love for Mrs
Mallow is compromised by his concealed contempt for her husband's
art. Brench learns, as soon as he breaks his rule and confesses
his love for Mrs Mallow, that she had 'always, always known' her
husband's sculpture to be third-rate, but loves him faithfully in
spite of that. It dawns on Brench that he had actually been striv-
ing to keep it a secret to protect himself from the knowledge that,
even if the wife knew the poor quality of her husband's work she
would still love him - which kills forever this tiny hope Brench
had maintained that she would leave her husband and perhaps
come to him once she learned she was married to a third-rater.
   There is surely an echo of Fleda Vetch's thrice avowed 'I cared,
I cared, I cared' in a strikingly similar scene between Kate Croy
and Densher in 'The Wings of the Dove'. Kate and Densher are
alone in an upper room at Lancaster Gate, and in one of the most
direct scenes in what is one of James's most obscure works, he
declares his love for her: (76)
   He laid strong hands upon her to say, almost in anger,
   'Do you love me, love me, love me?' and she closed her
   eyes as with the sense that he might strike her but that
   she could gratefully take it . . . the long embrace in which
   they held each other was the rout of evasion . . . .
Again the direct avowal of love is associated with pain, punishment and an end of evasion which is the beginning of vulnerability.
It is the single moment in the novel when Kate is, in Densher's
words, 'sublimely sincere', but, as we might expect, it is bonded
in irony and pathos to the moment of betrayal. The passage continues: (77)
   It seemed in fact only now that their questions were put on
   the table. He had taken up more expressly at the end of five
   minutes her plea for her own plan, and it was marked that

the difference made by the passage just enacted was a
difference in favour of her choice of means.
'Her choice of means' refers to her design on Milly's money which
leads to the hopeless compromising of Densher and the extinguish-
ing of their passion - the passion, precisely, which by its open
declaration here precipitates its own destruction. Densher had
intended in the above scene to ask Kate to marry him immediately
even though he had so little money ('Will you take me just as I
am?'), but the consequence of his passionate demand brings desolation. In all these cases, the fact of love had been a continuous
'steady state' in the narrative, a mute presence which had not
been at risk until the moment of direct avowal.

It would be wilful not to see the relation of this double interdiction (governing the scene of confrontation with the object of
desire) to the process described in psycho-analysis as 'foreclosure'
('Verwerfung'). This term is used to describe the relatively common act of repudiation or rejection at the instant when a desire is
about to be realized.

Foreclosure is used in somewhat disparate senses (78) but it
clearly centres on not symbolizing what ought to be symbolized:
it is 'symbolic abolition', and Freud saw foreclosure as a refusal
to acknowledge a desire by excluding it from the realm of signification, which is very close to Fleda's frightened words 'It isn't
for us to talk about.... Don't speak of it, don't speak.' Other
terms used by Freud in a context which would seem to authorize
their being linked to foreclosure are 'Ablehnen' (to fend off),
'Aufheben' (notoriously untranslatable into English but usually
given as 'to sublate', simultaneously to abolish and preserve at a
higher level) and also 'Verleugnen' (to disavow), all of which, for
readers of James, are verbs resonant with the remembrance of
countless narrative moments. Fleda, Peter Brench, Locksley,
Strether, Densher, Ralph Touchett, Maud Blessingbourne (in The
Story in It) and Rowland Mallet, all endeavour at some crucial
moment to foreclose a scene of avowal by a self-imposed inhibition
which, whilst not abolishing the substance of the wish, tries desperately to leave it in vague, unfulfilled suspension. Obscurity
of immediate need is so constant a feature of James's characters
that sometimes the given rationalizations for self-denial appear
perfunctory, perverse or infuriatingly inadequate. In the case of
Strether's refusal of Maria Gostrey, his rejection seems wilful and
arbitrary (79) and others - Ralph, Densher and Maggie - seem to
achieve satisfaction by denying themselves the symbolic expression
and enjoyment of immediate pleasure: they frustrate expression in
fulfilment of some distant, transcendent refusal which invites them
to take refuge in its private solace.

Failure to foreclose the scene of direct encounter leads to loss,
and the frequency of loss and disappointment makes the extraordinary success of Maggie Verver in 'The Golden Bowl' stand out
all the more. There is an important scene in 'The Golden Bowl'
which closely parallels the avowal scenes in 'The Spoils of Poynton'
and 'The Wings of the Dove' except that the rule is invoked and

then *kept*. Shortly after the symbolic destruction of the bowl,
Maggie and Amerigo are alone together, and Maggie feels almost
overcome in her physical desire for the Prince. But James has
made it (relatively!) clear that her success in winning him back
is conditional on her not surrendering to him. In this, one of the
most notoriously obscure of fictions, the encounter breaks through
all the clever talk and evasiveness with the unexpected clarity of
romance:(80)

> The sensation was for the few seconds extraordinary: her
> weakness, her desire, so long as she was yet not saving
> herself, flowered in her face like a light or darkness. She
> sought for some word that would cover this up.... He was
> so near now that she could touch him, taste him, smell him,
> kiss him, hold him; he almost pressed upon her, and the
> warmth of his face - frowning, smiling, she mightn't know
> which; only beautiful and strange - was bent upon her with
> the largeness with which objects loom in dreams.... Then it
> was that from behind her eyes the right word came. 'Wait!'
> It was the word of his own distress and entreaty, the word
> for both of them all they had left, their plank now on the
> great sea.... He let her go - he turned away with this
> message, and when she saw him again his back was presented,
> as he had left her, and his face staring out of the window.
> She had saved herself and got off.

Maggie succeeds where Fleda, Maria Gootrey and Kate Croy had
failed, she restrains herself from her almost overwhelming passion
and succeeds in obscuring it ('She sought for some word that
would cover this up....') She averts the crisis with the same
word - 'Wait' - that Fleda had failed to use until too late, and the
direct encounter is deflected ('he turned away with this message.')
Maggie is one of the few Jamesian characters to succeed in finally
obtaining what she wishes, and I believe this is because she is
almost alone in not having broken the rule about the expression of
desire. She refines herself almost to a principle of pure passivity,
she does little but speak, spinning a web of hints and equivocations until everyone else loses their nerve. She, of all James's
characters, has mastered his almost impossible demand that satisfaction be achieved passively, by using language which never
makes overt mention of that which is most pressingly, achingly
significant for the speaker.(81)

Obscurity in James is thus a way of ensuring purity. Desire may
be fulfilled, but only by remaining behind the circuits of information and representation which might advertise its presence. It
is a matter of avoiding any direct encounter, both for those in
love and those who watch, each must move away from the dangerous places of confrontation.

The word 'confrontation' can be taken quite literally, for the
linguistic obscurity in James has its precise counterpart in visual
presentation, and it is above all in the 'turned back' that both the
desire for security and the pathos of exclusion find their perfect
image. In the long passage quoted above, it is only when Maggie

closes her eyes and Amerigo turns away that she escaped the
crisis: 'and when she saw him again his back was presented, as
he had left her, and his face staring out of the window. She had
saved herself and got off.'

There are numerous scenes in James in which figures are only
seen from the back, and indeed critics occasionally note as much,
usually with quizzical interest. The most detailed study is in an
essay of 1954 by Maurice Beebe, The Turned Back of Henry James,
in which Beebe argues that 'James was able to use the turned
back of the artist to symbolize "the artist *in triumph*".'(82)
Beebe's argument is based upon four examples which describe the
artist at his desk with his back bent over his work, and his central example is from the preface to 'The Tragic Muse':(83)

Any representation of the artist *in triumph* must be flat in
proportion as it really sticks to its subject - it can only
smuggle in relief and variety. For, to put the matter in an
image, all we then - in his triumph - see of the charm-
compellor is the back he turns to us as he bends over his
work.

But although the image of a turned back is associated with the
working writer in James, it is frequently associated with other
figures as well - Strether, Chad, Amerigo, Peter Quint,(84)
Cuthbert Frush (in The Third Person), Maud Lowder, and Maisie.
What is certainly part of the overall significance of this visual
arrangement is the position in which the 'observer' must be located
to describe the scene in such a way. For the Jamesian observer
can gather his evidence without confrontation or detection by remaining behind the object of his scrutiny. The narrator in 'The
Sacred Fount' suddenly sees a gentleman, 'whose identity was
attested by his back, a back somehow replete for us, at the moment, with a guilty significance. There *was* the evidence of relations.'(85)

The link between the two things here could hardly be clearer,
where the very act of collecting the evidence of 'relations' is vis-
ually obscured by the fortuitously turned back. But the obscurity
in James is dialectically constrained for both subject and object,
and as I have shown it relates its narrative and semantic opacities
both to the observer and the observed. Those observed have to
avoid being seen directly, and the turned back can become a security for them too, a visual equivalent of ellipsis. Near the end of
'The Wings of the Dove', when the desire to know is made an explicit test of vulgarity and precipitance, Kate's attention is caught
by Densher's turned back, her eyes 'rested on the back and
shoulders he thus familiarly presented.' But Densher's back will
tell her nothing, it becomes instead the somatic correlate to the
essential obscuring processes in the novel itself. The back was
'a reference to things unimparted, links still missing and that she
must ever miss, try to make them out as she would.'(86)

The turned back is nearly always associated with a protecting
sense that painful confrontation has been avoided and that observation itself has gone unnoticed. Thus, on learning of Milly's

'incurable pain', Densher can only satisfactorily obscure the facts
of her physical suffering by ensuring that Sir Luke Strett's back
metaphorically interpose itself to screen Milly from the public.(87)
Indeed the feeling of elation which James often describes in relation to the image is quite extraordinary. It is a back turned not
only to the narrator but the reader, and when it belongs to a
writer, it becomes a tangible and appropriate image of the kind of
artistic privatization discussed in chapter 2 (pp. 32-43). In The
Great Good Place, George Dane is a famous author who has been
driven almost to breaking point by the invitations and requests of
the public. He needs a private place, tranquil and remote, where
he can return to his work undisturbed. A young friend - also a
writer - arrives one morning with the exciting announcement that
such a place exists:(88)

> He suddenly sprang up and went over to my study-table -
> sat down there as if to write my prescription or my passport.
> Then it was - at the mere sight of his back, which was turned
> to me - that I felt the spell work. I simply sat and watched
> him with the queerest deepest sweetest sense in the world -
> the sense of an ache that has stopped. All life was lifted; I
> myself was somehow off the ground. He was already where I
> had been.... He was already me.

The passage is open to a certain very obvious kind of psycho-
analytical reading, but the homosexual connotations of the scene
are not apparent in the many other scenes in James which feature
the turned back. The 'sense that an ache had stopped' is linked
rather to the immense sense of relief afforded by the escape into
privacy ('The Great Good Place' of the title), which James always
associated with the image.

It is something which, in both serious and ironic ways, has been
connected with the position of the modern novelist. For Thomas
Mann, the modern writer was the 'creator of back-images' ('Rück-
bildler'), formations of a deliberately evasive 'behind-the-back'
kind. 'Felix Krull' was Mann's own version of this, the creator as
confidence trickster, and Felix is not so far removed from the
manipulative 'arrivistes' who haunt the background of James's
fiction. It is consonant with a modern sense that those aspects of
things which are central and foregrounded are perhaps a screen
for the less obvious and the marginal, in which the real significance may be hidden. Jung's amusing equivocation about Joyce's
'Ulysses' (was it, he asked, 'die Kunst der Rückenseite, oder die
Rückseite der Kunst')(89) was not, as he made clear, altogether
fatuous. The obscurity of modern writing is inseparable from a
widespread tendency for the novelist to turn away from the reader,
leaving him the odd, uncomfortable, or even insulting view of his
turned back. The most important element of any work, wrote
Nietzsche, was not its manifest discourse, but its 'Hinterfrage'
(its 'back-question'), the question which comes from behind, held
in reserve as an ambush or a trap. If it is one thing which Conrad,
Meredith and James often share, it is a universal wariness, an
alertness, almost an expectation of traps and pitfalls, in a world

which has its dangerous 'back-formation'. Their works are rarely
free of an insidious, threatening 'Hinterfrage'.

In James, the turned back can be taken as an 'embodiment' of
these modernist concerns compounded with his own private symbolism. The fact that it is someone's back which 'gets one off' (as
in the case of Maggie and Amerigo) is probably not unconnected
to the back injury which James sustained as a young man and
which saved him from having to go off and fight in the Civil War -
an incident which he referred to (in a phrase which nicely suits
my purpose) as my 'obscure hurt'.

But if the turned back in James offers a perfect image of visual
obscurity, of literal effacement, it also perfectly indexes the
exclusion which is the necessary and tragic corollary of that
position of safety. In his preface to 'The Wings of the Dove',
James described the subject of his novel as not being 'frank', it
did not, he said have its elements well in view and 'its whole
character in its face'. Nevertheless he wanted the reader to see
the dangers and difficulties confronting Milly whilst at the same
time obscuring the dangers of 'the operatic death scene', the vulgarity of a public (Dickensian?) and sentimental theme. The sense
of 'Hinterfrage' is strongly present when he writes that he wanted
Milly's world to 'bristle' with meanings, and his method of representation is likened to a medal of which the front and back may be
seen simultaneously:(90)

> so, by the same token, could I but make my medal hang
> free; its obverse and reverse, its face and back, would
> beautifully become optional for the spectator. I somehow
> wanted them correspondingly embossed, wanted them
> inscribed and figured with an equal salience....

'The Wings of the Dove' achieves this complex narrative task
with complete success, representation and reticence are balanced
in its structure with consummate skill. But even more significant
than this for me is the recurrent phrase used to describe Milly's
acquiescence in death: 'She has turned her face to the wall.' The
perfection of the phrase is not simply that death and the deepest
processes of James's art are brought together in a delicate
euphemism. When Milly Theale quietly turns her back upon the
reader and upon her friends, it is to preserve them, as well as
herself, from all taint of the mawkish, sentimental or vulgar. The
price paid for this sublime obscurity is her isolation from the
world and her lonely death. It is James's own price, but when
paid with such stoical dignity it does not seem unjust.

NOTES

Unless otherwise stated: all references to the novels of George Meredith are to the 'Standard Edition', 16 vols (London, 1914-19), the pagination of which corresponds to the 'Memorial Edition' (1909-11), all references to the poems are to 'Poems', ed. G. M. Trevelyan, after the 'Memorial Edition', with corrections (London, 1912); all references to the novels and stories of Joseph Conrad are to the 'Dent Uniform Edition', 22 vols (London, 1923-8); all references to the novels of Henry James are to 'The Bodley Head Henry James', 11 vols (London, 1967-74), all references to the tales and short stories are to 'The Complete Tales', 12 vols, ed. Leon Edel (London, 1962-4).

Introduction
1 Althusser attempts to reconstruct what he terms the 'problematic' or un-conscious of the text on the model of the Freudian analysis of a patient's utterance. This fusion of Marxist and psycho-analytical method is - as Althusser himself would say - not accidental. It is precisely to the degree that they both participate in the cultural moment which produces symptomatic reading that they can be brought together in this way. It is important to stress that the 'problematic' (which Terry Eagleton refers to as a kind of 'sub-text') is neither an essence nor is it a world-view, but concerns the absence of certain problems and issues as much as their presence. See Ben Brewster's useful glossary to his translation of Althusser's 'Pour Marx' (Harmondsworth, 1969), pp. 252-3.
2 For an excellent account of this see R. Jackson, 'Fantasy: The Literature of Subversion' (London, 1981), which analyses the function of gothic episodes in both containing and releasing overwhelming psychological forces as they threaten to break up narrative form. This is particularly true of Dickens's fiction, where gothic moments erupt quite unpredictably throughout his stories.
3 J.-P. Sartre, 'What is Literature?' (1948), trans. B. Frechtman, pp. 19-20.
4 T. Eagleton, Irony and Commitment, 'Stand', vol. 20, no. 3, pp. 24-7.
5 T. Eagleton, 'Criticism and Ideology', (London, 1976). The final chapter is an heroic attempt to provide a Marxist theory of literary value, but it cannot be counted a success. Eagleton nowhere accounts for the pleasure which is derived from a literary work other than in terms of the intellectual-critical pleasure of exploring its 'rifts', 'creases' and 'ambiguities' (see particularly his judgments on Wordsworth, p. 187).
6 J.-P. Sartre, 'What is Literature?', op. cit., pp. 20-1.
7 It is quite possible that Wilde had in mind the Renaissance aphorism 'ogni dipintore dipinge se', which may be found in a variety of Renaissance writing on art, including Poliziano, Savonarola, Leonardo, and which Vasari attributes to Michaelangelo ('ogni pittore ritrae se medesimo'). See A. Chastel, 'Art et humanisme à Florence au temps de Laurent le Magnif-ique' (Paris, 1961), pp. 102-3; M. Kemp, 'Ogni dipintore dipinge se', in 'Cultural Aspects of the Renaissance', ed. C.H. Clough (Manchester, 1976), pp. 311-23.

Chapter 1 Obscurity and enlightenment
1 J. Middleton Murry, 'The Problem of Style' (Oxford, 1922), p. 52. It is of course a common ideal. 'It would seem fair to take the symbols of Russell and Whitehead's 'Principia Mathematica', or the formulae of Carnap, as the nearest approach we have to the vocabulary of the semantic ideal' - K. Burke, Semantic and Poetic Meanings, in 'Classics and Semantics',

ed D. E. Hayden and E. P. Alworth (London, 1965), pp. 297-322, p. 308.

2   'He had a phrase, expressive of the view he took of all moral speculations to which his method had not been applied, or (which he considered as the same thing) not founded on a recognition of utility as the moral standard; this phrase was "vague generalities". Whatever presented itself to him in such a shape, he dismissed as unworthy of notice, or dwelt upon only to denounce as absurd.' J. S. Mill on Bentham (1838) in 'Mill on Bentham and Coleridge', ed and introd. F. R. Leavis (London, 1971), p. 59.

3   See Saint Augustine and the Debate about a Christian Rhetoric, in 'Readings in Rhetoric', ed Lionel Crocker and Paul A. Carmack (Springfield, 1965), pp. 203-19.

4   R. Descartes, Meditation Troisième (1641), 'Oeuvres philosophiques', vol. II (Paris, 1967), p. 431.

5   F. L. Lucas, review of 'The Waste Land', 'New Statesman', 3 November 1923. See also Seven Studies in the History of American Obscurantism, in Yvor Winters's 'In Defense of Reason' (1947) (London, 1960).

6   J. R. Sutherland, 'On English Prose' (Toronto, 1957), p. 77.

7   C. S. Peirce, How to Make Our Ideas Clear, 'Popular Science Monthly', January 1878. Reprinted in 'Classics in Semantics', ed D. E. Hayden and E. P. Alworth, op. cit., p. 154.

8   G. Steiner, 'After Babel' (Oxford, 1975), p. 178.

9   J. Habermas, Systematically Distorted Communication, in 'Critical Sociology', ed P. Connerton (Harmondsworth, 1976), p. 348.

10   A. Brien, The Child is Father of the Man, 'Sunday Times', 20 April 1980, p. 40.

11   M. Bowie, 'Mallarmé and the Art of Being Difficult' (Cambridge, 1978). This excellent study of Mallarmé has direct relevance to the present study, particularly in Bowie's insistence on the positive resistance of the poetry. Some parts are easy of access, but 'Others are mobile and stubbornly unsmooth patterns of meaning which, while yielding to pressure in some of their parts or aspects, leave us with an abiding residue of unsolved questions ... our most important collaboration with the poet begins when we ourselves agree to be uncertain.' (pp. ix, x).

12   Of course, both the terms difficulty and ambiguity are invoked at appropriate points, but they remain 'subsets' of the overall notion of discursive resistance.

13   The accusations of obscurity against Meredith were legion. An unsigned review of 1895 remarked, 'The fact is that Mr Meredith has devoted himself to the study of obscurity with baneful success' (Mr Meredith's Novels, 'Edinburgh Review', 181, 1895, pp. 33-58, p. 34). Another reviewer in the 'Pall Mall Gazette' (28 March 1885) remarked upon 'the Cretan mazes and Gordian knots of phrase which he takes such pleasure in devising,' whilst yet another unsigned review in the 'Pall Mall Gazette' (20 July 1894) talked about Meredith's dialogue as 'always puzzling, sometimes unintelligible,.... The style is so tortured and elaborate that scarcely for half-a-page are you unconscious of the means.' Ioan Williams has collected an excellent anthology of contemporary criticism in 'Meredith: The Critical Heritage'.

Conrad's 'Nostromo' was considered by most reviewers to be rather obscure ('detail absorbs the position of outline, which becomes impossibly blurred,' wrote an anonymous reviewer in the 'Daily Telegraph' (9 November 1904)), but the accusations of obscurity against Conrad apply more to his enigmatic insubstantiality than to stylistic difficulty. In an early review of 'Almayer's Folly', H. G. Wells was probably the first critic to fire the common shot (unsigned, 'Saturday Review', 16 May 1896, pp. 509-10):

Mr. Conrad is wordy; his story is not so much told as seen intermittently through a haze of sentences. His style is like river mist; for a space things are seen clearly, and then comes a great, grey bank of printed matter, page on page, creeping round the reader, swallowing him up.

This 'foggishness', as Conrad himself called it in reference to 'Heart of
Darkness', was also referred to much later by E. M. Forster in his well-
known essay. Forster remarks that Conrad 'is misty in the middle as well .
as at the edges... the secret casket of his genius contains a vapour rather
than a jewel' ('Abinger Harvest', p. 135).

James was attacked endlessly over his late style, not least by his brother
William: 'For gleams and innuendos and felicitous verbal insinuations you
are unapproachable, but the core of literature is solid. Give it to us once
again!' Letter to Henry James, May 1907, in F. O. Matthiessen, 'The James
Family' (New York, 1947), pp. 341-2. E. C. Brownell wrote in the 'Atlantic'
(April 1905) that 'The loss of interest involved in obscurity is, to begin
with, enormous. Such elaborate care as that of Mr. James should at least
secure clearness. But with all his scrupulousness, clearness never seems
to be an object of his care.... The reader's pleasure becomes a task, and
his task the torture of Tantalus.' Many further examples of the same tenor
are collected in 'Henry James: The Critical Heritage', ed Roger Gard
(London, 1968).

14   L. Wittgenstein, 'Philosophische Untersuchungen', trans. G. G. M. Ans-
combe, 'Philosophical Investigations', 2nd edn (Oxford, 1958), p. 34.

15   E. Husserl, 'The Paris Lectures', trans. and introd. P. Koestenbaum
(The Hague, 1970), p. xiii.

16   For an excellent critique of this response to Joyce, see S. Heath,
Ambiviolences, 'Tel Quel', no. 50 (Summer 1972), pp. 22-43; 'Tel Quel',
no. 51 (Autumn 1972), pp. 64-77.

17   D. Hayman, 'Joyce et Mallarmé' (Paris, 1956), p. 13.

18   Jean-Noël Vuarnet, Dialogisme et vérité in 'Socialité de L'ecriture, le discours social', nos 3-4 (Paris, Cahiers de l'Institut de littérature et de
techniques artistiques de masse, 1975), p. 149.

19   One must ask how a critic expects to get an answer to the question
about intention. How is he to find out what the poet tried to do? If
the poet succeeded in doing it, then the poem itself shows what he
was trying to do. And if the poet did not succeed, then the poem
is not adequate evidence, and the critic must go outside the poem -
for evidence of an intention that did not become effective in the
poem.
W. K. Wimsatt, 'The Verbal Icon' (Lexington, Ky, 1954), edn used (London, 1970), p. 4. But that was only the beginning of the debate for recent
times. See 'On Literary Intention', ed and introd. D. Newton-de-Molina
(Edinburgh, 1976) for further development of this debate.

20   The anecdote is related by Charles Whibley in his early review, Stéphane
Mallarmé, 'Blackwood's Magazine', no. 164 (November 1898), pp. 692-7,
p. 696.

21   A. Fowler, Intention Floreat, 'On Literary Intention', ed and introd. D.
Newton-de-Molina (Edinburgh, 1976), pp. 242-55. The close parallel between Virginia Woolf and Joseph Conrad in their conception of the 'fore-
idea' of the text is quite striking. Woolf's 'It will never be so good as it is
now in my mind - unwritten,' recalls Conrad's remarks about 'The Rescue'
in a Letter to Hueffer (November 1898):
I get on dreamily with 'The Rescue'... it is sad to think that even
if all this came to pass - even then it could never be so fine to
anybody as it is to me now, lurking in the blank pages in an
intensity of existence without voice, without form - but without
blemish.

22   A. Fowler, Intention Floreat, op. cit., p. 245.

23   E. D. Hirsch, Jr, 'Validity in Interpretation' (New Haven, 1967).

24   Wittgenstein ('Philosophical Investigations', op. cit., p. 217) produced the
following useful musical analogy to describe this aspect of intention and
continuity:
The intention *with which* one acts does not 'accompany' the action
any more than the thought 'accompanies' speech. Thought and
intention are neither 'articulated' nor 'non-articulated'; to be

compared neither with a single note which sounds during the
acting or speaking, nor with a tune.

25 Ideology is to be understood in its widest sense as the form of thought and
belief currently and commonly held by a social group, and I do not confine
the use of the word to systematic 'strong' conceptual fields (Christianity,
Freudianism etc.). Thus I call the change from a belief in 'sincerity' to a
belief in 'authenticity' charted in Lionel Trilling's brilliant book 'Sincerity
and Authenticity' (London, 1972) an *ideological* transformation.

26 A. Jolles, 'Einfache Formen' (1930) trans. into French as 'Formes Simples'
by A. M. Buguet (Paris, 1972).

27 J. Cocteau, Poetry Lecture at Oxford, 1956, quoted by S. Ullmann,
'Language and Style' (Oxford, 1964), p. 99. Cocteau continues:
Elle [la poésie] est la proie de l'exégèse qui est sans conteste une
muse puis qu'il lui arrive de traduire en clair nos codes d'éclairer
nos propres ténèbres et de nous renseigner sur ce que nous ne
savions pas avoir dit.

28 G. Steiner, 'On Difficulty and Other Essays' (Oxford, 1978), p. 18.

29 C. Bally, 'Linguistique générale et linguistique française', 2nd edn (Bern,
1944), p. 37.

30 F. Schlegel, Philosophie der Sprache und des Wortes, Zweite Vorlesung
(1828), in 'Kritische Ausgabe', ed and introd. Ernst Behler (Zürich, 1969).
Band X, pp. 351-2, trans. A. J. Morrison in F. Schlegel, 'The Philosophy of
Life and the Philosophy of Language' (London, 1847), p. 389:
So profound, moreover, and lasting is this our intrinsic dualism and
duplicity - (and I use the term here, not in its usual moral sense,
but in a higher signification, which is purely psychological and metaphysical) - so deeply is this dualism rooted in our consciousness,
that even when we are, or at least think ourselves, alone, we still
think as two, and are constrained as it were to recognise our inmost
profoundest being as essentially dramatic.
The idea is further elaborated in Hegel's description of 'the unwon unity of
the two selves' in 'The Phenomenology of Spirit'.

31 M. Blanchot, 'L'Entretien infini' (Paris, 1969), pp. 581-2.

32 See M. Bakhtine's brilliant work on Dostoevsky for a full discussion of
dialogic form in fiction: 'Problems of Dostoevsky's Poetics', trans. R. W.
Rotsel (Ann Arbor, 1973).

33 P. Macherey, 'Pour une Théorie de la production littéraire' (Paris, 1970),
p. 105.

Chapter 2 Obscure writing and private life, 1880-1914

1 R. W. Emerson, Culture, in 'The Conduct of Life', 1883 (reprinted London,
1905) p. 126. The popularity of this book is evidenced by the fact that it
had been reprinted seven times in England by 1905.

2 R. A. Lanham, 'Style, An Anti-Textbook' (New Haven and London, 1974),
p. 32.

3 For an extremely intelligent attempt to analyse the meshing of social,
textual and psychic changes in the period, see J. Kristeva, L'État et le
Mystère, Section C of 'La Révolution du language poétique' (Paris, 1974),
pp. 361-435.

4 The standard works (R. D. Altick, 'The English Common Reader: A Social
History of the Mass Reading Public, 1800-1900' (Chicago, 1957), and
Q. D. Leavis, 'Fiction and the Reading Public' (London, 1932)), give
scant coverage to this period and particularly to the specific problems
facing Meredith and James with respect to a 'dual addressee'.

5 See G. L. Griest, 'Mudie's Circulating Library and the Victorian Novel'
(Bloomington, 1970), for the best study of the forms of distribution of the
three-decker.

6 Ibid., p. 3.

7 Louis James, 'Fiction for the Working Man, 1830-1850' (London, 1963);
M. Sadleir, 'XIX Century Fiction: a Bibliographical Record' (London, 1951).
See also n. 4 above.

8   Unsigned review, 'St. James Gazette', vi, 25 June 1883; unsigned review
    in 'Temple Bar', xcvii, April, 1893. Both are reprinted in 'Meredith: The
    Critical Heritage', ed Ioan Williams (London, 1971), pp. 241; 368.
9   Ibid., p. 428.
10 L. Stevenson, 'The Ordeal of George Meredith' (New York, 1953).
11 S. Sassoon, 'Meredith' (London, 1948), p. 125.
12 Meredith described 'The Adventures of Harry Richmond' to his friend
    Augustus Jessop in 1864 as 'a spanking bid for popularity'.
13 S. Sassoon, 'Meredith', op. cit., p. 74.
14 G. Meredith, 'Sandra Belloni' (entitled 'Emilia in England' until the 1886
    reprint), p. 483.
15 Meredith even went so far as to write chapters of his novels to be read
    differently by different sections of the audience. In chapter 8 of 'The
    Amazing Marriage' when Gower Woodseer and Lord Fleetwood (two comple-
    mentary versions of 'sylvan' man, the seer and the man of action)
    encounter one another and discuss Carinthia Jane. It is requested that
    the male reader 'bear in mind what wild creature he was in his youth,
    while the female should marvel credulously.' And indeed, the passionate
    and idealized male versions of Carinthia which draw the two men together
    would, I think, elicit different responses from men and women.
16 G. Meredith, 'One of Our Conquerors', p. 120.
17 L. Johnson, review of 'One of Our Conquerors', the 'Academy', xxxix
    (13 June 1891), cited in 'Meredith: The Critical Heritage', op. cit., pp
    360-3.
18 G. Meredith, 'Modern Love', stanza XLVIII.
19 Meredith wrote of himself in 'Beauchamp's Career': 'Back I go to my wil-
    derness, where, as you may perceive, I have contracted the habit of
    listening to my own voice more than is good.'
20 J. Fletcher and M. Bradbury, The Introverted Novel, 'Modernism', ed
    M Bradbury and J. McFarlane (Harmondsworth, 1976), p. 365.
21 L. Johnson, in his review of 'One of Our Conquerors', ('Meredith: The
    Critical Heritage', op. cit., p. 360), asked:
        Is there no danger that, in a kind of unconscious defiance and
        challenge, they [the artists] will have gone too far, and grown
        enamoured of that in their work which the world did well to blame?
        If the world cried out upon their obscurity, where there was some
        obscurity but not much, was it not natural in them to have replied
        with worse obscurities, out of an impatient contempt and exasperation?
22 In an unsigned review of Meredith's poem 'The Empty Purse' the reviewer
    spoke of 'this new cryptographic style', indicating the degree to which
    the age was becoming conscious of the new obscurity. It is a function, in
    many instances, of increasing heterogeneity in the fiction, a dissociation
    of private experiences from a realm of shared meanings which do not con-
    tain the experiences but encroach upon them.
23 This junction of two modes of subjectivity, this 'in mixing of subjects',
    refers to the kinds of plural subjectivity which became an important feature
    of modernist writing. Perhaps the clearest example is in 'Les Chants de
    Maldoror' by Lautréamont, in which 'characters' are no longer kept sep-
    arate as stable and discrete entities, but constantly melt into each other
    in protean, shifting transformations.
24 G. Meredith, 'The Tragic Comedians', pp. 198-9.
25 H. James, 'The Sacred Fount', ed and introd. Leon Edel (London, 1959),
    pp. 50-1.
26 G. Meredith, 'The Tragic Comedians', preface, p. i:
        The word 'fantastical' is accentuated in our tongue to so scornful
        an utterance that the constant good service it does would make it
        seem an appointed instrument for reviewers of books or imaginative
        matter distasteful to those expository pens. Upon examination,
        claimants to the epithet will be found outside of books and of poets,
        in many quarters, Nature being one of the most prominent, if not
        the foremost. Wherever she can get to drink her fill of sunlight
        she pushes forth fantastically.

27   J. Conrad, 'Heart of Darkness', p. 126.
28   J. Laforgue, 'Oeuvres' (Paris, 1925-62) ed G. Jean-Aubry, II, p. 26.
29   C. Photiades, 'George Meredith: sa vie - son imagination' (Paris, 1910),
      cited in I. Williams, 'Meredith: The Critical Heritage', op. cit., p. 18.
      Meredith seems to have been deeply stung by the image of himself as har-
      lequin and he never forgot the term. In a letter of reply (22 July 1887) to
      a young American critic who had praised his work, Meredith wrote:
         In England I am encouraged but by a few enthusiasts. I read in a
         critical review of some verses of mine the other day that I was 'a
         harlequin and a performer of antics'. I am accustomed to that kind
         of writing, as our hustings orator is to the dead cat and the brick-
         bat flung in his face - at which he smiles politely.
30   J. Conrad, The Informer, p. 93.
31   R. Roussel, 'The Metaphysics of Darkness' (Baltimore, 1971), p. 4.
32   'Joseph Conrad's Letters to R. B. Cunninghame Graham', ed C. T. Watts,
      (Cambridge, 1969), p. 117.
33   'Letters from Joseph Conrad, 1895-1924', ed E. Garnett (London, 1928),
      p. 142.
34   Ibid., p. 59.
35   This and the following extracts from Dickens and Thackeray discussing
      their relationship to their readers are cited in K. Tillotson, 'Novels of the
      Eighteen-Forties' (Oxford, 1954), pp. 33 ff.
36   J. Conrad, The Return, in 'Tales of Unrest', p. 119.
37   'Joseph Conrad: Life and Letters', 2 vols, ed G. Jean-Aubry (New York,
      1927), I, p. 227.
38   J. Conrad, Alphonse Daudet, 'Notes on Life and Letters', p. 22.
39   Joseph Conrad, 'Letters to Cunninghame Graham', op. cit., p. 65.
40   Meredith misled the public about his private life in many ways, even ex-
      tending to his place of birth. See the opening chapter of David Williams's
      excellent study, 'George Meredith: His Life and Lost Love' (London, 1977);
      and D. Johnson, 'Lesser Lives' (London, 1973), p. 97. The calculated
      reticence of both Conrad and James is discussed below, chapters 5 and 6
      respectively.
41   J. Conrad, Books, 'Notes on Life and Letters', p. 6.
42   E. M. Forster, Joseph Conrad: A Note, in 'Abinger Harvest' (1936);
      reprinted (Harmondsworth, 1974), pp. 151-2.
43   J. Conrad, A Familiar Preface, in 'A Personal Record', p. xv.
44   J. Conrad, 'A Personal Record', p. 95.
45   O. Elton, A Note on Mysticism, 'Fortnightly Review', 76 (1904), pp. 462-77,
      p. 475.
46   Mrs E. L. Linton, Our Illusions, 'Fortnightly Review', 49 (1891), pp.
      584-97, pp. 595-6.
47   The following were among the most significant contributions to the period-
      ical literature on the subject: W. J. Corbet, The Increase of Insanity,
      'Fortnightly Review', 59 (1896), pp. 431-4; T. Drapes, Is Insanity In-
      creasing?, 'Fortnightly Review', 60 (1896), pp. 483-93. The growing
      uncertainty of the barrier between sanity, criminality and madness is
      expressed by Vernon Lee, Deterioration of the Soul, 'Fortnightly Review',
      59 (1896), pp. 928-43: 'I think that it is dangerous to draw a hard and
      fast line between ourselves and any of our fellow creatures, even when we
      may be obliged, for sheer self-defence, to shut some of them up and
      chastise them' (p. 931).
48   'One of Our Conquerors' (1891) is Meredith's remarkable portrayal of
      mental breakdown, and the work even led to a periodical discussion of the
      clinical forms of Victor Radnor's breakdown - see chapter 4 (pp. 106-7).
      Of Conrad's severed depression of 1897-8, Frederick Karl ('Joseph Conrad:
      The Three Lives', (London, 1979), pp. 424-5) writes:
         On March 29, as he was poised to begin something - anything - he
         wrote a desperate letter to Garnett, demonstrating possibly a more
         hopeless state of mind than any since his suicide attempt twenty
         years earlier...Conrad began to split into pieces,....

Leon Edel ('Henry James, A Biography', 5 vols, London, 1953-72) has documented Henry James's terrible period of depression and despair under the title of The Black Abyss, 1895, in vol. 4 of his biography, 'The Treacherous Years 1895-1900' (London, 1969), pp. 75-100.

49   H. Zimmern, Professor Lombroso's New Theory of Political Crime, 'Blackwood's Magazine', 149 (1891), pp. 202-11.

50   A. E. Hake, 'Regeneration, a reply to Max Nordau', (London, 1895).

51   For an attack on Lombroso's slipshod scholarship and blundering errors of fact see Musing Without Method, 'Blackwood's Magazine', 186 (1909), pp. 843-9. The date of this article should remind us however that the influence and topicality of Lombroso were spread over twenty years or more.

52   M. Nordau, 'Degeneration' (trans. from the 2nd German edn) (London, 1913), pp. vii-viii. The 1st English edn in 1895 went through seven new reprints in the same year and in September 1898 a 'popular' edn was published.

53   C. Lombroso, 'The Man of Genius' (London, 1891), pp. 359-60.

54   J. F. Nisbet, 'The Insanity of Genius' (London, 1891), Preface, p. xv.

55   G. Moreau, 'La Psychologie morbide' (Paris, 1859).

56   F. W. Hagen, Ueber die Verwandtschaft des Genies mit dem Irresein, 'Allgemeine Zeitschrift für Psychiatrie' (1877); P. Radestock, 'Genie und Wahnsinn' (Breslau, 1884).

57   Vernon Lee, Beauty and Sanity, 'Fortnightly Review', 58 (1895), pp. 252-68, p. 253.

58   T. Clifford Allbut, Nervous Diseases and Modern Life, the 'Contemporary Review', 67 (1895), pp. 210-31, p. 225.

59   A. Machen, 'Hieroglyphics: A Note upon Ecstacy in Literature' (London, 1902), p. 120. Essentially a plea for mystical romanticism, it contains some remarkable passages, particularly on the relation of conscious to unconscious expressed in the literary use of the 'Doppelgänger'.

60   The first work of Freud to be translated into English, A New Histological Method for the Study of Nerve-Tracts in the Brain and Spinal Cord, was contributed to 'Brain' in 1884. In 1893, Dr F. W. H. Myers, one of the leading members of the Society of Psychical Research where he was known as the Spiritualist Don, gave an account of the Freud-Breuer hysteria experiments at a meeting of the Society, the report of which was published in the 'Proceedings' of the Society in its issue of June 1893. In 1896, Dr M. Clarke, a leading British neurologist, published a long review of Freud's study of hysteria in 'Brain'. This review drew the attention of Havelock Ellis to Freud's work. Ellis published a paper, Hysteria in Relation to the Sexual Emotion, in 'The Alienist and Neurologist' in 1898. Ellis was really the prime English mediator of Freud at this time and vol. 1 of his 'Studies in the Psychology of Sex' (1904) referred to Freud's 'fascinating and really important researches'. By contrast Helen Zimmern stated that, by 1891, Professor Lombroso's books had an influence as 'immediate and decisive' as 'The Origin of Species'.

61   Oscar Wilde, The Sphinx (1891), in 'The Works of Oscar Wilde', introd. V. Holland (London, 1966), p. 842.

62   H. Zimmern, Professor Lombroso's New Theory of Political Crime, 'Blackwood's Magazine', 149 (1891), pp. 202-11, p. 211.

63   J. Conrad, 'Under Western Eyes', p. 52.

64   Cited in G. Markow-Totevy, 'Henry James', trans. J. Cummings (London, 1969), pp. 98-9.

65   H. James, The Figure in the Carpet, 'Cosmopolis', 1 (1896), p. 50.

66   Ibid., p. 49.

67   Ibid., pp. 47-8.

68   These descriptions are taken at random from dozens such in Lombroso and Nordau.

69   J. Conrad, 'Life and Letters', op. cit., II, p. 204.

70   A. Symons, Stephane Mallarmé, 'Fortnightly Review', 64 (1898), pp. 677-85, p. 678.

71   Ibid., p. 685.

72   Vernon Lee, Beauty and Sanity, op. cit., p. 260.
73   H. H. Statham, The Writings of Wagner, 'Edinburgh Review', 189 (1899),
     pp. 96-118, p. 96.
74   For an excellent discussion of the importance of music in 'One of Our
     Conquerors' see G. Beer, ' "One of Our Conquerors": Language and Music',
     in 'Meredith Now', ed I. Fletcher (London, 1971), pp. 265-80.
75   A. Symons, Stephane Mallarmé, op. cit., pp. 677, 682.
76   Modernist fiction adopted contrasting strategies in avoiding the dilemma of
     symptomatic reading and its crisis of intimacy: on the one hand it played
     up the 'make-believe', it forced fiction further towards radical playfulness
     (Borges, Nabokov, Beckett, Barth), it concealed the links between writer
     and written under the formal, ludic elements of structure; on the other
     hand it positively embraced the idea of fiction as the display of intensely
     private fantasies and desires, it pushed the psycho-dramatic and confes-
     sional nature of writing to extreme limits (Strindberg, Lawrence, Plath,
     Burroughs).

Chapter 3 Truth and impurity
1   Robert Bridges, Oh Youth Whose Hope is High (1890), 'Poetical Works'
     (London, 1936), p. 280.
2   There is certainly a link between the arguments made in this chapter and
     Lionel Trilling's thesis, in 'Sincerity and Authenticity' (Oxford, 1972),
     that in the late nineteenth century there was a movement away from the
     notion of sincere, honest, 'open' workmanlike relationships towards the
     exigent idea of personal 'authenticity'. 'Authenticity' takes very little
     account of communicating with the other. It is an introverted ideology and,
     as such, the move from sincerity to authenticity is consonant with the
     movement away from a fully integrated public life, documented in Richard
     Sennett's brilliant study, 'The Fall of Public Man' (Cambridge, 1976). A
     fascinating critique of this movement towards authenticity is Theodor
     Adorno's book, 'The Jargon of Authenticity' (1964), trans. from the Ger-
     man by K. Tarnowski and F. Will (London, 1973).
3   J. S. Mill, 'Letters' ed and introd. Hugh S. R. Elliot, with a note on Mill's
     private life by Mary Taylor, 2 vols, (London, 1910), vol. 1, p. 92. The
     operation of the metaphor of the (lonely) epistemological journey is quite
     clear in this further extract (vol. 1, p. 98):
        But I, too, have what for a considerable time was quite suspended
        in me, the feeling of growth. I feel myself made more *knowing*,
        more *seeing*, having a far greater experience of *realities*, not
        abstractions, than ever before.... One feels more and more that
        one is drifting so far out of the course of other men's navigation
        as to be altogether below their horizon; not only they will not go
        with us, but they cannot see whither we are steering.... However,
        this must be, and may be borne with, borne with when one's own
        path is clear - and mine is always becoming clearer.
4   J. McKechnie, 'Meredith's Allegory, "The Shaving of Shagpat"' (London,
     1910), p. 28.
5   G. Meredith, 'The Shaving of Shagpat', p. 301.
6   Ibid., p. 163.
7   W. Thackeray, 'Pendennis' (published serially, 1848-50), ed G. Saints-
     bury, Oxford, 1912, p. 801.
8   G. Eliot, 'Letters', ed G. S. Haight, (London, 1954-56), vol. 1, p. 125.
9   T. Carlyle, Life in London, 'Critical and Miscellaneous Essays' (London,
     1838), vol. II, pp. 16-17.
10   W. Iser, Indeterminacy and the Reader's Response, in 'Aspects of Nar-
     rative: Selected Papers from the English Institute', ed with a foreword
     by J. Hillis Miller (New York and London, 1971), pp. 1-46, pp. 30-1.
11   In his sonnet Internal Harmony, Meredith associates inner unity and self-
     control with the assurance that one is valued and has 'station' within
     society. The sonnet is itself contradictory, because its willed assertion
     that the poetic voice has remained harmonious despite social rejection is

at odds with the poet's remark that 'my place is here or there,' - the free substitution of these shifters (it doesn't matter which) gives an insubstantiality to the location of the poetic 'I'. See also the two sonnets, The discipline of Wisdom and The Garden of Epicurus, in which the domain of rational thought 'fenced from passion and mishap' appears as a prelapsarian ideal degraded in a fallen world.

12 G. Meredith, The Spirit of Shakespeare, p. 184.
13 G. Meredith, The World's Advance, and My Theme, pp. 186; 189.
14 G. Meredith, The State of Age, p. 186.
15 G. Meredith, Sense and Spirit, p. 182.
16 G. Meredith, A Later Alexandrian, p. 187.
17 Milly's lies almost all relate to the concealment of her illness - at first by the outright denial that she is ill at all, and later by a stoical concealment of her pain. Kate is right when she says to Densher that Milly 'never wanted the truth - she wanted *you*.'
18 F. Nietzsche, 'Werke' (Leipzig, 1899-1912), vol. XIV, p. 45; vol. X, pp. 171, 194. See also n. 37.
19 Oscar Wilde, The Decay of Lying was published in the 'Nineteenth Century' in January 1889, and subsequently published in book form in 1891.
20 J. Conrad, 'Heart of Darkness', p. 82.
21 Ibid., p. 161.
22 J. Conrad, 'The Nigger of the "Narcissus" ', p. 138.
23 G. Meredith, The Discipline of Wisdom, p. 185.
24 Mrs E. L. Linton, Our Illusions, 'Fortnightly Review', 49 (1891), pp. 584-97, p. 594.
25 H. James, Guy de Maupassant, 'Fortnightly Review', 43 (1888), pp. 364-86, p. 365.
26 R. B. Cunninghame Graham, 'Thirty Tales and Sketches', selected and introd. Edward Garnett (London, 1929), Introduction, pp. viii-ix.
27 F. Marion Crawford, 'Marzio's Crucifix', 2 vols (London, 1887), reprinted in 1 vol. (London, 1888), p. 1.
28 W. H. Mallock, 'The Veil of the Temple' (London, 1904), p. 46.
29 J. Galsworthy, 'The Island Pharisees' (London, 1904), p. 57.
30 J. Conrad, 'Notes on Life and Letters', p. 134.
31 J. Lester, 'Journey Through Despair 1880-1914: Transformations in British Literary Culture' (Princeton, 1968), p. 21.
32 H. James, The Tree of Knowledge (1900), 'The Complete Tales', vol. 11, pp. 93-100.
33 'In some deep zone within, an act of unfaithfulness may be an alliance' (my translation). Robert Musil, 'Tagebücher, Aphorismen, Essays und Reden' (Hamburg, 1955), p. 131.
34 R. L. Stevenson, The Story of a Lie in 'Tales and Fantasies' (printed in 1882 but not distributed until much later owing to a disputed copyright).
35 F. Paulhan, 'Le Mensonge de l'art' (Paris, 1907), p. 1.
36 The idea that social life as such was structured like a lie, and that lying was not merely a matter of individual moral turpitude, became very common on the Continent in the latter half of the nineteenth century. Not only Ibsen but Strindberg too, constantly spoke of language as something intended to conceal, not reveal, man's thoughts. Strindberg spoke of society as a 'tapestry of lies' ('Samlade skrifter' vol. 5, p. 19). He read Nordau with enthusiasm and was fond of quoting Talleyrand's 'apercu': 'La parole a été donnée à l'homme pour déguiser sa pensée.' He even came to believe that it is only when the child learns to lie that he is ready to enter adult life ('Samlade skrifter', vol. 45, p. 246). The key work however is surely Nietzsche's 'Über Wahrheit und Lüge im aussermoralischen Sinne' (1873), an essay in which he deliberately 'de-constructs' the moral and personal understanding of lying and replaces it within a universal philosophical framework.
37 Lee M. Whitehead, The Active Voice and the Passive Eye: 'Heart of Darkness' and Nietzsche's 'The Birth of Tragedy', 'Conradiana', vol. VII, no. 2 (1975), pp. 121-36; E. Said, Conrad and Nietzsche, in 'Joseph Conrad:

A Commemoration', ed N. Sherry (London, 1976), pp. 65-76. The influence of Ibsen on Henry James is explored by M. Egan, 'Henry James: The Ibsen Years' (London, 1972), but Egan pays scant attention to the important issue of lies and 'social' falsehoods.

38   V. Lee, 'Vital Lies: Studies of Some Varieties of Recent Obscurantism', 2 vols (London, 1912), vol. 1, p. vii.
39   J. Conrad, 'Lord Jim', p. 306.
40   H. Ibsen, 'The Wild Duck' (1884), Act V. A slightly different translation is given by J. W. McFarlane (Oxford, 1971), p. 204, but it does not affect the argument here.
41   J. Conrad, An Outpost of Progress, pp. 105-6.
42   Ibid., p. 89.
43   J. Conrad, The Return, p. 134.
44   G. Meredith, 'The Egoist', p. 35.
45   M. Proust, 'Remembrance of Things Past', trans. C. K. Scott-Moncrieff (London, 1944), vol. 11, The Sweet Cheat Gone, p. 266.
46   H. James, 'The Golden Bowl', p. 468.
47   Ibid., p. 585.
48   J. Wilt, 'The Readable People of George Meredith' (Princeton, 1975).
49   J. Conrad, 'Victory', p. 222.
50   Ibid., p. 167.
51   H. James, 'The Golden Bowl', p. 396.
52   H. James, 'The Sacred Fount', p. 45.
53   J. Conrad, 'Lord Jim', p. 93.

Chapter 4 *'Godiva to the gossips': Meredith and the language of shame*

1   This is the Shorter Oxford Dictionary definition: for an excellent detailed study of the problems caused to character development see E. Goffman, 'Stigma: Notes on the Management of a Spoiled Identity' (Harmondsworth, 1973).
2   'Sandra Belloni', ch. XXXVII, p. 392.
3   C. Ricks, 'Keats and Embarrassment' (Oxford, 1974). By a compounding irony which links Meredith's shame to Keats's embarrassment, William Michael Rossetti said that he saw signs in Meredith's Love in a Valley, of a 'cut-price Keats'.
4   J.-P. Sartre, 'Critique de la Raison Dialectique' (Paris, 1960), pp. 90-1.
5   The precise facts of the affair are not well known, and it is the relation of public knowledge to the affair which is precisely in question. See D. Johnson, 'Lesser Lives' (London, 1973), pp. 104-31. See also D. Williams, 'George Meredith, His Life and Lost Love' (London, 1977), pp. 54-5.
6   'Letters of George Meredith', ed C. L. Cline, 3 vols (Oxford, 1970), vol. 1, pp. 31-43.
7   Ibid., p. 42.
8   D. Williams, op. cit., pp. 41-2.
9   Ibid., p. 1.
10   C. Berg, 'The Unconscious Significance of Hair' (London, 1951); E. Leach, Magical Hair, 'Journal of the Royal Anthropological Institute', vol. 88, no. 2, (1958), pp. 147-64; S. Sassoon, 'Meredith', (London, 1948), p. 19.
11   'The Shaving of Shagpat', Conclusion, p. 301.
12   D. Williams, op. cit., p. 2.
13   'Evan Harrington', ch. XXI, p. 277.
14   Ibid., ch. XXIII, p. 290.
15   Ibid., ch. XXVII, p. 345.
16   Ibid., ch. XLIII, p. 531.
17   L. Trilling, 'Sincerity and Authenticity' (Oxford, 1972), pp. 141-2.
18   G. Beer, 'Meredith: A change of Masks' (London, 1970), p. 70.
19   Viscountess Milner (Talks with George Meredith, 'National Review', CXXXI (1948), pp. 454-6) gives an account of Meredith's description of 'The Knight-errant of the Nineteenth Century' as it was told to H. G. Wells in 1904 and part of her description is worth quoting at length:

For a while, & for long after the First of heroes had performed his
main and most unsavoury task there clung to him such pervasions
of the Augean reek as knocked down men more emphatically than
the trained fist of their champion; ladies, on a visit of admiration,
fell swooning within a league; kings of the countries he traversed,
despatched messengers entreating him to hurry onward his feet; &
it was with a roar of melancholy laughter that this glory and this
pest of men betook himself to his repeated plunge-bath, & submitted
to the pouring on of ointments, unguents, essences, fine scents,
hateful to his manly nostrils;.... Nevertheless, for the sake of
living among his fellows, also, one surmises, in compassion for his
legitimate wife, who tottered in his presence, he went through the
processes of purification.

A champion with body odour is a marvellous burlesque symbol of the hero
struggling against humiliation, pursued by his own stench. But beyond
its energetic amusement the episode brings out yet again the Meredithian
preoccupation with 'covering up' the shameful in a context of heroic endeavour.

20 'Double-bind' is a term used by Gregory Bateson to describe a case in
     which someone is confronted with a dual set of rules, both sets of which
     he must obey, but which are mutually exclusive – hence, whatever he does,
     he will be in the wrong.
21 Napoleon, 'Poems', IV, p. 480.
22 J. Wilt, 'The Readable People of George Meredith' (Princeton, 1975), p. 218.
23 'The Amazing Marriage', ch. XXXIII, p. 345.
24 'Sandra Belloni', ch. XXXVIII, p. 420.
25 'One of Our Conquerors', ch. XX, p. 226.
26 'Lord Ormont and his Aminta', ch. XXV, p. 293.
27 The Empty Purse, 'Poems', p. 443.
28 Modern Love, 'Poems', stanza XXII, p. 142.
29 G. Deer, op. cit., p. 176.
30 'Evan Harrington', ch. XXXVIII, p. 481.
31 S. Freud, 'Standard Edition', trans. J. Strachey (London, 1953-66), vol.
     XIX, p. 162.
32 J. Calder, 'Women and Marriage in Victorian Fiction' (London, 1976). She
     writes: 'Meredith was always in danger of losing the sharpness of his com-
     ment in sheer density of language, as he tends to do in "One of Our Con-
     querors" (1891), or in idiosyncrasies of plot, and sometimes momentarily
     in both' (p. 192). But I hope it is clear from what has been said so far
     that it is impossible to dissociate the formal difficulties of Meredith's work
     from the 'feminist' content. The two are deeply interrelated on the basis
     of an afflicted subjectivity which identifies itself as feminine and self-
     concealing. See also E. Sönmez, 'The Novelist George Meredith: Woman's
     Champion' (Hacettepe, 1972).
33 'One of Our Conquerors', ch. XI, p. 120.
34 'Emilia in England' ('Sandra Belloni'), ch. XXXVIII, p. 419.
35 P. Aulagnier-Spairani, La Féminité, in 'Le désir et la perversion', ed J.
     Lacan (Paris, 1966), pp. 53-89, p. 65. My translation.
36 'The Egoist', ch. XI, p. 131.
37 A. Welsh, The Allegory of Truth in English Fiction, 'Victorian Studies',
     vol. IX, no. 1, (September 1965), pp. 7-27, p. 24.
38 M. Proust, 'Remembrance of Things Past', trans. C. K. Scott-Moncrieff
     (London, 1944), vol. 9, The Captive, p. 237.
39 'Diana of the Crossways', ch. XII, p. 134.
40 Ibid., ch. XIV, p. 148.
41 'Lord Ormont and his Aminta', ch. XXIV, pp. 285-6.
42 'The Amazing Marriage', ch. XXVIII, pp. 295-6.
43 Ibid., p. 288.
44 Ibid., ch. XIII, pp. 132-3.
45 J. Wilt, op. cit., pp. 210-40.
46 'The Amazing Marriage', ch. III, p. 32.

47   Ibid.
48   Ibid.
49   'Lord Ormont and his Aminta', ch. XXIV, p. 286.
50   Meredith went to the Moravian School at Neuwied (on the Rhine, near
     Cologne) in August 1842, and remained for almost two years, without
     returning for holidays. The school and the Rhineland subsequently became
     positive and important memories for him.
51   'Lord Ormont and his Aminta', ch. XXX, p. 347.
52   F. Nietzsche, 'Beyond Good and Evil' (1886), trans. Marianne Cowan
     (Chicago, 1955), pp. 46–7.
53   D. Howard, George Meredith: Delicate and Epical Fiction, in 'Literature
     and Politics in the Nineteenth Century', ed J. Lucas (London, 1971), pp. 131–
     72, pp. 135, 160.
54   E. Goffman, 'Stigma: Notes on the Management of a Spoiled Identity',
     op. cit.; and Embarrassment and Social Organization, 'American Journal
     of Sociology', vol. LXII (1956), pp. 264–75.
55   'The Amazing Marriage', ch. I, p. 7.
56   'The Egoist', ch. XLVI, p. 574.
57   T. Carlyle, 'Sartor Resartus' (1833–4); reprinted (London, 1967), p. 54.
58   Ortega y Gasset, 'The Dehumanization of Art' (New York, 1956), p. 31.
59   'One of Our Conquerors', ch. XVII, p. 179.
60   The Problem of Enigma in Narrative Structure (forthcoming, in 'Poetics
     and Theory of Literature').
61   'Lord Ormont and his Aminta', ch. XXX, p. 351.
62   'The Amazing Marriage', ch. IX, pp. 97–8.
63   G. Beer, 'One of Our Conquerors': Language and Music, in 'Meredith Now',
     ed I. Fletcher (London, 1971), pp. 265–80, p. 266.
64   H. M. Lynd, 'On Shame and the Search for Identity' (London, 1958), p. 64.
65   'Schizoid' is not to be confused with clinical schizophrenia. See R. D. Laing,
     'The Divided Self' (London, 1959), pp. 78–93: W. Ronald D. Fairbairn,
     'Psychoanalytic Studies of the Personality' (London, 1952), pp. 3–27.
66   D. Holbrook, Lawrence Revalued, 'Books and Issues', vol I, no. 1 (1979),
     p. 7.
67   'The Adventures of Harry Richmond', ch. XVI, p. 197.
68   'One of Our Conquerors', ch. XVII, p. 183.
69   Ibid., ch. XLI, p. 495.
70   Of course, guilt is not identical with shame, but it seems nevertheless a
     deliberate pun, for Meredith gives us a generous clue (ibid., ch. XLI,
     p. 491): "'Strange, touching, terrible, if really the silly gilt figure sym-
     bolized! ...", thinks Victor, forcing it out of mind.'

Chapter 5 Conrad and the rhetoric of enigma
1   The best study is E. Said's excellent essay on 'Nostromo' in his book
     'Beginnings' (New York, 1975); but also see J. McLauchlan, 'Conrad:
     Nostromo', Studies in English Literature, 40 (London, 1969), for a further
     discussion of the chronological complexity of the narrative.
2   M. C. Bradbrook, 'Joseph Conrad: Poland's English Genius' (Cambridge,
     1941), p. 77.
3   J. Conrad, 'A Personal Record', A Familiar Preface, p. xxi.
4   For an excellent and exhaustive study of the symbolism of darkness in
     Conrad, see R. Roussel, 'The Metaphysics of Darkness: A Study in the
     Unity and Development of Conrad's Fiction' (Baltimore, 1971).
5   The Planter of Malata, 'Within The Tides', p. 79.
6   F. R. Leavis, 'The Great Tradition' (1948), reprinted (Harmondsworth,
     1972), p. 207.
7   Ibid., p. 204.
8   In 'Victory' for example. See R. Secor, 'The Rhetoric of Shifting Perspec-
     tives: Conrad's "Victory" ' (Pennsylvania, 1971), p. 3.
9   D. Thorburn, 'Conrad's Romanticism' (New Haven and London, 1974),
     p. 117.
10   J. Hawthorn, 'Joseph Conrad: Language and Fictional Self-Consciousness'
     (London, 1979), p. 31.

11   Conrad in a letter to E. Garnett (23 March 1896), 'Letters from Conrad, 1895-1924', ed Edward Garnett (London, undated, 1928?), p. 23.
12   'Lord Jim', chapter 20, p. 216.
13   Letter to R. B. Cunninghame Graham (5 August 1897), in 'Joseph Conrad: Life and Letters', ed G. Jean-Aubry (London, 1927), 2 vols, I, p. 208.
14   J. Conrad, Guy de Maupassant, 'Notes on Life and Letters', p. 27.
15   'Under Western Eyes', Part Second, chapter 1, p. 104.
16   The Planter of Malata, 'Within the Tides', p. 86.
17   W. Benjamin, 'Illuminations', ed and introd. H. Arendt, trans. H. Zohn (London, 1973). See The Work of Art in the Age of Mechanical Reproduction, pp. 222-5, and On Some Motifs in Baudelaire, p. 190.
18   W. Benjamin, op. cit., p. 245.
19   'Heart of Darkness', p. 100.
20   Ibid., p. 127.
21   'Victory', Part Four, chapter 8, p. 350.
22   'Heart of Darkness', p. 48.
23   G. Meredith, 'Poems', The Empty Purse, p. 454.
24   W. Benjamin, op. cit., p. 190.
25   'Heart of Darkness', p. 45.
26   Ibid.
27   Jules Vallès, L'enfant, 'Oeuvres' (Paris, 1950), vol. I, p. 238.
28   'Heart of Darkness', p. 45.
29   'Inter-textuality' is a term used to describe the network of texts, literary and otherwise, which inform a given work. It is not the same as allusion or 'echo-hearing', in that the discourses are transformed within the work and are often not direct quotations, but adaptations of the codes and languages available in the culture and its traditions.
30   E. J. Charpier and P. Seghers, 'L'Art poétique' (Paris, 1957), Salon de 1867, p. 182.
31   Ian Watt, Impressionism and Symbolism in 'Heart of Darkness', in 'Joseph Conrad: A Commemoration', ed N. Sherry (London, 1976), pp. 37-53.
32   Conrad was initially derisive about Impressionist painting, but Eloise Knapp Hay (Impressionism Limited, in ibid., pp. 54-64) shows that, perhaps through the influence of Brunetière, Conrad does adopt certain Impressionist ideas later in his career, when he 'began to aim for the same effects that he had earlier questioned.'
33   I. Watt, op. cit., p. 39.
34   'Heart of Darkness', p. 46.
35   Ibid., p. 47.
36   W. Benjamin, op. cit., p. 190.
37   'Heart of Darkness', p. 81.
38   W. Benjamin, op. cit., p. 190.
39   'Heart of Darkness', p. 129.
40   'Heart of Darkness', p. 52.
41   G. Bachelard, 'La Poétique de l'espace' (Paris, 1974), p. 170.
42   'Heart of Darkness', p. 105.
43   This does not apply to 'Nostromo' or 'The Secret Agent', where the women in the case are individualized more successfully than in the early work. The connection between 'wild, feral women' and this kind of cultivated mystery is quite evident in the novels and stories, from 'Almayer's Folly' through to 'The Arrow of Gold'.
44   I have looked at 112 'different' interpretations of 'Heart of Darkness', and they are indeed distinct in terms of tone, perspective and valuation, but strong patterns of interpretation soon become apparent. My analysis here is based upon the way that the interpretations cluster round each of the textual features (which are associative 'chains' in the story) designated as 'enigma', and the interpreter then tries to resolve the story along the line of that chain. 'Complex' interpretations may even try to account for a superimposition of two different symbolic domains as in Cedric Watts's recent book, 'Conrad's "Heart of Darkness": A Critical and Contextual Discussion' (Milan, 1977). My analysis takes as its starting point the interpretative

plurality of the text; that at a strictly hermeneutic level, many of the interpretations are interchangeable. What is chiefly interesting is the medium of exchange, which I take to be 'enigma', since it is this which mediates the different interpretative fields.

45   L. Feder, Marlow's Descent into Hell, 'Nineteenth-Century Fiction', 9 (1955), pp. 280-92; R. O. Evans, Conrad's Underworld, 'Modern Fiction Studies', 2 (1956), pp. 56-62.

46   A. Jolles, 'Einfache Formen' (1930), trans. into French as 'Formes Simples' by A. M. Buguet (Paris, 1972), pp. 105-6.

47   See W. Iser, 'The Implied Reader' (Baltimore, 1974).

48   'The Arrow of Gold', Author's Note, ix.

49   'Heart of Darkness', p. 151.

50   The concept of a 'transcendental signified', developed by Roland Barthes in the 1960s, is that the sign is often believed to have some designated entity within it which is both the origin and end of language as such, something which is 'transcendent' of language. 'God' is the obvious example, but any term which refers to such a semiotic entity (Heidegger's 'Dasein' would be another example) is called by Barthes a transcendental signified.

51   For the phenotext/genotext distinction, see 'Théorie d'ensemble', ed P. Sollers (Paris, 1968), p. 308. The genotext is the (infinite?) interpretative field of the text, and would, I think, correspond to 'hermeneutic potential'. The phenotext is any specifically constituted interpretation.

52   'Heart of Darkness', p. 162.

53   W. B. Stein, Buddhism and 'Heart of Darkness', 'Western Humanities Review', 9 (1957), pp. 281-5; see n. 45 above.

54   Letter from Conrad (24 April 1922), 'Conrad to a Friend', ed R. Curle (London, 1928), p. 142.

55   J. Bayley, 'The Romantic Survival' (London, 1957), p. 72.

56   The Shadow-Line, p. 23.

57   'Life and Letters', op. cit., vol. II, pp. 83-4. Conrad's remark recalls the mystical incompletion evoked by George Moore in 'Conversations in Ebury Street' (1924), edn used (London, 1930), p. 145: 'The beginning and end of things are hidden from us. We know only that everything is being re-formed, reshapen, but never wholly remade.'

58   'Heart of Darkness', p. 93.

59   'Lord Jim', ch. 21, p. 225.

60   'A Personal Record', p. 35.

61   'Within The Tides', Author's Note, p. x.

62   J. Lacan, 'Le Discours de Rome', trans. A. Wilden in 'The Language of the Self' (Baltimore, 1968), p. 21.

63   'Lord Jim', chapter 33, p. 313.

64   J. Hawthorn, op. cit., p. 7.

65   Ideology: see n. 25, chapter 1.

66   Kurtz seems to me like an attempt to regenerate a mythical concept of evil in a secular world. 'La vraie civilisation', wrote Baudelaire, 'n'est pas dans le gaz, ni dans la vapeur, ni dans les tables tournantes. Elle est dans la diminution des traces du péché originel.' Kurtz is precisely the embodiment of 'péché originel' in a civilized world which denies such things.

67   F. Kermode, 'The Genesis of Secrecy' (Cambridge, Mass., 1979), p. 45.

68   Russell's paradox, simply stated, is the question: 'Is the class of all classes a class of itself?' In terms of interpretation we may ask: 'Is the reading of all readings a reading of itself?' That is, an attempt to account for all the interpretations of a text is itself an interpretation, and logically this series (n+1 + (n+1) + ...) can never be closed.

69   'Heart of Darkness', p. 51.

70   See J. A. Arnold, The Young Russian's Book in Conrad's 'Heart of Darkness', 'Conradiana', vol. VIII, no. 2 (1976), pp. 121-6.

71   'Gefühlter Eindruckspunkt': a felt, central point of impression (my translation) in a text. The notion is Dilthey's, who takes it as the intuitive starting-point for interpretation as a way out of the hermeneutic circle. It is quoted by Kermode in 'The Genesis of Secrecy' (op. cit., p. 147) who

rejects its usefulness as an interpretative device whilst wishing to conserve its value as an interpretative fiction.

72 'Heart of Darkness', pp. 160-1.
73 The Return, 'Tales of Unrest', p. 176.
74 'A Personal Record', p. 18.

Chapter 6 'The deterrent fact': vulgarity and obscurity in James
1 S. Chatman, 'The Later Style of Henry James' (Oxford, 1972); T. Laitinen, Aspects of Henry James's Style, 'Annales Acad. Scientiarum Fennicae'. 'Dissertationes Humanarum Litterarum', 4 (Helsinki, 1975); R. Ohmann, Generative Grammars and the Concept of Literary Style, 'Word', 20 (1964), pp. 423-39. See also the work on ambiguity in James in nn.2-7, below.
2 S. Rimmon, 'The Concept of Ambiguity - The Example of James' (Chicago and London, 1977).
3 Wayne Booth, 'The Rhetoric of Fiction' (Chicago, 1961), p. 361.
4 C. T. Samuels, 'The Ambiguity of Henry James' (Urbana, Illinois, 1971), p. 5.
5 J. F. Blackall, 'Jamesian Ambiguity and "The Sacred Fount" ' (New York, 1965), p. 36.
6 C. T. Samuels, op. cit., p. 4.
7 E. Wilson, The Ambiguity of Henry James, 'Hound and Horn', VII (1934), pp. 385-406.
8 See chapter 1, pp. 25-6.
9 T. Todorov, Le Secret du récit, in 'Poétique de la prose' (Paris, 1971), pp. 151-85; C. Brooke-Rose, The Squirm of the True, 'Poetics and Theory of Literature', 1 (1976), pp. 513-46, p. 513.
10 (i) 'The Golden Bowl', II, 41, p. 591; (ii) 'The Golden Bowl', II, 41, p. 591; (iii) 'The Sacred Fount', p. 127; (iv) 'The Wings of the Dove', VI, 3, p. 272; (v) 'The Sacred Fount', p. 21; (vi) 'The Sacred Fount', p. 139.
11 S. Spender, 'The Destructive Element' (London, 1935), p. 39.
12 S. Kappeler, Writing and Reading in Some Works by Henry James (unpublished dissertation, University of Cambridge, 1977), p. 69.
13 The 'actant' is the underlying role and structural location of an acting subject in a narrative. In James, the observer is such an actant, and various actors or characters are the surface particularization of the actantial position. See A. J. Greimas, 'Sémantique structurale' (Paris, 1966), pp. 172-89.
14 M. Geismar, 'Henry James and his Cult' (London, 1964), p. 6.
15 The Art of Fiction, 'Partial Portraits' (London, 1888), p. 8.
16 H. James, On Some Pictures Lately Exhibited (1875), reprinted in 'The Painter's Eye: Notes and Essays on the Pictorial Arts', ed J. L. Sweeney (London, 1956), p. 89.
17 S. Ullmann, 'Semantics' (1951), 2nd edn (Glasgow, 1959), p. 122.
18 'The Sacred Fount', p. 44.
19 H. James, Gabriele D'Annunzio (1904), reprinted in 'Notes on Novelists' (New York, 1914), pp. 292-3.
20 Ibid., p. 292.
21 Ibid., pp. 292-3.
22 R. Ohmann, op. cit., pp. 436, 437.
23 The opening sentence of James's tale The Bench of Desolation, which Ohmann takes as his example.
24 Edmund Wilson notes that perhaps the most striking use of ellipsis in James is his early story Rose-Agathe (1878), in which a man falls in love with a hairdresser's dummy and eventually purchases it and takes it home to live with him. The dummy is cut off at the waist.
25 The 'scene of seduction' is defined as a real or phantasied scene in which the subject, generally a child, submits passively to the advances or sexual manipulations of another person. Although Freud subsequently abandoned the theory, its relevance for James (particularly in 'What Maisie Knew' and The Turn of the Screw) is fairly evident.
26 P. Macherey, 'A Theory of Literary Production', trans. Geoffrey Wall (London, 1978), pp. 96-7.

27   T. Todorov, op. cit., p. 160: 'la vérité elle-même, bien qu'elle provoque
le mouvement tout entier, restera absente.'

28   R. B. Yeazell, 'Language and Knowledge in the Late Novels of Henry
James' (Chicago, 1976), p. 20.

29   F. R. Leavis, 'The Great Tradition' (1948), republished (Harmondsworth,
1972). Of the late James, Leavis remarks (p. 192), 'That there really was
incapacity, essential loss of power, that something had gone wrong in his
life....'

30   'The Europeans', pp. 132-3.

31   'The Princess Casamassima', II, 19, p. 264.

32   See particularly ch. XVIII of 'Evan Harrington', In Which Evan Calls himself Gentleman.

33   'The Princess Casamassima', Preface, p. xxx.

34   Ibid., II, 21, p. 293.

35   'James treats the energetic projects of revolutionaries and social reformers
with the distrust he reserves for all forms of direct pursuit.' - Leo Bersani's remark here seems directly confirmative of the notion, examined in
this chapter, of James's fear of both confrontation and 'forwardness' at
both the general social level and between individuals. L. Bersani, 'A Future for Astyanax' (Toronto, 1976), ch. 5, The Jamesian Lie, p. 139.

36   A clear index of James's inability to understand the political nature of the
British class structure is the Princess's sojourn in Madeira Crescent. A
less likely home of anarchistic ferment is unimaginable, and it really seems
that James shared his Princess's blindness to class distinction below the
level of the 'haute-bourgeoisie'.

37   I agree with Edmund Wilson that there is really only one 'charged and convincing scene' which amounts to a substantial encounter between a man
and a woman - that between Nick Dormer and Julia Dallow in 'The Tragic
Muse'.

38   L. Edel, 'Henry James, A Biography', 5 vols (London, 1953-72), vol. 4,
pp. 77-130.

39   'The Ambassadors', IV, 1, p. 143.

40   E. Wilson, op. cit., p. 394.

41   L. Edel, Introduction, 'The Sacred Fount', p. 7.

42   Quoted by Wilson, op. cit., p. 123; and Edel, Introduction, 'The Sacred
Fount', p. 5.

43   Quoted by Edel, Introduction, 'The Sacred Fount', p. 7.

44   'The Sacred Fount', p. 57.

45   The degree of 'fit' between the story and Freud's account of artistic sublimation in 'Leonardo da Vinci and a Memory of his Childhood' (1910), is
striking, and connects with the idea of the 'scene of seduction' in James
in the degree to which James makes 'the sublime' the almost transparent
form of his own sublimation.

46   See S. Kappeler, op. cit., p. 48.

47   In Conrad the isolation concomitant upon obscurity is experienced as an
existential loneliness, but in James it finds social expression and justification as 'discretion'.

48   'The Sacred Fount', p. 127.

49   Ibid., p. 184.

50   It is similar to that used by Marlow, but works in the opposite direction
to that of the narrator here. Marlow is always gesturing vaguely towards
some immense enigma, whilst in James the intangible 'solution', never
quite made clear, is a further discrimination of particularity.

51   'The Sacred Fount', p. 156.

52   This is clearly similar to the creation of 'aura' in Conrad. Without pur-
suing the economic metaphor too far, there does seem to be a general
principle of textual economy involved here, which creates value through
scarcity of meaning at the same time as indicating that possession of the
meaning is desirable. A full exploration of this economy is beyond my
scope here.

53   'The Sacred Fount', p. 188.

54 Instincts are said to be sublimated in so far as they are diverted towards a new, non-sexual aim and in so far as their objects are socially valued ones. Freud, 'Standard Edition', trans. J. Strachey (London, 1953-66), vol. IX, p. 187; vol. XXI, p. 79.

55 'The Sacred Fount', p. 161.

56 These words are known as 'intangibles' or 'immeasurables'. See S. Chatman, op. cit., p. 7.

57 Ibid., pp. 7-12.

58 'The Sacred Fount', p. 77.

59 The Turn of the Screw, I, p. 89.

60 This process, which is a simultaneous abstraction and mediation of the object of desire through a formal aesthetic object, has its analogues on the lexical level (Chatman identifies abstract nouns as a key stylistic feature in the late works of James) and on the level of novel production. It is in this way that the Jamesian innocent is mediated in the writing of fiction.

61 It is interesting to note that Chillon and the Colosseum should both be connected with the imprisonment and 'containment' of Byron. It is quite possible that James is making a subtle point, in this double choice of locale, about the suppression of 'Byronic' passion, for when Winterbourne enters the Colosseum, 'he began to murmur Byron's famous lines out of *Manfred*'. (See 'Manfred', Act III, sc. 4, 37-41)

62 'The Ambassadors', XI, 3, 411.

63 Ibid., XI, 4, 426.

64 'The Sacred Fount', pp. 36-7.

65 The Story of A Masterpiece, 'The Collected Tales', I, pp. 295-6.

66 A yellowback was a cheap Victorian novel named after the usual colour of its jacket, which normally had a lurid print on the front cover.

67 See Anna Freud on abstract thought as defence, in 'The Ego and the Mechanisms of Defence' (London, 1937).

68 'The narrator of "The Sacred Fount" is', says Leon Edel, 'addicted to... the intellectualizing of every human situation; he seems to be a prey to anxieties unless he can achieve a kind of intellectual superiority and omniscience over those around him.' L. Edel, 'The Psychological Novel, 1900-1950' (New York, 1955), p. 71.

69 M. Banta, 'Henry James and the Occult', (Bloomington, 1972).

70 This seems to me a result of reading James's theoretical pronouncements as accurate accounts of his own fictional practice, and the chief error in O. Segal's 'The Lucid Reflector: the Observer in Henry James's Fiction', (New Haven, 1969).

71 'The Spoils of Poynton', XVI, p. 153.

72 Ibid., pp. 153-4.

73 A Landscape Painter, 'The Complete Tales', I, p. 127.

74 Ibid., p. 138.

75 The Tree of Knowledge, 'The Complete Tales', XI, pp. 108-9.

76 'The Wings of the Dove', VI, 2, p. 259.

77 Ibid., p. 260.

78 S. Freud, 'Standard Edition', op. cit., vol. III, p. 58, writes apropos of psychosis: 'There is, however, a much more energetic and successful kind of defence. Here, the ego rejects the incompatible idea together with its affect and behaves as if the idea had never occurred to the ego at all.' But the idea of foreclosure is only fully developed in Lacan. See 'The Language of Psycho-analysis', J. Laplanche and J.-B. Pontalis, trans. D. Nicholson-Smith (London, 1973), pp. 166-9.

79 'The Ambassadors', XII, 5, p. 468.

80 'The Golden Bowl', II, 41, pp. 591-2.

81 By foreclosing the possibility of expressed desire, one avoids the danger of vulgarity, hence achieving the Jamesian aim of satisfaction without overt signification.

82 M. Beebe, The Turned Back of Henry James (1954), reprinted in 'Henry James: Modern Judgements', ed Tony Tanner (London, 1969), p. 78.

83 'The Tragic Muse' ('New York Edition', 1909), preface, I, p. xxi.

84   C. Brooke-Rose, The Squirm of the True, op. cit., Part II, pp. 517-28.
85   'The Sacred Fount', p. 40.
86   'The Wings of the Dove', X, 4, p. 515.
87   Ibid., IX, 4, p. 462.
88   The Great Good Place, 'The Complete Tales', XI, p. 29.
89   C. G. Jung, 'Ulysses': Ein Monolog, 'Wirklichkeit der Seele' (Zürich, 1934) p. 148.
90   'The Wings of the Dove', preface, p. 19.

SELECT BIBLIOGRAPHY

General
Adorno, T., 'The Jargon of Authenticity' (1964), trans. K. Tarnowski and
    F. Will (London, 1973).
Altick, R. D., 'The English Common Reader' (Chicago, 1957).
Bachelard, G., 'La Poétique de L'espace' (Paris, 1974).
Balfour, A. J., 'The Foundations of Belief' (London, 1895).
Barthes, R., 'Essais critiques' (Paris, 1964).
Barthes, R., 'S/Z' (Paris, 1970).
Bayley, J., 'The Romantic Survival' (London, 1969). First published 1957.
Benjamin, W., 'Illuminations', ed Hannah Arendt, trans. Harry Zohn (London,
    1973).
Bersani, L., 'A Future for Astyanax. Character and Desire in Literature'
    (London, 1978).
Besant, W., Mrs E. L. Linton, and T. Hardy, Candour in English Fiction,
    'New Review', II (January, 1890), pp. 6-21.
Blanchot, M., 'Le Livre à venir', new edition (Paris, 1969).
Blanchot, M., 'L'Entretien infini' (Paris, 1973).
Bowie, M., 'Mallarmé and the Art of Being Difficult' (Cambridge, 1978).
Bradbury, M., and J. McFarlane (eds), 'Modernism' (Harmondsworth, 1976).
Bridges, R., 'Poetical Works' (London, 1936).
Bridgewater, P., 'Nietzsche in Anglosaxony' (Leicester, 1972).
Carlyle, T., Life in London, 'Critical and Miscellaneous Essays' (London, 1838).
Charlesworth, B., 'Dark Passages: The Decadent Consciousness in Victorian
    Literature' (New York, 1965).
Charpier, E. J., and P. Seghers, 'L'Art poétique' (Paris, 1957).
Cixous, H., L'Ecriture comme placement, 'Poétique', I (1970), pp. 35-50.
Corbet, W. J., The Increase of Insanity, 'Fortnightly Review', 59 (1896),
    pp. 431 ff.
Crocker, L., and P. A. Cormack, 'Readings in Rhetoric' (Springfield, Illinois,
    1965).
Drapes, T., Is Insanity Increasing?, 'Fortnightly Review', 60 (1896), pp.
    483-93.
Eliot, G., 'Letters', 7 vols, ed G. S. Haight (London, 1954-6).
Eliot, T. S., Baudelaire (1930), in 'Selected Essays' (London, 1969), pp.
    419-30.
Ellenberger, H. F., 'The Discovery of the Unconscious' (London, 1970).
Emerson, R. W., 'The Conduct of Life' (New York, 1883).
Fairbairn, W. R. D., 'Psychoanalytic Studies of the Personality' (London, 1952).
Forrest-Thomson, V., 'Poetic Artifice' (Manchester, 1978).
Freud, S., 'Traumdeutung', trans. James Strachey as 'The Interpretation of
    Dreams' (1953), reprinted (Harmondsworth, 1976).
Galsworthy, J., 'The Island Pharisees' (London, 1904).
Garnett, R., 'Twilight of the Gods and Other Tales' (London, 1888).
Gibson, R., 'Modern French Poets on Poetry' (Cambridge, 1961).
Gosse, E., The Tyranny of the Novel, 'National Review', XIX (April, 1892),
    pp. 163-75.
Griest, G. L., 'Mudie's Circulating Library and the Victorian Novel'
    (Bloomington, 1970).
Gunn, P., 'Vernon Lee' (Oxford, 1964).
Hagen, F. W., Ueber die Verwandtschaft des Genies mit dem Irresein,
    'Allgemeine Zeitschrift für Psychiatrie' (1877).
Hake, A. E., 'Regeneration, a reply to Max Nordau' (London, 1895).

Hayden, D. E., and E. P. Alworth (eds), 'Classics in Semantics' (London, 1965).
Hogarth, J. E., Literary Degenerates, 'Fortnightly Review', 57 (1895), pp. 586-92.
Holbrook, D., Lawrence Revalued, 'Books and Issues', vol. 1, no. 1 (1979), pp. 7-8.
Holland, V. (ed), 'The Works of Oscar Wilde' (London, 1966).
Husserl, E., 'The Paris Lectures', trans. and introd. Peter Koestenbaum (The Hague, 1970).
Iser, W., 'The Implied Reader' (Baltimore, 1974).
James, L., 'Fiction for the Working Man, 1830-50' (London, 1963).
Jolles, A., 'Einfache Formen' (1930), trans. into French as 'Formes simples' by Antoine Marie Buguet (Paris, 1972).
Jung, C. G., 'Ulysses': Ein Monolog, 'Wirklichkeit der Seele' (Zürich, 1934).
Keary, C. F., The Philosophy of Impressionism, 'Blackwood's Magazine', 163, (May 1898), pp. 630-6.
Kermode, F., 'The Genesis of Secrecy' (Cambridge, Mass., 1979).
Kesting, M., 'Vermessung des Labyrinths: Studien zur modernen Ästhetik' (Frankfurt, 1965).
Knighton, W., Suicidal Mania, the 'Contemporary Review', XXXIX (1881), pp. 81-90.
Kristeva, J., 'La Révolution du langage poétique' (Paris, 1974).
Laforgue, J., 'Ésthétique', Oeuvres complètes, ed G. Jean-Aubry (Paris, 1925-62).
Langbaum, R., 'The Mysteries of Identity: a Theme in Modern Literature' (Oxford, 1977).
Lanham, R. A., 'Style: An Anti-Textbook' (New Haven, 1974).
Laing, R. D., 'The Divided Self' (Harmondsworth, 1965).
Laplanche, J., and J.-B. Pontalis, 'The Language of Psycho-Analysis', trans. D. Nicholson-Smith (London, 1973).
Leach, E., Magical Hair, 'Journal of the Royal Anthropological Institute', vol. 88, no. 2 (1958), pp. 147-64.
Leavis, F. R., 'The Great Tradition' (London, 1948).
Lee, Vernon, (pseud. of Violet Paget), Beauty and Sanity, 'Fortnightly Review', 58 (1895), pp. 252-68.
Lee, Vernon, Deterioration of the Soul, 'Fortnightly Review', 59 (1896), pp. 928-43.
Lee, Vernon, 'Vital Lies: Studies of Some Varieties of Recent Obscurantism', 2 vols (London, 1912).
Lester, J. A., 'Journey through Despair 1880-1914' (Princeton, 1968).
Linton, Mrs Eliza L., Our Illusions, 'Fortnightly Review', 49 (1891), pp. 584-97.
Lucas, F. L., review of 'The Waste Land', 'New Statesman' (3 November 1923).
Lucie-Smith, E., 'Symbolist Art' (London, 1977).
Lynd, H. M., 'On Shame and the Search for Identity' (London, 1958).
Machen, A., 'Hieroglyphics: A Note Upon Ecstacy in Literature' (London, 1902).
Macherey, P., 'Pour une Théorie de la production littéraire' (Paris, 1970); trans. into English as 'A Theory of Literary Production', by Geoffrey Wall (London, 1978).
Manheim, L. F., 'Hidden Patterns - Studies in Psychoanalytic Literary Criticism' (London, 1966).
Mill, J. S., 'Letters', 2 vols, ed and introd. Hugh S. R. Elliot (London, 1910).
Mill, J. S., 'Mill on Bentham and Coleridge', ed and introd. F. R. Leavis (London, 1971).
Moore, G., 'Conversations in Ebury Street', new edn (London, 1930).
Moreau, G., 'La Psychologie morbide' (Paris, 1859).
Murry, J. Middleton, 'The Problem of Style' (Oxford, 1922).
Myers, F. W. H., A New Eirenicon, 'Fortnightly Review', 32 (1882), pp. 596-607.
Nietzsche, F., The Case of Wagner, Letter from Turin, May 1888, 'Fortnightly Review', 58 (1895), pp. 367-79.
Nisbet, J. F., 'The Insanity of Genius' (London, 1891).
Ohmann, R., Generative Grammars and the Concept of Literary Style, 'Word', XX (1964), pp. 436-7.

Ortega y Gasset, 'The Dehumanization of Art' (New York, 1956).
Parke, H. W., 'Greek Oracles' (London, 1967).
Pinkney, J. V., 'Tacita Tacit' (London, 1860).
Radestock, P., 'Genie und Wahnsinn' (Breslau, 1884).
Read, Sir Herbert, 'The Cult of Sincerity' (London, 1968).
Ricks, C., 'Keats and Embarrassment' (Oxford, 1974).
Ryle, G., Systematically Misleading Expressions, 'Proceedings of the Aristot-
    elian Society', XXXII (1932), pp. 139–70.
Sadleir, M., XIX Century Fiction: a Bibliographical Record' (London, 1951).
Said, E., 'Beginnings' (Baltimore, 1975).
Sarraute, N., 'The Age of Suspicion', trans. Maria Jolas (London, 1963).
Sartre, J.-P., 'Critique de la raison dialectique' (Paris, 1960).
Schilder, P., 'Wahn und Erkenntnis' (Berlin, 1918).
Sennett, R., 'The Fall of Public Man' (Cambridge, 1977).
Shils, E., 'Centre and Periphery: Essays in Macrosociology' (Chicago, 1975).
Sollers, P. (ed.), 'Théorie d'ensemble' (Paris, 1968).
Statham, H. H., The Writings of Wagner, 'Edinburgh Review', 189 (1899),
    pp. 96–118.
Steiner, G., 'After Babel' (Oxford, 1975).
Steiner, G., 'On Difficulty' (Oxford, 1978).
Stevenson, R. L., 'Tales and Fantasies' (London, 1893).
Stuart Hughes, H., 'Consciousness and Society: The Reorientation of European
    Social Thought 1890-1930' (London, 1959).
Sutherland, J. R., 'On English Prose' (Toronto, 1957).
Symonds, J. A., 'The Letters of John Aldington Symonds', 3 vols, ed H. M.
    Schueller and R. L. Peters (Detroit, 1967-9).
Symons, A., The Problem of Gérard de Nerval, 'Fortnightly Review', 63 (1898),
    pp. 81–91.
Symons, A., Stéphane Mallarmé, 'Fortnightly Review', 64 (1898), pp. 677–85.
Taylor, U., Some Aspects of Modern Art, 'Edinburgh Review', 190 (1899),
    pp. 48–69.
Thomson, J., 'The City of Dreadful Night' (London, 1874).
Tillotson, K., 'Novels of the Eighteen-Forties' (Oxford, 1954).
Todorov, T., 'Poétique de la prose' (Paris, 1971).
Trilling, L., 'Sincerity and Authenticity' (London, 1972).
Ullmann, S., 'Semantics' (1951), 2nd edn (Glasgow, 1959).
Winters, Y., 'In Defense of Reason' (1947), reprinted (London, 1960).
Yeats, W. B., The Celtic Element in Literature, 'Cosmopolis', 10 (1898),
    pp. 675–86.
Zimmern, H., Professor Lombroso's New Theory of Political Crime, 'Blackwood's
    Magazine', 149 (1891), pp. 202–11.

George Meredith
Beer, G., 'Meredith: A Change of Masks' (London, 1970).
Beer, G., 'One of Our Conquerors': Language and Music, in 'Meredith Now',
    ed I. Fletcher (London, 1971), pp. 265–80.
Booth, T. Y., 'Mastering the Event: Commitment to Fact in George Meredith's
    Fiction', Monograph Series, Utah State University, XIV, 2 (Logan, Utah,
    May, 1967).
Calder, J., 'Women and Marriage in Victorian Fiction' (London, 1976).
Cline, C. L. (ed.), 'Letters of George Meredith', 3 vols (Oxford, 1970).
Collie, M., 'George Meredith: A Bibliography' (Toronto, 1974).
Ellis, S. M., 'George Meredith: His Life and Friends in Relation to His Work'
    (New York, 1920).
Fletcher, I. (ed.), 'Meredith Now' (London, 1971).
Gretton, M. S., 'The Writing and Life of George Meredith. A Centenary Study'
    (London, 1926).
Hewett-Thayer, H. W., Ferdinand Lassalle in the Novels of Spielhagen and
    Meredith, the 'Germanic Review', XIX, 3 (1944), pp. 186–96.
Johnson, D., 'Lesser Lives, The True History of the First Mrs Meredith'
    (London, 1973).

Kelvin, N., 'A Troubled Eden: Nature and Society in the Works of George Meredith' (Stanford, 1961).
Kruppa, J. E., Meredith's Late Novels: Suggestions for a Critical Approach, 'Nineteenth-Century Fiction', XIX (1964), pp. 271-86.
Lee, Vernon, (pseud. of Violet Paget), The Handling of Words: Meredith, Henry James, 'English Review', 5 (June 1910), pp. 427-34.
McKechnie, J., 'Meredith's Allegory, the Shaving of Shagpat' (London, 1910).
Meredith, G., 'Poems', ed G. M. Trevelyan, after the 'Memorial Edition', with corrections (London, 1912).
Meredith, G., 'Works, Standard Edition', 16 vols (London, 1914-19).
Milner, Viscountess, Talks with George Meredith, 'National Review', CXXXI (1948), pp. 454-6.
Priestley, J. B., 'George Meredith' (London, 1926).
Robinson, A. E., Meredith's Literary Theory and Science: Realism Versus the Comic Spirit, 'PMLA', LIII, 3 (1938), pp. 857-68.
Sassoon, S., 'Meredith' (London, 1948).
Sönmez, E., 'The Novelist George Meredith: Woman's Champion' (Hacettepe, 1972).
Stevenson, L., 'The Ordeal of George Meredith: A Biography' (New York, 1953).
Stone, D. D., 'Novelists in a Changing World: Meredith, James and the Transformation of English Fiction in the 1880s' (Cambridge, Mass., 1972).
Sturges, I. M., George Meredith: A Study in Theory and Practice, unpublished dissertation (University of Utah, 1960).
Williams, D., 'George Meredith: His Life and Lost Love' (London, 1977).
Williams, I. (ed.), 'Meredith: The Critical Heritage' (London, 1971).
Wilt, J., 'The Readable People of George Meredith' (Princeton, 1975).
Wright, W. F., 'Art and Substance in George Meredith: A Study in Narrative', (Nebraska, 1953).

Joseph Conrad
Arnold, J. A., The Young Russian's Book in Conrad's 'Heart of Darkness', 'Conradiana', VIII, 2 (1976), pp. 121-6.
Baines, J., 'Joseph Conrad' (London, 1960).
Bender, T. K., Conrad and Literary Impressionism, 'Conradiana', X, 3 (1978), pp. 211-24.
Birdseye, L. E., The Curse of Consciousness: A Study of Conrad's The Return, 'Conradiana', IX, 2 (1977), pp. 171-8.
Bradbrook, M. C., 'Joseph Conrad: Poland's English Genius' (Cambridge, 1941).
Conrad, J., 'Works', 'The Dent Uniform Edition', 22 vols (London, 1923-8).
Coy, J. J., Oscuridad y Subconsciente en Joseph Conrad, 'Critica Literaria Actual: Metodo y Sistema' (Madrid, 1966), pp, 302-25.
Curle, R., 'Conrad to a Friend: 150 Selected Letters from Joseph Conrad to Richard Curle' (New York, 1928).
Emmett, V. J., Jr, Carlyle, Conrad, and the Politics of Charisma: Another Perspective on 'Heart of Darkness', 'Conradiana', VII, 2 (1975), pp. 145-54.
Forster, E. M., Joseph Conrad: A Note, in 'Abinger Harvest' (1936), reprinted (Harmondsworth, 1974).
Galsworthy, J., Joseph Conrad: A Disquisition, 'Fortnightly Review', 83 (1908), pp. 627-33.
Glassman, P. J., 'Language and Being: Joseph Conrad and the Literature of Personality' (New York and London, 1976).
Gose, E. B., Jr, 'Cruel Devourer of the World's Light': 'The Secret Agent', 'Nineteenth-Century Fiction', XV (1960), pp. 39-52.
Guerard, A., 'Conrad the Novelist' (Cambridge, Mass., 1958).
Guetti, J., 'The Limits of Metaphor: A Study of Melville, Conrad and Faulkner' (New York, 1967).
Hawthorn, J., 'Joseph Conrad: Language and Fictional Self-Consciousness' (London, 1979).
Jean-Aubry, G., 'Joseph Conrad: Life and Letters', 2 vols (New York, 1927).
Karl, F. R., 'Joseph Conrad: The Three Lives'(London, 1979).
Low, A., 'Heart of Darkness': The Search for an Occupation, 'English Literature in Transition', vol. 12, no. 1 (1969), pp. 1-9.

Martin, D. M., The Diabolic Kurtz: The Dual Nature of his Satanism in 'Heart of Darkness', 'Conradiana', VII, 2 (1975), pp. 175-7.
Najder, Z., 'Conrad's Polish Background: Letters to and from Polish Friends' (Oxford, 1964).
Nettels, E., 'James and Conrad' (Athens, 1977).
Said, E., Conrad and Nietzsche, in 'Joseph Conrad: A Commemoration', ed N. Sherry (London, 1976), pp. 65-76.
Saveson, J. E., Conrad, 'Blackwood's', and Lombroso, 'Conradiana', VI, 1 (1974), pp. 57-62.
Schleifer, R., Public and Private Narrative in 'Under Western Eyes', 'Conradiana', IX, 3 (1977), pp. 237-54.
Sherry, N., 'Conrad's Eastern World' (Cambridge, 1966).
Sherry, N., 'Conrad's Western World' (Cambridge, 1971).
Sherry, N., 'Joseph Conrad: The Critical Heritage' (London, 1973).
Sherry, N (ed.), 'Joseph Conrad: A Commemoration' (London, 1976).
Stein, W. B., Buddhism and 'Heart of Darkness', 'Western Humanities Review', II (1957), pp. 281-5.
Stephens, R. C., 'Heart of Darkness': Marlow's 'Spectral Moonshine', 'Essays in Criticism', 19 (1969), pp. 273-84.
Watts, C. T. (ed.), 'Joseph Conrad's Letters to Cunninghame Graham' (Cambridge, 1969)
Whitehead, L. M., The Active Voice and the Passive Eye: 'Heart of Darkness', and Nietzsche's 'The Birth of Tragedy', 'Conradiana', VII, 2 (1975), pp. 121-36.
Willy, T. G., The 'Shamefully Abandoned' Kurtz: A Rhetorical Context for 'Heart of Darkness', 'Conradiana', X, 2 (1978), pp. 99-112.
Yarrison, B. C., The Symbolism of Literary Allusion in 'Heart of Darkness', 'Conradiana', VII, 2 (1975), pp. 155-64.

Henry James
Anderson, Q., 'The American Henry James' (New Brunswick, 1956).
Banta, M., 'Henry James and the Occult: The Great Extension' (Ontario, 1972).
Beach, J. W., 'The Method of Henry James', revised edn (Philadelphia, 1954).
Beebe, M., The Turned Back of Henry James, 'South Atlantic Quarterly' (1954), reprinted in 'Henry James: Modern Judgements', ed Tony Tanner (London, 1969), pp. 71-88.
Blackall, J. F., 'Jamesian Ambiguity and "The Sacred Fount" ' (New York, 1965).
Blackmur, R. P. (ed.), 'The Art of the Novel: Collected Critical Prefaces of Henry James' (New York, 1934).
Bowden, E. T., 'The Themes of Henry James' (New Haven, 1956).
Brooke-Rose, C., The Squirm of the True, 'Poetics and Theory of Literature', 1 (1976), two parts, pp. 265-94, 513-46.
Chatman, S., 'The Later Style of Henry James' (Oxford, 1972).
Clair, J., 'The Ironic Dimension in the Fiction of Henry James' (Pittsburgh, 1965).
Crews, F. C., 'The Tragedy of Manners: Moral Drama in the Late Novels of Henry James' (New Haven, 1957).
Edel, L., 'Henry James: A Biography', 5 vols (London, 1953-72).
Edel, L. (ed.), 'The Complete Tales of Henry James', 12 vols (London, 1962-4).
Egan, M., 'Henry James: The Ibsen Years' (London, 1972).
Gale, R. L., 'The Caught Image: Figurative Language in the Fiction of Henry James' (Chapel Hill, 1964).
Geismar, M., 'Henry James and the Jacobites' (Boston, Mass., 1963).
Goode, J. (ed.), 'The Air of Reality: New Essays on Henry James' (London, 1972).
Grover, P., 'Henry James and the French Novel' (London, 1973).
James, Henry, 'The Bodley Head Henry James', 11 vols, ed Leon Edel (London, 1967-74).
James, Henry, 'The Complete Tales', 12 vols, ed Leon Edel (London, 1962-4).
James, Henry, 'Guy Domville' (1895), ed Leon Edel (London, 1961).

James, Henry, 'Hawthorne' (London, 1879).
James, Henry, 'The Painter's Eye, Notes and Essays on the Pictorial Arts', ed J. L. Sweeney (London, 1956).
James, Henry, 'The Reverberator' (1888), reprinted (London, 1949).
James, Henry, 'The Sacred Fount' (1901), ed L. Edel (London, 1959).
Kappeler, S., Reading and Writing in Some Novels of Henry James, unpublished dissertation (University of Cambridge, 1977).
Krook, D., 'The Ordeal of Consciousness in Henry James' (New York, 1962).
Lee, Vernon (pseud. of Violet Paget), The Handling of Words: Meredith, Henry James, 'English Review', 5 (June 1910), pp. 427-34.
Levy, L. B., 'Versions of Melodrama: A Study of the Fiction and Drama of Henry James 1865-1897' (Berkeley, 1957).
Lowery, B., 'Marcel Proust et Henry James' (Paris, 1964).
Mackenzie, M., 'Communities of Honor and Love in Henry James' (Cambridge, Mass., 1976).
Markow-Totevy, G., 'Henry James', trans. J. Cummings (London, 1969).
Matthiessen, F. O., and K. B. Murdock (eds), 'The Notebooks of Henry James' (New York, 1961).
Nettles, E., 'James and Conrad' (Athens, 1977).
Norrman, R., Techniques of Ambiguity in the Fiction of Henry James, With Special Reference to In the Cage and The Turn of the Screw, 'Acta Acad. Aboensis', A54 ii, (Abo, 1977).
Powers, L. H., 'Henry James's Major Novels' (Michigan, 1973).
Putt, S. G., 'A Reader's Guide to Henry James' (New York, 1966).
Rimmon, S., 'The Concept of Ambiguity - The Example of James' (Chicago and London, 1977).
Samuels, C. T., 'The Ambiguity of Henry James' (Urbana, 1971).
Sharp, M. S., 'The Confidante in Henry James: Evolution and Moral Value of a Fictive Character' (Notre Dame, Ind., 1963).
Stevenson, E., 'The Crooked Corridor: A Study of Henry James' (New York, 1949).
Stone, D. D., 'Novelists in a Changing World: Meredith, James, and the Transformation of English Fiction in the 1880s', (Cambridge, Mass., 1972).
Tanner, T. (ed.), 'Henry James: Modern Judgements', (London, 1969).
Ward, J. A., 'The Imagination of Disaster: Evil in the Fiction of Henry James' (Nebraska, 1961).
Wilson, E., The Ambiguity of Henry James, 'Hound and Horn' (April, 1934), reprinted in 'A Casebook on Henry James's Turn of the Screw', ed G. Willen (New York, 1959).
Wright, W. F., 'The Madness of Art: A Study of Henry James' (Nebraska, 1962).
Yeazell, R. B., 'Language and Knowledge in the Late Novels of Henry James' (Chicago, 1976).

INDEX

accomplices, 73-5
Allbut, T.C., 46, 48
Althusser, L., on 'symptomatic' reading, 4, 163n
Altick, R., 31
ambiguity, 17-18, 83, 130-2
anarchism, 41; 'The Princess Casamassima' and, 141-2
Apollinaire, G., 61
aura, 111; in 'Heart of Darkness', 111-13, 115, 116, 119

Bachelard, G., 118
Bally, C., 26
Barth, J., 103
Baudelaire, C., 45, 47, 111, 115
Bayley, J., 121, 122
Beebe, M., and the turned back in James, 160
Beer, G., 85, 90, 94, 104
Benjamin, W., and 'aura', 111-12, 113, 117
Bennett, A., 5
Berkeley, G., 15
Bianchi, A.G., 46
Blackall, J.F., 130
Blanchot, M., on 'dialogic' form, 27
Booth, W., 130
Borges, J.L., 20; 'The Mirror of Enigmas', 116
Bradbury, M., 36

Cage, J., 26
Calder, J., 91; 'Women and Marriage in Victorian Fiction', 173n
Carlyle, T., 56, 59; and heroism, 98; 'Sartor Resartus', 102
Cartesian ego, 29, 39
Cecil, H.M., 32
Chomsky, N., 14
Clark, Barrett H., 52
clowns, 37-9, 83, 89
Cocteau, J., 25
Conrad, J., 1, 61, 93; accused of obscurity, 18, 164-5n; alienation and, 40-1; civilization in, 65-6, 70; creativity, 121-2; Cunninghame-Graham and, 65, 110; Curle, letter to, 121; dual voice in, 48, 73-5;

Fascism and, 125; Galsworthy, essay on, 67; guilt and, 41; harlequins in, 37; hermeneutics and, 108-9, 113, 118-20, 123-4, 126-8; Impressionism in, 115; indefinite boundaries and, 25, 110-14; lies in, 62, 63-4, 72; mental breakdown, 39, 44; opacity and, 24; privacy, 38-9, 40, 42-3; romanticism, 1, 122, 124; secrecy in, 6, 49, 114, 116; Symbolism and, 52-3, 115, 120; unconscious and, 69-71, 124-5, 128-9; women in, 127-8
Works: 'Almayer's Folly', 71, 112; 'The Arrow of Gold', 119; 'Heart of Darkness', 9, 16, 37, 39, 62, 65, 74, 108-22; The Informer, 38; The Inn of the Two Witches, 115; 'Lord Jim', 65, 73-4, 109, 110; 'The Nigger of The "Narcissus"', 63, 68, 109, 124; 'Nostromo', 111; An Outpost of Progress, 65, 70, 120; 'A Personal Record', 42, 123, 128, The Planter of Malata, 109, 111, 122; The Return, 40, 71, 109, 122, 128; The Secret Sharer, 26, 74, 109; The Shadow Line, 39, 121; 'Under Western Eyes', 49, 69, 109-10, 122, 128; 'Victory', 52, 62, 72, 110, 128; Within the Tides, 123
'Cosmopolis', 50
Crawford, M., 66
cult, 116; initiation and, 119

Darwin, C., 47
Daudet, A., 22, 41
'Death of Chatterton', 79-82, illustration, 81
degeneration, 44
Descartes, R., 14, 24, 25
Dickens, C., 32, 40, 57; London as portrayed by, 114, 141-2
Donne, J., 17
Dostoevsky, F., 47

Eagleton, T., 7, 163n
Edel, L., 143
Egg, A., 80
Eliot, G., 27, 32, 45, 57, 59, 60, 150

Eliot, T.S., 15
Elton, O., 43
embarrassment, 41, 79, 100, 140, 145
Emerson, R.W., 30, 39, 41
Empson, W., 17, 18
enigma, 117–20, 124, 125, 128, 133, 175n

Flaubert, G., 47, 59
Gletcher, J., 36
Forster, E.M., 42
'Fortnightly Review', 43, 44, 47
Fowler, A., 23–4
'Free Review', 32
Freud, S., 49, 91; and foreclosure, 158; and 'the scene of seduction', 138; and sublimation, 150

Galsworthy, J., 5, 66–7
Gasset, Ortega y, 102
Gautier, T., 115
Geismar, M., 133, 142
Gissing, G., 5, 32
Goethe, J.W., 6
Goffman, E., 100
Goncourt, The Brothers, 47
Gosse, E., 5, 31, 65
gothic, 5
Graham, R.B.Cunninghame, 39, 65, 110
Grundyism, 35
guilt, 6, 41, 107

Habermas, J., 16
hair, 82, 172n
Hake, A.E., 44
Hardy, T., 104
harlequin, 37–8, 168n
Hawthorn, J., 110, 125
Hay, E.Knapp, 115
Hegel, G.W.F., 7
hermeneutics, 15, 16–23, 108–9, 113, 118–20, 123–4, 126–8, 133
Hirsch, E.D.Jr, 23
Holbrook, D., 105
Hopkins, G.M., 61
Howard, D., 100
Husserl, E., 18–19

Ibsen, H., 32, 45, 52, 69, 70, 71
Impressionism, 115
insanity, 39, 44–8
intention, 5, 6, 22–5, 47
Iser, W., 59

James, H., 1, 3, 9, 25, 31, 54, 57, 113; accomplices in, 73; accused of obscurity, 18, 165n; ambiguity in, 17, 130–2; clown and, 37; communication and, 20–2; critics, relation to, 49–52; dual voice in, 26, 48; embarrassment and, 41, 53, 138, 145–6; foreclosure in, 158–9; guilt and, 6; illusion in, 65, 71, 95; interdiction in, 154–9; lies and, 62, 67–9, 72; privacy and, 32, 41, 160–2; realism and, 2–4; sublimation and, 149–50; 'turned back' in, 4, 159–62; voyeurism and, 133, 135–6, 142; vulgarity and, 28, 75, 130–62
Works: 'The Ambassadors', 4, 25, 28, 62, 73, 75, 132, 151–2; 'Art of Fiction', 143; 'Daisy Miller', 151; The Death of the Lion, 51; The Figure in the Carpet, 22, 50–2, 119; 'The Golden Bowl', 7, 16, 62, 71–3, 132, 138, 158–60; The Great Good Place, 161; John Delavoy, 22, 50–1, 53, 119; A Landscape Painter, 155–6; The Lesson of the Master, 49; The Liar, 67; Notes on Novelists (D'Annunzio), 135–6; 'The Princess Casamassima', 38, 140–2; The Private Life, 26; 'The Sacred Fount', 5, 28, 37, 73, 135, 143–50, 153; The Story of a Masterpiece, 153; 'The Tragic Muse', 160; The Tree of Knowledge, 21, 67, 156–7, 'The Wings of the Dove', 4, 8, 20–2, 62, 90, 157–8, 160
James, L., 31
James, W., 43, 44, 165n
Johnson, L., 35
Jolles, A., 25, 119
Joyce, J., 36
Jung, C.G., 161

Kafka, F., 36
Keats, J., 79
Kermode, F., 126
Koestenbaum, P., 19

Lacan, J., 124; on enigma and sexuality, 132–3
Laforgue, J., 38, 120
Lamb, C., 47
Lassalle, F., 36, 38, 142
Leavis, F.R., 109–10, 139
Lester, J., 67
lies, 62–4, 67–9, 71, 72, 83–5, 94–6, 171n
Linton, E.L., 43, 64
Lombroso, C., 5, 44, 45, 46, 47–8
Lowry, M., 72
Lubbock, Sir P., 32
Lucas, F.L., 15
Lukács, G., 59
Lynd, H., 104

Machen, A., 48
Macherey, P., 28, 138
McKechnie, J., 57
Mallarmé, S., 2, 5, 16, 22, 52, 53, 54, 69

Mallock, W.H., 66
Mann, T., 36; and 'Rückbilder', 161
Marlow, 8, 38, 39, 62, 63, 65, 71, 73, 112, 114, 116, 118, 120, 123-4, 127, 129
Marx, K., 91
Maupassant, G.de, 65; Conrad's essay on, 110
Meredith, A., 80
Meredith, G., 1, 2, 3, 5, 20, 24, 31, 48, 56, 75, 112; accomplices in, 73; accused of obscurity, 18, 32-3, 164n, 168n; ambiguity in, 17, 83; body, his relation to, 19, 80-2, 86-7, 98, 100-2, 105-7; concealment and, 25, 34-7, 53, 84, 90, 101-3, 105-7; dual voice in, 26-7, 33-7, 96-8; guilt and, 6, 107; harlequin and, 38, 168n; Henry Wallis, relations with, 79-82, imagery in, 74; lies and, 62, 64; 84-5, 89, 93, 95-6; Mallarmé and, 54; Mary Ellen, relations with, 79-80; mental illness, 44, 88, 105-7, 168n; Nietzsche and, 99-100; quest for truth in, 57-8, 60-1, 71; shame and, 7, 41, 53, 79-107, 172-3n; women and, 7, 84-6, 91-6
Works: 'The Adventures of Harry Richmond', 64, 105-6; 'The Amazing Marriage', 27, 64, 86, 87, 89, 96, 103; 'Beauchamp's Career', 34, 35, 85; 'Diana of the Crossways', 34, 35, 62, 64, 85, 93, 94, 95, 101; 'The Egoist', 34, 62, 71, 93, 101; The Empty Purse, 112-13; 'Evan Harrington', 34, 36, 62, 82-5, 90, 101; 'The Fair Frankincense', 60; A Later Alexandrian, 61; 'Lord Ormont and his Aminta', 64, 85, 86, 89, 90, 95, 98, 99, 103; Napoleon, 86; 'One of Our Conquerors', 16, 34, 35, 36, 43, 54, 62, 64, 82, 87, 88, 92, 93, 100, 101, 102, 104-7; 'The Ordeal of Richard Feverel', 34, 64, 98; 'Sandra Belloni' (Emilia in England), 26, 27, 33, 79, 88; 'The Shaving of Shagpat', 57, 82, 98, 99; 'The Tragic Comedians', 34, 36, 37, 38, 142
Meredith, Mary Ellen., 79, 80, 86
metaphor, 101-4
Metterlinck, M., 69
Mill, J.S., 56, 59
Modernism, 1, 9, 16-17, 24, 54, 72, 94, 161-2
Monet, C., 115
Moore, G., 65
Morley, J., 33
Morris, Sir L., 56
Mudie's Circulating Library, 31, 146
Murry, J. Middleton, 13-14
Musil, R., 34

Musset, A.de, 47

Nerval, G.de, 47
Neuwied, 99
New Criticism, 17-18
Newman, J.H., 58
Nietzsche, F., 45, 62, 69, 99; and 'Hinterfrage', 161
Nisbet, J.F., 5, 46, 47, 49
Nordau, M., 5, 44, 45, 46, 48, 49

Ohmann, R., 136
'Origin of Species, The', 44

Pascal, B., 25
Pater, W., 52
Paulhan, F., 69
Peacock, T.L., 79
petrifaction, 82, 104-6
Pierce, C.S., 15
Pinkney, J.V., 92
Poe, E.A., 47
Proust, M., 93, 111, 116
Pynchon, T., 119-20

regeneration, 44
riddle, 119
Roussel, R., 39
Royal Society, The, 14
Ruskin, J., 80
Russell's paradox, 127, 176n
Russian Formalism, 17

Sadleir, Sir M., 31
Samuels, O.T., 100-1
Sanderson, E.L., 40
Sarraute, N., 3
'Sartor Resartus', 102
Sartre, J.-P., 6, 7-8, 79
Savonarola, 4
Schlegel, F., 26-7; translated, 166n
Secor, R., 109
secrecy, 6, 49, 114, 116
shame, 7, 41, 79-107, 145
Souriau, E., 69
Southey, R., 47
Spender, S., 132-3
sphinx, 117, 128
Steiner, G., 16, 26
Stevenson, R.L., 32, 54, 68
Strauss, R., 53
Strindberg, A., 69, 171n
sublimation, 136, 149-50
Sutherland, J.R., 15
Swift, J., 14
Swinburne, A.C., 33
Symbolism, 52, 115; the displacement of religion and, 122; the mysterious and, 120
Symons, A., 5, 6, 53, 54, 122
symptomatic reading, 4-8, 43-6, 48, 50

170n

Thackeray, W.M., 31, 40, 57, 58, 60, 93
Thorburn, D., 109
Trilling, L., 56, 85
Trollope, A., 31, 57, 93

Ullmann, S., 134
unconscious, 43, 47-8, 53, 124, 129

Verlaine, P., 52
Vernon Lee, 5, 46, 47-8, 49, 53, 69
Vizetelly, F., 104
Vuarnet, J.-N., 22

Wagner, R., 32, 52, 53-4
Wallis, H., 79, 80, 82, 86

Watt, I., 115
Wells, H.G., 5
Welsh, A., 93
Whitman, W., 47
W.H. Smith's Circulating Library, 31
Wilde, O., 8, 45, 49, 62, 104
Williams, D., 80, 83
Wilson, E., 131, 143
Wilt, J., 87, 97
Wittgenstein, L., 18
women, 7, 35, 84-6, 90, 91-6, 102, 104, 127-8, 173n
Woolf, V., 23

Yeats, W.B., 61, 65, 95
Yeazell, R.B., 138

Zimmern, H., 44
Zola, E., 52, 104

British Military Policy
between the
Two World Wars